Why Bother with History?

Pearson Education

We work with leading authors to develop the
strongest educational materials in History, bringing
cutting-edge thinking and best learning practice to
a global market.

Under a range of well-known imprints, including
Longman, we craft high quality print and electronic
publications which help readers to understand and
apply their content, whether studying or at work.

To find out more about the complete range of our
publishing please visit us on the World Wide web at:
www.pearsoneduc.com

Why Bother with History?

Ancient, modern, and postmodern motivations

Beverley Southgate

An imprint of **Pearson Education**

Harlow, England · London · New York · Reading, Massachusetts · San Francisco · Toronto · Don Mills, Ontario · Sydney
Tokyo · Singapore · Hong Kong · Seoul · Taipei · Cape Town · Madrid · Mexico City · Amsterdam · Munich · Paris · Milan

Pearson Education Limited

Edinburgh Gate
Harlow
Essex CM20 2JE
United Kingdom

and Associated Companies throughout the world

Visit us on the World Wide Web at
www.pearsoneduc.com

First published in Great Britain in 2000

ISBN 0-582-42391-0 CSD
ISBN 0-582-42390-2 PPR

British Library Cataloguing in Publication Data
A CIP catalogue record for this book can be obtained from the British Library.

10 9 8 7 6 5 4 3 2 1
05 04 03 02 01 00

Typeset by 35
Produced by Pearson Education Asia Pte Ltd.
Printed by Singapore

For Sheila, who bothers but not too much

Contents

Preface

'Why bother with history?' That might seem a strange question to pose at a time when the subject has never seemed more popular. Books, journals, films, television programmes – all provide daily offerings of newly revised accounts of our past to students, scholars, and the general public; while the associated 'heritage industry' in its various forms continues to flourish and offer alternative visions of the past to an ever wider number of interested people.

Yet, despite its apparent popularity, history remains under threat from various quarters. Sniping from the outside, our political 'modernisers' sometimes seem to wish to eradicate all vestiges of a past that has supposedly become irrelevant under their new dispensation for the future: the trappings of tradition, it is claimed, need to be eliminated, as inconsistent with the newly fashioned image of ourselves that we are required to project; we should look less to our past, and more to our future; history may not quite be bunk, but at best it's untrendy. And from inside the subject itself, at its very heart, historians are obliged to come to terms with a postmodern challenge that questions, not only the validity of the subject as it has previously been practised, but (when pushed to an extreme) the very point of studying history at all.

The apparent paradox of the simultaneous threats to history and its ever greater popularity is not accidental. We all need our memories, or histories, in order (as one of Saul Bellow's characters put it) to 'keep the wolf of insignificance from the door'; and so long as we can take those memories and histories for granted, all remains well. But, when threatened with their loss, at times of personal or cultural upheaval, we may come to recognise our need for them even more acutely, and even more emphatically reassert that need. The present is just such a time, when history (and so our own significance) is under threat, and so it seems more than ever necessary to find some positive answers to the question of why we should bother with it – bother with the past and with representations of the past.

That question is not new: it has been asked by the more self-conscious practitioners of the subject from the very beginnings of historical study. So, in confronting the issues for today, this book will be concerned with the past – with history – as well as with the present and the future. It will introduce past answers to the question, and seek to evaluate those answers for ourselves; and it will thereby put our current discussions and concerns into some historical perspective. *argument*

My own position on the subject is partly revealed in that last sentence, for it implies that there is some benefit (as well as great interest) to be derived from viewing things – whether issues or events – in a wider chronological context; and that fundamental belief provides the point, the rationale, for the whole book. For we shall be looking at a variety of uses to which history not only has been, but also might be, put.

To set the scene, I look at Lord Acton's aspiration towards a study that should be 'all but purposeless', since that model still endures for those who recommend history 'for its own sake', and who seek to perpetuate the attitude of those members of the Light Brigade, charged on no account 'to reason "Why?"'. Despite its ancient credentials, I argue that, in the face of postmodern challenges, that model of a 'purposeless' study is now widely and properly discredited (as is unquestioning obedience). Indeed, in the context of historical study, purposelessness has been revealed as actually meaningless.

In the central sections of the book, I turn to various motivations (whether consciously or unconsciously adopted) for doing history, in relation to core themes. Thus, in chapter 2, I consider one of the earliest reasons given by historians for their work: that of providing examples – examples to be emulated or avoided. Originating again in antiquity, the ideal of exemplary history can be traced through the early modern period to (emphatically) the nineteenth century and our own time; role models may have changed in character, but not in their essential function. In chapter 3, I am concerned with some psychological motivations for historical study. In particular, I consider (a) our reliance on memory and on forgetting for our notions of self and identity (however unstable these remain), and (b) history's provision of meaning and purpose, at both personal and public levels. In chapter 4, I consider the long-lived relationship of history with politics and power. The way that new politics can require new history, or even the past's complete eradication, has long been widely recognised: history can be used to support or to subvert existing power structures, and I conclude that it is inevitably political, in the sense that 'political' motivations of one sort or another can never be avoided. In chapter 5, I go on to consider some inter-relationships of history with religion. One motivation for historical study has been that that study itself has sometimes been seen virtually *as* a religious activity; and other motivations have resulted in religion's incorporation into historical narratives, and in the use of history for important theological purposes.

The final three chapters are concerned with history and education and the (postmodern) future. Various skills have been claimed as deriving from historical study, ranging from the vocational to the social; and, despite numerous (and continuing) debates on the nature of what history should be taught, the subject has largely held its place in the curriculum. But I argue that traditional approaches to the role of history in education (particularly regarding the desirability of 'objectivity' and 'detachment') can be positively sinister, in the sense of fostering a dispassionate disengagement from what is going on. That leads directly to my concluding consideration of the role I believe history should have in the future. Contrary to some claims that 'the end of history' is nigh, I insist that postmodern history remains of crucial importance. By challenging existing structures and values, postmodernism itself imposes on history an ultimately moral role; for history is needed to underpin our future, and the definition of that future thereby becomes the responsibility of individual historians. It is they themselves who must define why we should bother with the subject.

In short, then, this interdisciplinary book (which draws in particular from psychology and literature) considers ancient, modern, and post-modern motivations for historical study, and it argues for a continuing, and important, and ultimately moral role for the subject. Far from seeing history as coming to an end or as irrelevant, I see it – after being 're-thought' no doubt, and re-vitalised – as having greater importance today than it has ever had.

Acknowledgements

I am grateful to those numerous students over the years who enrolled for my courses without apparently having much idea of why they were bothering to study history. They provoked me to re-assess my own motivations, and to consider further the question explicitly posed in the title of this book. I should like also to express my thanks to my editor, Heather McCallum, for her enthusiastic encouragement; to Dennis Brown (University of Hertfordshire), John Ibbett (Kingston University), Keith Jenkins (Chichester Institute) and Alun Munslow (Staffordshire University) for their generous encouragement and constructive comments on earlier drafts (which is not to say that they agree with me); to Lin Palmer for contriving actually to print those drafts from my obsolescent word-processing program; and to Sheila Lister for her physical and moral support throughout.

1

History for history's sake

I avoid, carefully, all occasions for being bothered.[1]

Introduction

The world-weary character in Aldous Huxley's novel, quoted above, would presumably have had little difficulty in responding to the central question to be considered in this book, of why we should be bothered with history – bothered, that is, both with the past and with our attempted representations of that past. 'Why indeed?' might well have been his rejoinder: 'in our brave new world, and poised as we are on the threshold of a new millennium, we have no occasion at all for being bothered with it. We should all be focusing firmly on the future, so if the past ever does seem to intrude, we should try even harder and more carefully to avoid being bothered with it.'

Huxley's unbothered hero would not lack supporters. 'The future, not the past' has been described as 'the favourite mantra' of Britain's modernising Prime Minister, who has been reported as having symbolically replaced a historic portrait of William Pitt the Younger in his official residence, with a canary-yellow image of a contemporary ballerina. At the same time, a Battle of Britain pilot, who had been invited to give a school talk, ascertained that the pupils in his audience hadn't heard of the momentous event in which he was involved in 1940 – and nor had their teacher; and other children, we are told, believe that Winston Churchill's fame derives from his invention of the compass, and don't even know who won the Second World War. Even more alarmingly, the organisers of an exhibition in a major museum in Barcelona do claim to know who won the war, and record how Britain capitulated to Nazi

Germany in 1939. And meanwhile, on the other side of the Atlantic, history has been recently described as 'the most despoiled and neglected subject in the curriculum'. As evidence, it is reported *inter alia* that, by 1994, 59 per cent of fourth-grade students were unable to assign any motive for the Pilgrim Fathers' transatlantic voyage; the same percentage of the eighth grade remained in ignorance of what conflict 'Hiroshima' referred to; and a majority of American schoolchildren don't know in what century their Civil War was fought. 'American students', according to one senior professor, 'have for a long time displayed an abysmal ignorance of history.'[2]

Yet on the other hand, plenty of people obviously *are* still bothered about the subject. Films and television documentaries compete to present alluring accounts of the past; history books not infrequently become best-sellers; popular newspapers report with concern on perceived threats to the history curriculum; museums and heritage centres entice increasing numbers of the general public, to the extent that one historian has written of 'Western societies . . . living through an era of self-archaeologising' – a point confirmed by reports that an English grocer's shop, which closed in 1973 but was never cleared of its stock, has re-opened (in 1999) as a museum.[3] And in academia more specifically, the ever-growing mountain of history books is challenged only by the number of books on historiography, discussing the nature of that history, or questioning what (if anything) history actually is.

Whether we see historical study as declining or increasing in importance, and whatever it is that we believe that history is, this book derives from my belief that it's time to take stock and ask why we should anyway be bothered with it – why we should be bothered with the past, and why we should be bothered with historians' representations and descriptions and assessments of that past. Unlike Aldous Huxley's hero, I *am* bothered with it, as something that's not only intrinsically interesting but also of enormous practical importance; and what I'm presenting here is itself in part an historical study. The central question I'm asking isn't by any means new: it doesn't suddenly appear at the end of the twentieth century, as a result of some heightened humanity or intellectual capacity in which we can take pride. But I believe that it's now of particular urgency. So before looking in the concluding chapters at some of our contemporary concerns about the purposes of historical study, I want to set the whole issue in a broader historical perspective.

In doing that, I'm conscious of looking back and plundering the past for my own purposes – of seeking to detect those antecedents which, while depriving me of any pretensions to originality, may add ballast to my case. And that already provides clues as to some of the functions history might perform, and as to why we might be bothered with it. By setting me and my opinions on a conveniently constructed trajectory that links the present with the past and future, it may provide some stability to my own identity and add weight to my position – prospective advantages that might be (and often have been) utilised not only on a personal but also on a public (political) level.

Those are points to which we'll obviously need to return. But it's also worth noting at the outset that the various purposes that historians have had, have helped to determine the various natures of the histories they've produced. Some have believed that their subject's primary purpose was to train those destined to wield political power and enable them to maintain that power, and they have naturally focused on political and diplomatic history; others, who have been more concerned with prospective military commanders, have sought to draw lessons in leadership and tactics from the history of warfare; some historians of religion have contrived to provide underpinning for theological and moral positions; educators in the fields of arts and sciences have prescribed the histories of their respective disciplines as useful foundations for future practitioners; and social scientists and students of literature have often shown an interest in the contextual material provided by the more colourful aspects of social history. There have been periodic fashions for the history of philosophy and of ideas, fuelled by such motivations as the acquisition of 'self-knowledge' and a recognition of intellectual alternatives; and numerous other interest groups, in attempts to establish their own identity and validity, have promoted the specialised histories of previous activities in their own back yards.

Different goals, then, have provoked different sorts of historical study, but pervading them all have been two motivations identified in classical antiquity by the Roman orator and philosopher Cicero: in the first place, history gives pleasure, and secondly it's actually useful. Those reasons for

Key *Goal.*

bothering with the subject are probably the most frequently cited through the following two millennia. During that time there were certainly those who viewed the subject with greater scepticism and even cynicism, and who claimed to detect more sinister objectives for historical study. But it wasn't until the 'professionalisation' of the subject in the later nineteenth century that the whole idea of having any underlying motive at all was explicitly repudiated, and 'purposelessness' was prescribed as an ideal. *Goal for reading history*

That ideal may be hard to envisage: it's surely difficult (if not impossible) to think of history being done without *some* goal in mind – some 'end', some purpose for it all. But that was the goal-less goal authoritatively set for historical study by the great British historian Lord Acton. His aspiration to an ideally 'purposeless' history seems to negate the very need for (or desirability of) so much as asking our central question, and might incidentally serve to justify the complaint of his historically aware contemporary, the Russian novelist Leo Tolstoy, when (in an epilogue devoted to that subject) he observes that 'modern history, like a deaf man, answers questions no one asks'.[4] But I'll argue anyway that even history that purports to be done without any avowed purpose, and entirely 'for its own sake', hasn't actually lacked its *raison d'être* or its 'end', and that in the end the aspiration to such purposelessness is literally meaningless.

That Huxleian-style ideal, though, as expressed by Lord Acton will serve our own purpose as a starting point.

The ideal of history as 'purposeless'

Our studies ought to be all but purposeless. – Lord Acton[5]

Lord Acton's ideal of an 'all but purposeless' study will sound ludicrous to many twenty-first-century readers – but for two quite different reasons. In the first place, rampant vocationalism and ubiquitous demands for 'accountability', make any aspiration to promote something 'purposeless' sound educationally and socially preposterous – a long outdated concept, associated with 'privilege' and 'élitism', twin horrors of an outgrown time. Historians can no longer afford that sort of decadence:

'we must', as Quentin Skinner has insisted, 'expect to be asked, and must not fail to ask ourselves, what is supposed to be the point of it all.'[6] Any vestige of 'purposelessness' is now anathema, offensive to our practical and utilitarian age.

There is another objection to it that will be raised by many others: that it is quite simply meaningless. However much we might like to promote 'art for art's sake', or history for history's, it's literally impossible. For it implies the enjoyment by artists or historians of a detached and value-free position, from which they are able to express themselves – or act as the medium for some higher power – without any ulterior artistic or historical, political or ideological, psychological or moral 'purpose'. And we now know that that is impossible: after Freud and Foucault, Lyotard and Hayden White, the prospect of enjoying any such privileged position is denied us.

Historians in the past may have confidently claimed, from some assumed position of Olympian detachment, to reveal the truth about the past, and for no other purpose than that such revelation was inherently good. But we are all more conscious now of those human limitations which prevent us from ever enjoying (or describing) more than a partial view of anything – a partial view derived from our inevitable adoption of a particular perspective which necessarily precludes the simultaneous adoption of alternatives. We remain as frustrated as Archimedes in our efforts to find an external point (an 'objectivity') from which we can lever the earth (or past) in its entirety. As things are, we have ourselves to stand somewhere on the earth (or in relation to the past); we can't ever quite remove ourselves from the work in which we're engaged. So historians are involved in something from which they can never entirely extricate themselves; and they choose their point of involvement for some reason, for some purpose – even if they themselves are not always conscious of what that purpose is.

Yet the idea and ideal of 'purposeless' knowledge 'for its own sake' have long historical pedigrees. In his series of lectures entitled 'On the Scope and Nature of University Education', delivered on his installation as Rector of the new Irish Catholic University in 1852, Cardinal Newman discoursed on the concept of 'liberal knowledge'. As distinct from knowledge which is to be applied in a business or professional context, 'liberal knowledge' is to be defined as being an end in itself, and is to be pursued entirely 'for its own sake'. That ideal Newman traces back again to Cicero, who enumerates various 'heads of moral excellence, [and] lays down the pursuit of Knowledge for its own sake, as the first of them'.[7]

Cicero here was following Aristotle's much earlier recognition that it is only after our basic material needs for food and shelter have been met, that we can hope to enjoy the luxury of theoretical speculations. When we have a little surplus time and energy left over from the demands of basic subsistence, we may start to *wonder* about those subjects – general questions of human life and the universe – that have come to form the essence of philosophical investigation. And those subjects, precisely because they don't pander to any extraneous needs, are to be esteemed as preferable – as free and 'pure' speculations which are intrinsically valuable for their own sake.

Cardinal Newman's mid-nineteenth-century vision of the ideal university, therefore, can be seen as perpetuating that classical evaluation: a 'liberal' education is superior to any more practically orientated training, and it equips the gentleman – the person unconcerned with the basic material necessities for survival – for a fulfilling life. 'Liberal knowledge ... stands on its own pretensions ... is independent of sequel, expects no complement, refuses to be *informed* (as it is called) by any end ...' Unlike 'mechanical' knowledge which is focused on particulars, 'liberal' knowledge aspires to transcend the 'particular and practical' in its quest for the universal; and so it is 'a knowledge worth possessing for what it is, and not merely for what it does'.[8]

That aspiration to a knowledge that elevates its recipient above the banal demands of practical everyday experience, has remained as a visionary motivation for some educationists even through the twentieth century. Inspired by philosophical, theological or political ideals, such theorists (and practitioners) have evaluated academic subjects, and attempted to define them, accordingly; and they have been active not least in the field – or minefield – of historical study. Writing on 'the practice of history' in the 1960s, Geoffrey Elton sees his subject's role as 'to understand the past ... *in its own right*'. By accepting the tenet 'that the past must be studied for its own sake' (which involves 'the deliberate abandonment of the present'), the historian 'contributes to the complex

[handwritten marginalia:] Is not just to understand past ... we just should understand it because we should study it

of *non-practical* activities which make up the culture of a society'. 'The search for truth' about the past, after all, as well as affording intellectual and 'emotional satisfaction of a high order', is really its own justification. J. H. Plumb similarly describes the historian's purpose as 'to see things as they really were', and records 'a growing determination for historians to try and understand what happened, *purely in its own terms*'. And following more recently (1987) in that same tradition, Alan Beattie once again distances historians from concern with anything as practical as moral judgements, and insists, against challenges that put the subject 'in peril', that 'history is the study of the past *for its own sake*'.[9]

Should we, then, be questioning the purpose of our studies anyway? The immortal phrase from Tennyson's poetic account of the charge of the Light Brigade in 1854 – 'Their's not to reason "Why?"' – seems to answer that question, in expressing an ideal which has been frequently applied in other, less obviously military contexts. 'Why should I?' is one of the earliest questions children ask, and the answer is likely to come back pat: 'Because I told you to!' Frank McCourt's account of his schooldays will resonate for many, when he recalls how the questioning pupil was reminded:

> That's none of your business. You're here to . . . do what you're told. You're not here to be asking questions. There are too many people wandering the world asking questions and that's what has us in the state we're in and if I find any boy in this class asking questions I won't be responsible for what happens . . .[10]

So the question 'Why?' becomes one of the earliest things we learn to avoid, or forget, or repress, or ignore. We tend to go on doing as we're told, consoling ourselves that that conformity is actually a virtue. And in an educational context, we're as unlikely, as in a military one, to find many people willing to risk the charge of philistinism (or cowardice, or good order) by questioning the 'reason why', or the purpose of what seems to be self-evidently a Good Thing.

A Good Thing, on the whole, is what history has been perceived to be. In an admittedly (and increasingly) attenuated form, and despite some challenges (as already noted), it still seems to have a reasonably secure place in the school curriculum, and universities respond to a continuing (though recently decreasing) student demand for the subject. It seems, strangely, to have been a subject that has seldom needed to justify itself. With ever-increasing pressure on curriculum time, that may now be changing; but few people (other than recalcitrant schoolchildren) seem to have seriously questioned why we should bother to study history at all.

What history is – the nature of that study – is another matter altogether: that's a subject that has been increasingly debated, and often heatedly. *What is History?*, *The Nature of History*, *Re-Thinking History*, *Deconstructing History*, *Reconstructing History* – these and many, many more titles provide ample evidence for a continuing interest in what it is that we do, or should be doing, when we claim to be studying history. That interest, and that debate, recently re-fuelled by postmodernist pressures, will undoubtedly go on – not least because there can never be a single conclusive or satisfactory answer to the question 'What is history?'

But to indicate that it 'ought to be all but purposeless' gives us a helpful clue as to its ideal nature, according at least to Acton and his followers. For it implies that history is somehow to be removed from the concerns of the wider world: Clio, as the muse of history, should remain chaste, unblemished, and untouched by such humdrum considerations as might afflict less aetherial creatures; like a guest at an old-fashioned English dinner party, she should remain aloof from such contentious issues as politics, religion and ethics (or anything that matters). Avoiding any unseemly passion or prejudice, she should strive only to be true – true to the past, true to herself.

In this way, though, 'purposelessness' itself paradoxically assumes a moral dimension. For by purporting to stand in the best traditions of a discipline that aspires to the sanctity of 'scientific' status, Acton implies that there is a positive virtue in *not* having a standpoint or a purpose or a moral position; he subscribes to the supposed virtues of standing detached and objective, of remaining unmoved by extraneous and irrelevant considerations, and of repudiating anything that stands in the way of the historian's essential quest for the truth about the past.

And that in itself has moral implications, for an ideally 'purposeless' history requires a certain sort of practitioner – an ideal historian, who lacks any purpose. Historians will clearly need to be a certain sort of person, in order to do the sort of job they need to do in the way that it needs to be done. And the sort of person whom Lord Acton might have had in mind is actually described in the writings of a much earlier historian, Lucian of Samosata, in the second century AD. Attempting to describe the ideal historian, 'the sort of man the historian should be', Lucian insists that he needs to be:

> fearless, incorruptible, free, a friend of free expression and the truth, intent, as the comic poet says, on calling a fig a fig and a trough a trough, giving nothing to hatred or to friendship, sparing no one, showing neither pity nor shame nor obsequiousness, an impartial judge, well disposed to all men up to the point of not giving one side more than its due, in his books a stranger and man without a country, independent, subject to no sovereign, not reckoning what this or that man will think, but stating the facts.[11]

Lucian's ideal historian has had many imitators, and we'll be looking again at his required characteristics in relation to other writers and issues. But it's worth noting here the close correspondence of his approach with that of Lord Acton. Lucian's emphasis on absolute impartiality implies the historian's freedom from any external and even internal constraints; it presupposes an independence which precludes any personal or political loyalties, commitments, obligations. The historian, in short, must be a free spirit, whose only concern is truth and 'stating the facts'. His mind, as Lucian goes on to describe, has to be 'like a mirror, clear, gleaming-bright, accurately centred, displaying the shape of things just as he receives them, free from distortion, false colouring, and misrepresentation'. Having passively received the image of what happened – the historical truth about the past – the historian (so the story goes) reflects it back, just as it is, or was, and without intruding anything extraneous that might derive from the present. There is no underlying *point* about the history that is transmitted in this way: the historian has no *motive*, other than to reveal the truth; the work is inherently (using Acton's word again) 'purposeless'.

That, of course, is not the only view of history and historians that came from antiquity: equally influential (as I indicated earlier) has been the Ciceronian vision of history as both pleasurable and actually useful. But Lucian's ideal has certainly persisted through the years. Early in the eighteenth century, for example, John Hughes published his ambitiously entitled *Complete History of England*. Reflecting in his Preface on the 'extreme difficulty of writing history', he defines the 'perfect historian' in terms that recall Lucian, and make such universal men as Leonardo da Vinci sound positively limited. In addition to all the intellectual qualities required, and the breadth of practical experience in every field of life at every level, 'he must have no passions or prejudices, but be a kind of deity that from a superior orb looks unmoved on parties, changes of state, and grand revolutions'; for his readers must be confident that they are enabled to see 'things in their own light and colours, and not in those which the art or mistake of the writer has brought upon them'.[12]

Lucian's ancient ideal, then, was alive and well on the threshold of modernity; and it survives to this day. The most quoted job-description for historians remains that they should tell it (their story of the past) how it actually was. Formulated by Leopold von Ranke in the nineteenth century, and repeated *ad nauseam* as a model to aspire to or to mock, the belief in a Lucian-like passive intermediary between the past and present lives on against the odds.[13] Not only conservative traditionalists like Geoffrey Elton, with his belief that, through 'studying the past for its own sake . . . a true past has a chance to emerge'[14], but even the more left-inclining and equally respected E. P. Thompson asserts the historian's need to *listen* to his sources – without, that is, imposing his own self or sense upon them. 'If', we are assured by Thompson, 'he listens, then the material itself will begin to speak through him.'[15] He just needs to become an open ear, and hear what's there if only he will listen, and then report it back to the less well aurally endowed, 'displaying the shape of things just as he receives them'.

More recently still, Richard Evans, in an attempt to defend his subject against the perceived ravages of postmodernists, has written of the historian properly describing 'in factual terms' what people did, while 'avoiding explicit moral judgements'. A historical fact, he believes, 'really is there entirely independently of the historian', and 'the real historical world . . . has to be established' from the traces it has left – the evidence. So he strongly re-affirms that historians are indeed still 'engaged in the pursuit of truth'. To catch it, they will, of course, need to have 'detachment', or 'to develop a detached mode of cognition'. For 'they have to be objective', and to refrain from 'distorting or manipulating the reality of the past'.[16]

Ideally, then, historians develop into a sort of priestly caste – a superhuman type which lacks the characteristics generally ascribed to mortal men and women. Above all, they can remain above it all – pure and uninvolved and purposeless. Their ability to stand quietly aloof, awaiting inspiration from their sources, resembles that of priests and religious mediums, who await messages from gods or spirits for onward transmission to the earthbound; like Moses, they are privileged to act as intermediaries, to relay messages from god to humans. They are just the mirror, which has to be clean enough, pure enough, perfect enough, to reflect the truth – 'the reality of the past'.

That this is still a well-respected model is indicated, not only by the relief with which Evans' book was widely received (defending, as it did, a traditional view of history while claiming to assimilate the less threatening aspects of postmodernism) but also by closely parallel proclamations made by news reporters – who are, after all, essentially contemporary historians. Recalling Herbert Butterfield's cry, that 'above all, it is *not* the role of the historian to come to what may be called judgements of value'[17], John Simpson wrote an article in September 1997 under the headline, 'Save me from news reporters who pass judgements'. Provoked by Martin Bell's conversion to a 'journalism of attachment', rather than of the traditional 'detachment' in which he had been trained, Simpson re-defines his 'duty' as being 'to present things as they are'.[18] To become personally involved or committed in his work is, he believes, a form of 'self-indulgence'; and his credo's close resemblance to that of Ranke (who would present the past as it was) presupposes a belief that it is actually possible for a human being to act like Lucian's mirror – bringing no personal input to a situation, making no judgement about what is seen, but simply reflecting and expressing it. 'London as it happens', claim advertisements for the *Evening Standard* newspaper in 1999. Presumably, that's how the readers want it, and how some still think that they can get it: just tell it 'how it is'.

Purposelessness as meaningless

What is the use of a baby? – Faraday

When the inventor Michael Faraday asked his question about the 'use' of a baby, he was implying that something that originally seems quite useless, and quite devoid of any conceivable purpose, can actually have enormous potential, and can come in time to be seen as having an extraordinary range of unsuspected uses. Babies may not seem to be of any use initially, but they embody infinite possibilities. And so it is with history: its apparent uselessness, or purposelessness, should not be taken at face value. As even Geoffrey Elton noticed, 'No one reads or writes history in a fit of total absentmindedness.'[19]

History has been more than adequately 'deconstructed' over the last decade, and there is no need to rehearse the well-known arguments about its nature here. But 'purposelessness' does still require some attention, since it impinges so directly on the question of my title: whatever it is, why should we bother with history? And the continuing promotion of a purposeless history reveals a fundamental misunderstanding about what history actually is. There's nothing new, or essentially 'postmodern', in recognising that what it isn't is a straight and unadulterated description of what happened in the past: the past is far too complex for that to be a practicable possibility, and that has been realised for centuries. In his own essay on the use of history, Nietzsche quotes with approval from a little-known Austrian critic, Franz Grillparzer, who emphasised the historian's responsiblity for imposing his own orderly models on an inherently impenetrable past:

> What is history but the way in which the spirit of man apprehends *events impenetrable to him*; unites things when God alone knows whether they belong together; substitutes something comprehensible for what is incomprehensible; imposes his concept of purpose from without . . .[20]

Grillparzer thus realises the very active role played by historians, in their coming to terms with the chaos of the past. Even 'events', which seem to be the building-blocks of history, are only 'events' when rather more amorphous 'happenings' are perceived as such.[21] Comprehensibility and order is not just there, waiting to be found by historians; it has to be imposed by them. And that, of course, implies their own purpose: they must have some rationale for imposing in the way they do.

Others, too, in the later nineteenth century articulate the problem of seeming to aspire to a purposeless history 'for its own sake'. In his inaugural lecture as Regius Professor of Modern History at the University of Oxford in 1884, E. A. Freeman spoke fervently of calling students 'to the pursuit of learning for its own sake'; and he reiterated his belief in his own academic function as being to do what he could 'for the promotion of historic truth for its own sake'. But his difficulty with that simplistic view immediately emerged with his eulogy to his predecessor, Professor Thomas Arnold, as a 'great teacher', not only of 'historic truth', but also of 'moral right'; and Arnold's great achievement, he emphasised, was 'to show . . . that history is *a moral lesson*'. Freeman went on to consider again whether there might not be some further point to it all – some 'object beyond, higher than, the search after truth for its own sake'; and he concluded that historical study might indeed have some practical use and moral purpose:

> Our studies of the past may be found to have after all their use in the living present, that we may at least not play our part the worse in the public life of our own day if we carry about us a clear knowledge of those earlier forms of public life out of which our own has grown.[22]

A century and more since Professor Freeman's idealistic words were spoken, we have further reason to question the model of the 'purposeless' historian – and indeed the whole concept of purposelessness. For the Actonian aspiration to such purposelessness implies the virtue and the possibility of a study undertaken in a detached, impartial, objective way, and adopted without any ulterior motive (other than simply to record things as they are or were). That ideal derived, in part and in its modern form, from attempts in the nineteenth century to establish academic credentials for historical study. To be respectable, it had to be a 'science', and so the assumed methods of the sciences were aped, on the assumption explicitly recognised by Lord Acton (in the letter already quoted) that 'science is valueless unless pursued without regard to consequences or application'. The intrusion of any political or moral agenda had to be avoided: history should be done as physics is supposedly done, or geography – in an impersonal, detached, objective way, which carries no 'subtext' or hidden meaning and purpose. And to that scientific model, a theological dimension was added; for to be emotionally satisfying, history had to be not only a science but a 'religion'. Acton, again, describes it as his 'profession of *faith*', that purposeless historical studies 'be pursued *with chastity*, like mathematics'.[23] The value of striving towards 'truth', then, and of studying the past 'for its own sake' became a quasi-theological tenet, with any divergence liable to be treated as heresy.

The validity of that model, based on 'science' as then understood, and supported by religious-like props, has been totally eroded. Physicists have to decide which little bit of the physical world they're going to be concerned with, and which tools, out of many, they will use. Like anyone else, they have to make choices and selections before they can start to work effectively. Even geographers have to sit somewhere before they can draw their maps, and they have to choose which aspects of the world to represent and which, for the moment and for their current purposes, to ignore. Their maps of the earth, like all maps of any territory (physical or mental), will inevitably display their own perspective. And that perspective – that chosen standpoint – must depend on what their ultimate purposes are, whether these are overtly practical or supposedly concerned, as we say, with 'pure' theoretical understanding.

Those choices derive in part from a consideration of what it seems appropriate to reveal in any given situation. We'll later discuss the whole ideal of being – or appearing to be – professionally 'dispassionate', but it's worth noting here, in this introductory chapter, that debates about that, too, go back at least to the sixteenth century. Jean Bodin, for example, argues that historians are well-advised to refrain from adding their own moral conclusions. He criticises Agathias of Smyrna (*c.* 536–582) for asserting that 'history unadorned [or without such moral comment] seemed to him like the idle speech of old women'. Much better, Bodin thinks, to leave the moral judgements to the reader: when Appian described how Mithridates had murdered his mother, brother, sons and daughters, it was hardly necessary to add (as he had), 'Bloody and cruel towards all was he.' In fact, it was actually counter-productive, since it had the effect of undermining our faith in his reporting.[24]

Quite why we should be suspicious of authors who are, like Appian, open in their praise and condemnation, isn't clear, for we are all well aware that we come to any subject with our own pasts, preconceptions and purposes. For better or worse, humans are not – as Lucian and Bodin and Acton might have wished – unblemished mirrors, designed to reflect perfectly whatever is put in front of them, any more than they are (in the language of an alternative analogy) *tabulae rasae*, or blank sheets of paper. They are, in their various ways, and no doubt to various degrees, positive forces in the world, making their own contributions to whatever experiences, or natural phenomena, or historical evidence, they confront. As the eighteenth-century historiographer Richard Rawlinson noted, we might think we are simply reading pure 'history', but soon realise that that history has some underlying 'purpose' after all. That happens most obviously in the case of history written by public figures (from Julius Caesar to our own contemporaries), where we often find an attempted self-justification, or a retrospective defence of a previous career: such writers 'think more of justifying themselves, than instructing their Readers'; so it can frequently happen that 'we imagine we are reading a History, and find nought but an Apology [i.e. self-defence], in which are related sometimes very improbable Facts'.[25] But all historians (however seemingly remote from such public affairs) confront the past with some purpose, and have a relationship of some sort with the past they represent. Indeed, that relationship is usually – and necessarily – extremely intimate, with historians often acting out, as Michael Roth has suggestively argued, 'their unconscious or hidden investments in the objects of their research, which can be objects of complex longing and loathing'.[26]

Historians themselves, then, no less (and arguably more) than other people, need to be aware of what they're doing, and why: they bear an enormous responsibility; they wield extraordinary power. There have been numerous well-publicised revelations of how history in the past has been used and abused for blatantly political purposes. The manipulation of German history for ideological purposes in the Nazi era is one of many examples; another, more recently surfacing, concerns the politically implicated post-war re-construction (as late as 1967) of the holocaust, and its subsequent place in American life.[27]

In short, it is now widely accepted that all history is inevitably 'ideological', in the sense of being written from some standpoint and with some agenda; and postmodern theorists in particular have stripped away any pretensions that historians might have had to be providing simply a truthful account of the past 'as it was'. But that implies a need for greater 'transparency' about the motivations of historians. If all history is just a contingent, temporary, relative, semi- (or even wholly) fictional construction, what then is its point? Why even do we need to bother with what's past at all? What is our purpose?

Discussion of that very practical matter is what this (far from purposeless, but blatantly moralising) study is intended to promote. After all, as Voltaire insisted in the context of historical writing: 'Life is too short, time too valuable, to spend it in telling what is useless.'[28]

Conclusion

In the following chapters, I'll consider historians who have agreed with Voltaire's proposition, and worked at their histories with a variety of motivations – whether moral or political or religious or whatever. But before leaving 'purposelessness' behind as an unachievable and ultimately meaningless goal, we should note that consistency requires some purpose to be assigned to purposelessness itself.

This is something that we'll consider further in chapter 6, where some of the educational aspects of historical study are discussed. But it's worth noting here already that 'own sakism' is not without its own (sometimes hidden) agenda. It results in a need for students to be inducted into something akin to a religious community. They are encouraged to become members of that community, whose members are engaged in a search for truth for its own sake; and, not surprisingly, some personal sacrifices need to be made in pursuit of that objective. Indeed, what is ideally required is the ultimate sacrifice of 'self': the historian needs to be drained of such personal (human) characteristics as subjectivity and emotion, in order to cultivate the professional characteristics of objectivity and detachment – of being just a 'mirror'.

Those characteristics are the ideal attributes of the conformist – of the functionary who is committed to the existing institutional (imperial or corporate) ethos, and who is not required to question its foundations or even its prospective path and destination. The editors of the inaugural issue of the *English Historical Review* in 1886 wrote of the desirability of pursuing history 'for its own sake, in a calm and scientific spirit'; and, as we have seen, that desire with some persists. The overcoming of a more natural passionate involvement may have to be carefully learnt, but the

Why history in schools not why history ~ (handwritten margin note)

renunciation of 'self', in what is perceived to be a good cause, can be an enormously attractive proposition – removing as it does the need to make difficult decisions, and liberating the individual from personal responsibility. As has been often repeated in a more explicitly Christian context, 'In thy service is perfect freedom'; and historians have been pleased to sacrifice their subjective personalities and selves, for the sake of the cause. And that – the renunciation of personal responsibility – is the purpose of purposeless history 'for its own sake'.

Notes

1 Aldous Huxley, *Eyeless in Gaza*, Harmondsworth, Penguin, 1955, p. 13.

2 *Sunday Telegraph*, 19 September 1999; *The Sun*, 27 October 1995; *Daily Telegraph*, 7 June 1999; Museu D'Història de la Ciutat, September 1999; Christopher Hitchens, 'Goodbye to All That: Why Americans are not taught history', *Harper's Magazine*, November 1998, pp. 37–47; Diane Ravitch, in Elizabeth Fox-Genovese and Elisabeth Lasch-Quinn (eds), *Reconstructing History*, London, Routledge, 1999, p. 243.

3 C. S. Maier, *The Unmasterable Past: History, Holocaust, and German National Identity*, Cambridge, Mass., Harvard University Press, 1997, p. 123; *Sunday Telegraph*, 28 November 1999.

4 Leo Tolstoy, *War and Peace*, transl. Louise and Aylmer Maude, London, Oxford University Press, 1941, vol. 3, p. 493.

5 Letter xxvi, dated Aldenham, 19 January 1859, in F. A. Gasquet (ed.), *Lord Acton and his Circle*, London, George Allen, 1906, p. 57.

6 Quentin Skinner, *Liberty Before Liberalism*, Cambridge, Cambridge University Press, 1998, pp. 107–8. (I am indebted to this work for the reference to Lord Acton's letter cited in note 5 above). Skinner's words are quoted with approval by David Cannadine, who takes as the starting-point for his own inaugural lecture as Director of the Institute of Historical Research Winston Churchill's question, 'What is the worth of all this?' *Making History Now*, London, University of London Institute of Historical Research, 1999, p. 2, n. 4.

7 Cardinal John Henry Newman, *On the Scope and Nature of University Education*, London, J. M. Dent, 1915, pp. 94, 95. Newman refers to Cicero's *De Officiis*; cf. Aristotle, *Metaphysics* A.

8 Newman, *University Education*, pp. 103–4, 106.

9 G. E. R. Elton, *The Practice of History*, London, Fontana, 1969, pp. 65–8; J. H. Plumb, *The Death of the Past*, London, Macmillan, 1969, p. 13; A. Beattie, *History in Peril*, London, Centre for Policy Studies, 1987, pp. 13, 11 (my emphases).

10 Frank McCourt, *Angela's Ashes*, London, Flamingo, 1997, p. 130. Cf. Graham Swift, *Waterland*, London, Pan, 1992, p. 6, where the central character refers to 'the familiar protest that every history teacher learns to expect (what is the point, use need, etc. of History)'.

11 Lucian of Samosata (*c.* AD 125–200), quoted by D. R. Kelley (ed.), *Versions of History*, New Haven and London, Yale University Press, 1991, p. 66.

12 John Hughes, *A Complete History of England*, London, Brab. Aylmer, 1706, Preface.

13 It should be noted that Ranke's injunction was 'not . . . a naive commitment to the impossible goal of constructing a plain narrative, but rather a repudiation of the slogan *historia magistra vitae*' (history as life's teacher): see Alex Callinicos, *Theories and Narratives*, Cambridge, Polity, 1995, p. 58.

14 G. E. R. Elton, *Return to Essentials*, Cambridge, Cambridge University Press, 1991, p. 52.

15 Quoted by Richard J. Evans, *In Defence of History*, London, Granta, 1997, p. 116.

16 Evans, *Defence*, pp. 51, 76, 112, 219, 251, 252, 223.

17 Herbert Butterfield, *The Whig Interpretation of History* (1931), Harmondsworth, Penguin, 1973, p. 57 (my emphasis). Cf. Croce: 'Those who on the plea of narrating history bustle about as judges, condemning here and giving absolution there, because they think that this is the office of history, are generally recognised as devoid of historical sense.' (Quoted by A. L. Rowse, *The Use of History*, London, Hodder & Stoughton, 1946, p. 150.

18 *Sunday Telegraph*, 14 September 1997. Cf. George Rodger, who gave up war photography after realising the growth of his own detachment (see further ch. 6, p. 125).

19 Elton, *Practice*, p. 56.

20 Franz Grillparzer (1791–1872) is quoted by Nietzsche in *Untimely Meditations*, transl. R. J. Hollingdale, Cambridge, Cambridge University Press, 1983, pp. 91–2 (emphasis in original).

21 So for the nineteenth-century cultural historian Jacob Burckhardt, 'something that happens becomes an event only when it is mentally and emotionally perceived and registered.' Erich Heller, *The Disinherited Mind*, Harmondsworth, Penguin, 1961, p. 63.

22 E. A. Freeman, *The Office of the Historical Professor*, London, Macmillan, 1884, pp. 8, 10, 59, 60.

23 Gasquet (ed.), *Acton*, p. 57 (my emphasis).

24 Jean Bodin, *Method for the Easy Comprehension of History* (1566), transl. B. Reynolds, New York, Columbia University Press, 1945, p. 53.

25 Richard Rawlinson, *A New Method of Studying History*, 2 vols, London, W. Burton, 1728, I, 222–3. This work was originally written in French by Langlet du Fresnoy, translated into Italian 'with considerable additions', and then 'made English, with variety of Improvements and Corrections' (title-page).

26 Michael S. Roth, *Psycho-Analysis as History: Negation and Freedom in Freud*, London, Cornell University Press, 1995, p. 196.

27 See Peter Novick, *The Holocaust in American Life* (Houghton Mifflin, 1999). This book appeared too late for me to consider here, and I rely on Norman Finkelstein's review in *London Review of Books*, 6 January 2000.

28 Voltaire, Letter to Abbé Jean Baptiste Dubos, 1738, quoted by Fritz Stern (ed.), *The Varieties of History from Voltaire to the Present*, New York, Meridian, 1956, p. 40.

2

History and historical examples

History is philosophy teaching by examples.
Dionysius of Halicarnassus, 1st century BC[1]

Introduction

Lord Acton's affected ideal of an 'all but purposeless' history contradicted a long-standing tradition – dating back, as we have seen, at least to Cicero – that the subject should give pleasure and instruct. Its practical usefulness in instructing (and ideally its pleasure too) would be likely to derive from the provision of appropriate examples from the past. Jean Bodin, in the sixteenth century, claimed that the pleasure to be derived from history was 'such that sometimes it alone can cure all illnesses of the body and the mind'; and he cited a particular example of how a military commander, bent on destroying a city that he had just captured, had been so moved by reading about some earlier victims' heroic actions, that he had relented, spared the city, and made friends with his erstwhile enemies. But that sort of therapeutic and moral benefit was only a part of history's main didactic value, and Bodin went on to re-emphasise the paramount usefulness of past examples as models for the future: 'This, then, is the greatest benefit of historical books, that some men, at least, can be incited to virtue and others can be frightened away from vice.'[2]

Even in pre-literate societies, where the 'benefit of books' is still unknown, an oral tradition can fulfil a similar moral function. Thomas Bewick (the wood engraver) recorded his experiences in his English village in the mid-eighteenth century, when

> the winter evenings were often spent in listening to the traditionary tales and songs, relating to men who had been eminent for their prowess and bravery ..., and of others who had been esteemed for better and milder qualities, such

as their having been good landlords, kind neighbours, and otherwise in every respect being bold and honest men.[3]

The promulgation of those physical and moral virtues indicates that history, whether orally transmitted or inscribed in books, is to be seen as a subject with a very practical outcome. It's not just an intellectual exercise: in the words of the seventeenth-century historian Degory Wheare, 'the principal end of History is Practice, and not Knowledge or Contemplation . . . We must learn, not onely that we may know, but that we may doe well and live honestly.'[4] The trouble with philosophy is that it's all so abstract: the benefit of history is that it illustrates philosophy's precepts with particular examples; and those examples provide a shorter, more effective route to moral guidance. As Seneca had long since proclaimed, 'the journey is long by way of precepts, but short and effective through examples'; and, unlike examples that might be found in that other great moral teacher, poetry, those provided by history are all the more persuasive for actually being 'true'.

Few historians today would be likely to justify their subject in that way – in terms of providing examples for a practical moral purpose. History is no longer meant to tell a moral tale, and often we're no longer expected to learn from the subject anything more than rudimentary skills that can be readily transferred to 'real' (by which is meant working, rather than academic) life situations. Yet for centuries the provision of examples from the past, that might help us for the future, seemed to be the paramount point of it all, and historians themselves were quite unapologetic about adopting a didactic tone: some of the objects of their study were to be emulated, while others provided dire warnings about what had to be avoided. Or, as Dionysius of Halicarnassus implied in the oft-quoted words heading this chapter, the point of history is to provide particular examples of general moral principles.

Teaching by examples

History should include the lives of great men and women, and the lessons to be learnt therefrom. – National Curriculum, 1922[5]

That history can best achieve its moral aim by recording the lives of the great and the good has been an assumption motivating numberless historians and educationists, from antiquity to the formulators of the first English national curriculum quoted above. Indeed, that motivation persists even up to our own time. Concern has recently been expressed in the USA that newly proposed standards for history teaching had no place for traditional national heroes, and represented the 'neglect or discrediting of most of the people . . . that had been taken to embody American ideals of greatness'. And in England, similarly, in the face of alleged government proposals to eliminate 'landmark . . . personalities' from the national curriculum in August 1999, the History Curriculum Association launched a manifesto demanding their reinstatement, in a 'final attempt to restore to the children of this country [England] their birthright'.[6]

The foundations for that biographical birthright were laid in the first/ second centuries AD, when Plutarch described the lives of eminent Greeks and Romans who for him exemplified virtues that deserved applause and imitation. Introducing his life of the great Athenian leader Pericles, he notes how 'virtue has this peculiar property, that at the same time that we admire her conduct, we long to copy the example . . . The beauty of goodness has an attractive power . . . even in an historical description.' So while he is by no means blind to some of his subject's alleged faults, Plutarch concludes by emphasising Pericles's 'mild and dipassionate behaviour, his unblemished integrity, and irreproachable conduct'; these characteristics made him well worthy of emulation.[7] Similarly with the Roman Brutus: his 'principles were reason, and honour, and virtue; and the ends to which these directed him, he prosecuted with so much vigour, that he seldom failed of success'. As a leading conspirator, Brutus (in Plutarch's portrayal) saw it as his duty to speak out against the monarchical ambitions of his erstwhile ally, Julius Caesar, and if necessary 'to sacrifice my life for the liberties of Rome'. 'Caesar', he publicly insisted, 'neither does, nor shall hinder me from acting agreeably to the laws.'[8]

That idealised picture of Brutus proved highly influential. Historians may have to wait many centuries to be vindicated, but some of Plutarch's representations can be seen to have come into their own in periods of later European revolutions. Following the civil wars and execution of King Charles I in mid-seventeenth-century England, Thomas Hobbes laid much of the blame for what he saw as an anti-monarchical 'rebellion' at the doors of the 'histories of the ancient Greeks and Romans', with their pro-republican messages newly translated into English[9]; and in the later French Revolution, such men as Brutus were again held up (by those who favoured revolution) as the very embodiments of heroic virtue and as models to be emulated, just as Plutarch would have wished.

Throughout the Middle Ages, moralising chroniclers continue to present their models, often in the form of Christian saints, believing, in the words of one, that an attentive reader would thereby learn 'both what he ought to imitate, and what he ought to eschew'; for the main point of history is that it 'frequently leads to moral improvement'.[10] Political improvement too can be encouraged. The famous fourteenth-century chronicler Froissart claimed to write in order to preserve for posterity 'the honourable enterprises, noble adventures and deeds of arms which took place during the [hundred years] wars . . . so that brave men should be inspired thereby to follow such examples'; but, writing under royal patronage, he used episodes such as the Peasants' Revolt in England to confirm the need for political and social order. The 'uprisings of the common people' in 1381, he warns, almost ruined the country 'beyond recovery', and he leaves his readers in no doubt that the rebels were 'bad people', who were 'encouraged originally by a crack-brained priest . . . called John Ball' and later led by another 'wicked and nasty fellow', Wat Tyler, who incited them to go 'raging about in wild frenzy, committing many excesses'. The rebellion was finally crushed, its leaders executed, and 'over fifteen hundred . . . put to death by beheading and hanging', so that Froissart is able to present his record to 'serve as a lesson to all good men and true'.[11]

Later, though in a rather different context, that same approach of providing exemplary models was adopted by the Renaissance historian Giorgio Vasari. In his biographical accounts of such eminent artists as Giotto and Michelangelo, Vasari wrote with a quite practical motivation: precisely 'to serve as a spur' to others – on the assumption that his lofty examples would inspire emulation and so result in yet more artistic achievement. And, following Machiavelli's lead, a number of historians applied the same idea to politics, presenting models from the past in order to provide practical guidance for contemporary rulers. Ben Jonson, for example, in his historical play *Sejanus* (1603), depicted the rise and fall of the Roman Emperor Tiberius's confidant, in the context of imperial corruption and depravity that both reflected on Queen Elizabeth's court, and served as a warning to her successor, James I. And Francis Bacon, similarly, was motivated by a desire to modify his own king's behaviour when he wrote his critical biography of Henry VII.[12]

That sort of practical moralistic aim became particularly fashionable once again in nineteenth-century Britain, when potential pupils were not confined to royalty, and nor was the advice confined to politics. Ordinary people could be inspired to better themselves, intellectually, economically, and morally; and in that educational task, history in the form of 'biography is the most useful, and the most instructive of all studies'. Those quoted words are taken from an early nineteenth-century collection of 'the lives of men, who, by their industry, or by scientific inventions and discoveries, etc. have raised themselves to opulence and distinction, and essentially promoted the welfare of mankind'. Through his examples of 'British Genius', Cecil Hartley (the author also of other educational tracts on punctuation and elocution) wanted to inspire his readers to 'persevere and prosper'. His idealistic aims as stated in the Preface are worth quoting, as illustrating nineteenth-century historians' optimistic belief in the practical utility of presenting their examples:

> to display the advantages of early exertion, of unwearying perseverance, of inflexible integrity, of unstained honour; to shew the necessity of improving and employing, to the utmost, the talents with which it may have pleased Heaven to endow us; to point out the value of those self-resources, which, in the hour of difficulty, of danger, or of distress, enable their possessor to rise superior to every ill; and, by proving that virtue alone can lead to all that is great, and noble, and estimable, in society, to offer a salutary stimulus to youth, in every sphere of life.[13]

Better known in this context than Cecil Hartley is Samuel Smiles. Later in the century, Smiles produced biographies of those whose lives, as he believed, illustrated the Victorian values of thrift, perseverance, and self-help. Such men as Isaac Newton and James Watt did not make their discoveries and inventions by chance: 'fortune is usually on the side of the industrious'; and, while 'Watt was one of the most industrious of men', Newton is recorded as having modestly claimed to have solved his problems 'by always thinking unto them'. It is perseverance, rather than some mystical quality of 'genius' that marks out the successful: 'the most distinguished inventors, artists, thinkers, and workers of all kinds, owe their success, in a great measure, to their indefatigable industry and application'; and the point about that is that it can be emulated by anyone and everyone.[14] To recount the lives of such people, then, has again a very practical point: history is to teach, as Dionysius had proposed, by the provision of appropriate examples. And Smiles would no doubt have been much gratified to learn that his best known work, *Self-Help*, when republished in 1996, met with a positive response from a critic in the *Financial Times*, where the reviewer emphasised the continuing relevance of the book's 'central precept – the value of hard work, ingenuity, perseverance, thrift, a solid education . . .'[15]

Such exemplary or moralising histories do not have to be literary or written down: the past can be mined by practitioners in other fields, for the same good reason. In the context of the visual arts, for instance, the equivalent of biographies are portraits; and when the National Portrait Gallery was founded in London in 1856, its moral aims were made explicit. A quotation from a speech delivered by Lord Palmerston to Parliament is still displayed on the Gallery's wall. 'There cannot', we read, 'be a greater incentive to mental exertion, to noble actions, to good conduct on the part of the living than for them to see before them the features of those who have done things which are worthy of our admiration, and whose example we are . . . induced to imitate.' Portraits of past worthies, then, no less than their biographies, were intended to promote patriotic and moral ideals.

That message was confirmed a few years later by no less a figure than Queen Victoria herself. The grieving widow's approval of Sir George Gilbert Scott's design for the Albert Memorial was more than a mere rubber-stamping of an artistic commission, for that memorial was designed to teach a moral lesson, of which Albert, no less than Samuel Smiles, would have approved. Completed in 1872 (and recently restored), it incorporates more than two hundred statues, and those statues represent again the virtues in which Victorians were expected to take pride: Industry, Humility, Fortitude, Charity, and Temperance.

At different times, of course, there have been, and will be, different values – different lessons presented by historians to be learnt, and different exemplars from whom it seems appropriate to learn. But it has often been thought that there are also universal moral lessons to be taught through history – and in particular the ultimate truth that we are all equal in our mortality: death is the great leveller. 'Look on my works, ye mighty, and despair', proclaimed Ozymandias; but, for all his great power and magnificence, he too died and, before many years had passed, nothing of his empire remained. One of the great moral lessons of history is that empires and individuals may rise, but they then inevitably fall. Plutarch recorded how the great Roman general Pompey rose to a position of pre-eminence, only to fall in his later years. Having defeated Rome's enemies in a succession of campaigns, he was finally himself defeated by that younger rising star, Julius Caesar:

> He . . . who had been used for thirty-four years to conquer and carry all before him . . . now in his old age first came to know what it was to be defeated and to fly . . . In one short hour he had lost the glory and the power which had been growing up amidst so many wars and conflicts; and he who was lately guarded with such armies of horse and foot, and such great and powerful fleets, was reduced to so mean and contemptible an equipage, that his enemies, who were in search of him, could not know him.[16]

The story of Caesar himself soon reveals a similar pattern. Having risen to pre-eminence, he too aspires too far, and is laid low. Significantly, he falls, having been stabbed by the republican conspirators, at the very 'base of Pompey's statua,/Which all the while ran blood'; 'so that Pompey seemed to preside over the work of vengeance'.[17] Caesar's life too is thus used to exemplify the same moral point. And other great leaders inevitably meet their nemesis. So long as historians can outlive the subjects of their research (and here could be another argument against contemporary history), they can depict, not always without some satisfaction, how even the most powerful men and women in the end prove mortal. The Anglo-Saxon chronicler obviously enjoys recording the deserved death of William the Conqueror, as he describes how once again the uncertainty of political power is revealed:

> He that was before a rich king, and lord of many lands, had not then of all his land more than a space of seven feet! and he that was whilom [formerly] enshrouded in gold and gems, lay there covered with mould![18]

It's better, after all, to be a modest historian, who will never find it hard to choose examples to illustrate the vulnerability of humans and their mortality.

Heroes and hero-worship

History is at bottom the History of the Great Men who have worked here.
Carlyle[19]

History has often been written from the individualistic perspective expressed above by Thomas Carlyle, in his famous lecture on 'Heroes and Hero-worship'. Carlyle believed that we all needed our heroes, our objects of admiration, in order to elevate us, however momentarily, from our own mundane existence: 'nothing so lifts [man] from all his mean imprisonments, were it but for moments, as true admiration'.[20] But, whether or not we agree with that individualistic emphasis, we have to recognise that today's great men may not be yesterday's or tomorrow's; today's hero may well have been yesterday's villain, and vice versa. For there are fashions in greatness and in heroism, no less than in the length of skirts, and (as in the sartorial world) reputations can be seriously affected by new degrees of revelation – whether for better of for worse.

Heroes in traditional historiography have generally been identified in military and socio-political terms. They are assumed to be the people who have exerted some clear and practical influence on the course of historical events: the winners of wars, for example, or the builders of empire, or the reformers of society. Candidates for inclusion in any European list might thus include Alexander the Great and Julius Caesar, Napoleon and Bismarck, Wilberforce and Shaftesbury; while in a recent British survey, more nationalistic interests prompted the proposal of such heroic figures as Henry VIII, Nelson, Livingstone, and Winston Churchill.[21]

From other perspectives, though, other names emerge. Edward Gibbon, while in practice remaining somewhat ambivalent, professed to consider 'contemplative' heroes more worthy of remembrance than the traditional 'active' ones, and he gave a fair amount of coverage in his great work on the decline and fall of the Roman Empire to such intellectually orientated scholars as the mediaeval philosopher Boethius, and the Renaissance reviver of ancient learning Petrarch. Ideally, though, Gibbon liked his heroes to combine intellectual eminence with some more obviously practical activity, in the way achieved by Julian and Marcus Aurelius – two emperors who could claim to be philosophers as well as military commanders.[22] But qualifications for inclusion in the heroic canon do continue to be extended: in the United States, heated debate continues about the proposed replacement of such traditional heroes as Paul Revere, Robert E. Lee, Thomas Edison, Alexander Graham Bell and the Wright brothers, by less obviously achieving underdogs; and in the recent survey of English historians cited above, some less conventional candidates were offered, with the inclusion in some lists of Oliver Cromwell, Isaac Newton, Grace Darling and John Lennon.

We identify as 'heroic', those figures in the past who seem to lead to the present of which we personally approve, or to the future which we would wish to have. Luther believed that heroes – who for him included, above all, Jesus Christ – were actually given to the world by God; and their very successes, therefore, could be taken as an indication of their authenticity.[23] It's interesting to note that Luther himself, in turn, was described as a religious hero by Carlyle; and we can see how the people included in the list above can all be seen to represent various positions approved of by their sponsors. Cromwell, then, can be taken to demonstrate the possibility of a practical alternative to monarchy; Newton exemplifies a tradition of theoretical and non-commercial science; Grace Darling represents 'a heroine in humble life', and Lennon a musical ambassador.

There is thus a sense in which all these choices are 'political' and far from value-free. They are not made without a 'purpose', for all are inevitably linked with a variety of views about society and the sorts of people we admire. And the implications of those choices can be far-reaching, personally, politically and chronologically – at least in the estimation of one early-modern writer, Thomas Heywood, who speculated that 'had Achilles never lived, Alexander had never conquered the whole world'.[24] Heywood records how the philosopher Aristotle took his young pupil Alexander (later to be termed 'the Great') to an historical drama which told the story of the fall of Troy. Alexander was hugely impressed by the dramatic representation of the courageous hero Achilles – so impressed, in fact, that he used him thereafter as his own role-model; or, in Heywood's words, 'all his succeeding actions were meerly shaped after that patterne'. Mediaeval historians, such as Henry of Huntingdon, had assumed that Homer, like themselves, had deliberately assumed the role of moraliser – showing 'what is virtuous and what is profitable' through his depiction of his various characters.[25] And in this continuing tradition, Heywood is simply agreeing once more that Dionysius was justified in his belief that examples from history could teach practical lessons. Alexander is yet one more example of a man who, without an inspiring model from the past, would never have gone on to achieve his own future greatness.

Or he *might* not have achieved it. Heywood's claim may seem extravagant but, if Aristotle really did include that visit to the theatre in his pupil's education, then who can measure its importance for Alexander's subsequent development? And from Alexander, the chain goes on: Jean Bodin claims that Julius Caesar was driven in turn to emulate Alexander; Gibbon notes how Alexander's reputation, 'transmitted by a succession of poets and historians . . . kindled a dangerous emulation in the mind of Trajan'[26] (a later Roman emperor); and the American General Patton is alleged to have emulated Alexander in the Second World War. Many of us will have experienced crucial turning-points in our own life histories – plays that we've seen, books that we've read, or people that we've met; and we can acknowledge the influence of individuals with whom we've come into contact. Personal examples continue to have a crucial role in education and, when taken from history, they can enlarge our perception of what seems possible. And so, as in the case of Alexander, they can make some practical differences for our future.

Those differences may not be immediately apparent, and influences are always hard to assess. For one thing, effects may be far from immediate: we have already noticed the case of Plutarch's Brutus, and there was after all a considerable time-lag (of some centuries) between Achilles and Alexander. Some exemplary figures may have an obvious and immediate impact on their contemporaries, as in the case of military commanders such as Alexander himself. But others may die without, at that time, apparently leaving any trace at all – utterly powerless to have any influence whatever, as in cases of resistance to tyranny, when names such as those of Oskar Schindler are only unearthed and come to prominence decades (or even centuries[27]) later.

History's teams of 'winners' and 'losers', indeed, take some time to get sorted – even an indefinite time; and during that time they not infrequently change sides. Pontius Pilate, for example, has recently been reassessed. Described by early Christian historians as being personally responsible for Jesus Christ's execution, he has been automatically vilified ever since; but alternative and more sympathetic interpretations of his position are, of course, possible. Although Pilate may never become a 'hero', at least his villainy may be more qualified. Like the rest of us, he was free to act only within certain constraints, and his demonisation – as in many other cases – may have been more historiographically convenient than morally just. A Manichaean view of history, where absolute good is contrasted with absolute bad and each assigned its human representatives, can't possibly do justice to any aspect of the past (or present); and it's particularly problematic in the context of contemporary relativism.

That relativism has resulted in the fluctuating reputations of numerous erstwhile heroes. 'Poor Columbus!', exclaimed Frances Fitzgerald twenty years ago. Having enjoyed centre stage in accounts of America's discovery and origins, he had fallen victim to a new historical focus on the previously victimised. The indigenous Indians, who had effectively been written out of history by the 1930s, were retrieved to memory following the intellectual dislocations and relocations that were a function of the Vietnam War; and in relation to their restoration as significant players, Columbus's role was correspondingly diminished. Indeed, he was relegated to being merely 'a minor character . . . a walk-on [no longer at the beginning, but] in the middle of American history'.[28] And since Fitzgerald wrote, his performance, even in that diminished role, has seemingly suffered ever more critical reviews.[29]

Similarly arraigned at the bar of post-colonial revisionism has been that other once-heroic founding father, Captain Cook. After the death of the explorer at the hands of tribesmen in 1779, he was seen at first – at least by his fellow-countrymen – as a standard-bearer of the enlightened (Enlightenment) values of western civilisation. His supposedly humane approach was contrasted with that of the earlier Conquistadors; and even into the twentieth century he was often regarded as the founder of white Australia – a heroic figure whose life had been sacrificed for the empire. Increasingly, though, his motives, actions and historical reputation have been subject to re-evaluation. As early as the eighteenth century, some doubts were expressed (by Horace Walpole and others) about the propriety of European intrusions on the peoples of the south seas, to whom they brought western diseases and from whom they hubristically accepted divine honours. But more recently, post-colonial re-assessments have gone further. The first editor of Cook's Journals (in 1784) has been revealed as having re-ordered material with the deliberate aim of enhancing his subject's reputation; and Captain Cook himself has come to exemplify the imperial imposition of an alien culture on unsuspecting peoples, with its inevitable (if sometimes unwitting) implication of the destruction of an earlier paradise.[30] In the longer historical term, then, the last really can come first, and of course vice versa.

Exemplary essences

That which in the past was able to expand the concept 'man' and make it more beautiful must exist everlastingly. – Nietzsche[31]

Despite the assumed relativism of our choice of heroes and villains, winners and losers, perhaps, as Nietzsche indicates in the words above, there are some more universal values with which history might be concerned. 'Greatness' does not necessarily imply achievement in conventional political or social or military roles, but can be taken to apply to the whole concept of 'humanity'. The great or heroic person will then be the one who exemplifies the characteristics we associate with that concept; and, if it is argued that that concept is elusive, or itself only relative, then that only places an additional responsibility on historians – that of making their own personal definitions, their own personal moral judgements. So that history remains the moral teacher.

Nietzsche himself, like so many others, believed that history was a very practical subject, and was needed in particular by 'the man of deeds and power'. For such people need models, and those models may be lacking in their own contemporaries. They can then only be provided by history, and what they show is that greatness, though it may currently be absent, is nonetheless practically possible: it may not be any longer visible in the people around us, but it has existed, and it has been exemplified in the past; and that in itself can serve to encourage us in the present.

That aim of looking for what is essentially 'human' in past lives has been more recently proposed in the case of scientific biographies. Some benefit, it has been suggested, might result from viewing scientists, not just as professional agents, but as ultimately human beings – individual men and women. For in retrospect their professional contributions may have come to appear as virtually inevitable – a natural step in a continuously unfolding progressive development; that, at any rate, is how the history of science has often tended to get written. But scientists might more profitably be revealed as having had their own moments of anxiety and uncertainty, of existential doubt. They were, after all, ultimately fallible human beings like the rest of us: their problems were not so different from our own. And so, in their new, more human guise, they might provide more useful examples: we might, for instance, learn from them how human beings have previously responded to the sorts of problems by which we find ourselves presently confronted; their histories might teach us by their provision of practical examples.

There is in the end more to a human being than any biographer can ever reveal: there is a real sense in which historians fashion their subjects, deriving from them what they think is most important, and focusing on what tended, in Nietzsche's words again, 'to expand the concept "man"'. It was said by contemporaries of the painter Ingres, that his portraits presented people as more coherent than they actually appeared in real life: 'the portraits showed what, had they got themselves together, they might have been'.[32] And Vandyke's portraits of King Charles I, in the words of Professor E. H. Gombrich, 'show the Stuart monarch as he would have wished to live in history: a figure of matchless elegance, of unquestioned authority and high culture, the patron of the arts, and the upholder of the divine right of kings'.[33] Other portrait painters, working inevitably from their own perspectives, have caused offence by representing their subjects in a way that those subjects preferred not to see.

The German painter Max Liebermann responded to such a criticism from a banker, by whom he had been commissioned: 'My dear man, this is more like you than you yourself.'[34] As Virginia Woolf once concluded: 'it would seem that the life which is increasingly real to us is the fictitious life'.[35]

This is not just a question of including 'warts and all', as Oliver Cromwell insisted should be shown in his own portrait: the point is that portraits and biographies give an illusion of completeness, and of a stability of personal identity which is lacking in real life. There were no doubt many facets to Sir Winston Churchill's character, but his historical essence and identity has been caught in his photographic portraits of a single moment of personal and national triumph – smoking his cigar, and giving his characteristic V-sign. As Lord Herbert of Cherbury noted in the mid-seventeenth century, 'It is unpossible to draw his Picture well who hath severall countenances.'[36] So painters (or photographers or historians) have to fix on a definitive version of their subjects at a definite time, rather than try to represent the fluctuating moods of constantly evolving identities, that would necessarily reveal 'severall countenances'.

Both portraits and biographies, then, are aesthetic constructions. Their forms are imposed by the painter and biographer, and the form then determines the content, permitting entrance to some details, and denying it to others. When the mediaeval historian Bede wrote his Life of St Cuthbert, he declined to add material that he came across after his initial scheme had been completed, for it would have disrupted the form and argument that he had previously chosen. He concedes that the new material is important, and warranted inclusion, but he thinks it 'unmeet to insert new matter into a work, which, after due deliberation, I considered to be perfect'.[37] Aesthetic considerations prevail; and the writer of any essay, article or book – though perhaps from a more modest standpoint – would sympathise with Bede's predicament. We may sometimes speak, in complimentary mode, of 'definitive' accounts, as if there were nothing else that could be added; but we know that in practice 'definitiveness' is only relative. And we only have to look at the writings of Marcel Proust or Virginia Woolf, to see how very limited our own descriptions are; or to consider actual experience, and recall how often we wouldn't have recognised someone else's description of a mutual friend – or of ourselves. It's always, and inevitably, a question of what particular characteristics we choose to notice and pick out, from what is, quite literally, an infinitude of possibilities; or a question of what we believe still can and should 'expand the concept "man"'.

Conclusion

While, then, the old belief in the moral efficacy of historical examples may now sound rather quaint and outdated, history can still be seen to have some function of that sort. Without it, we seem to be rather lost. In a characteristically perceptive comment, the historian J. A. Froude noted in an essay of 1850 that 'Times have changed. The old hero-worship has vanished with the need of it; but no other has risen in its stead, and without it we wander in the dark.'[38]

Wandering in the dark is perhaps the quintessential human activity. Nietzsche portrayed a madman, with his lantern alight in the broad light of morning; and when challenged by amused bystanders he explained that he was looking for God – a God whom they had killed without any awareness. Even the morning seems dark, as we search for some replacement for what we have killed – whether God or the heroic. And as the madman saw, the only solution for the murderers of God is for them to become gods themselves.[39]

In the context of history, that means that historians have to make up their own minds about *who* is heroic. We may believe now that different things are 'worthy of our admiration', but we are still 'induced to imitate' appropriate examples; and in fact our own age seems to put an extraordinary emphasis on 'role models' for the young. So history is made to teach different things at different times and in different places, but the use of historical material to make a moral point remains as relevant as ever. Exemplary models continue to enlarge the boundaries of what seems humanly possible, so as David Harlan has recently argued, historians need to start 'ransacking the past for the men and women whose lives exemplify the moral values desired . . . What is at issue . . . is . . . our ability to find the predecessors we need.'[40]

Notes

1   Dionysius of Halicarnassus, *De arte rhetorica*, quoted by Donald R. Kelley (ed.), *Versions of History from Antiquity to the Enlightenment*, New Haven and London, Yale University Press, 1991, p. 54.

2   Jean Bodin, *Method for the Easy Comprehension of History* (1566), transl. B. Reynolds, New York, Columbia University Press, 1945, pp. 9, 12.

3   Thomas Bewick, *A Memoir* . . . quoted by Adam Fox, 'Remembering the Past in Early Modern England: Oral and Written Tradition', *Transactions of the Royal Historical Society*, Sixth Series, 9, 1999, p. 234.

4   Degory Wheare, *The Method and Order of Reading both Ecclesiastical and Civil Histories* (1635), transl. Edmund Bohun, London, Charles Brome, 1685, p. 299. Cf. J. H. M. Salmon, 'Precept, example, and truth: Degory Wheare and the *ars historica*', in D. R. Kelley and D. H. Sacks (eds), *The Historical Imagination in Early Modern England: History, Rhetoric, and Fiction, 1500–1800*, Cambridge, Cambridge University Press, 1997, from which (p. 12) the quotation from Seneca is taken.

5   Board of Education, Statutory Rules and Orders 1922, No. 1433 (HMSO, 1923), p. 13; quoted in R. Brooks, M. Aris, I. Perry, *The Effective Teaching of History*, London, Longman, 1993, p. 1. That first national curriculum lasted until 1926.

6   For a discussion of the American situation, see Elizabeth Fox-Genovese and Elisabeth Lasch-Quinn (eds), *Reconstructing History*, London, Routledge, 1999, Part IV; my evidence for England is a report in *The Daily Telegraph*, 4 August 1999.

7   Plutarch, *Lives*, transl. John Langhorne and William Langhorne, 6 vols, London, Lackington, Allen, 1803, vol. 1, pp. 349, 391.

8   Plutarch, *Lives*, vol. 5, pp. 276, 279, 282.

9   See Thomas Hobbes, *Leviathan* (1651), London, J. M. Dent, 1914, part 2, ch. 29; and cf. *Behemoth; or an Epitome of the Civil Wars of England, from 1640 to 1660*, London, 1679, p. 3. (*Behemoth* was written by 1668 but published posthumously.) In addition to Plutarch, pro-republican classical authors included importantly Cicero, Sallust, Livy and Tacitus.

10 Henry of Huntingdon (1109–55), *History of the English*, quoted by Kelley, *Versions*, p. 183.

11 Froissart, *Chronicles*, ed. Geoffrey Brereton, Harmondsworth, Penguin, 1968, pp. 37, 211–13, 218, 230.

12 See D. R. Woolf, *The Idea of History in Early Stuart England*, London, University of Toronto Press, 1990, p. 142. In this context, Woolf (p. 144) cites also Sir Robert Cotton's biography of Henry III, and William Habington's of Edward IV.

13 Cecil Hartley, *British Genius Exemplified*, London, Effingham Wilson, 1820, Preface.

14 Samuel Smiles, *Self-Help*, London, John Murray, 1890, pp. 94, 30, 95, 96.

15 Smiles's *Self-Help* was republished by Landmark Books for The Institute of Economic Affairs (London, 1996), from whose publicity the quotation is taken.

16 Plutarch, *Lives*, vol. 4, p. 120.

17 William Shakespeare, *Julius Caesar*, Act 3, sc. 2, ll. 193–4; Plutarch, *Lives*, vol. 4, p. 281.

18 *Anglo-Saxon Chronicle*, transl. James Ingram, London, J. M. Dent, 1912, p. 165.

19 Thomas Carlyle, *On Heroes, Hero-Worship and the Heroic in History*, London, Cassell, 1908, p. 11.

20 Thomas Carlyle, *Past and Present*, London, Ward Lock, n.d., p. 41.

21 See report in *The Guardian*, 19 September 1995.

22 I am here indebted to Patricia Craddock's essay 'Contemplative heroes and Gibbon's historical imagination', in Kelley and Sacks (eds), *Historical Imagination*, pp. 343–59.

23 See Lewis W. Spitz, 'Luther's view of history: a theological use of the past', in *The Reformation: Education and History*, Aldershot, Varium, 1997, pp. 139–54.

24 Thomas Heywood, *An Apology for Actors* (1612); facsimile New York and London, Garland, 1973, B3.

25 Henry of Huntingdon, quoted by Kelley, *Versions*, p. 181. Cf. p. 189, where Huntingdon's contemporary, Ordericus Vitalis, notes that the importance of moral examples has been recognised also in the Judaeo-Christian tradition of historiography from the time of Moses and Daniel.

26 Bodin, *Method*, p. 13. Gibbon is quoted by Craddock, 'Contemplative Heroes', p. 344.

27 See Thomas Carlyle, *Past and Present*, on the belated historical recovery, after seven hundred years, of the monk Jocelin of Brakelond. That prompts speculation of the 'regiments and hosts and generations . . . [that] Oblivion [has] already swallowed!' (p. 90).

28 Frances Fitzgerald, *America Revised: History Schoolbooks in the Twentieth Century*, Boston, Little, Brown, 1979, pp. 8, 92–3.

29 These culminate in David E. Stannard, *American Holocaust: Columbus and the Conquest of the New World*, New York, Oxford University Press, 1992.

30 I rely here on a lecture by Prof. Glyndwr Williams (University College London, 1 February 1999). See also Alan Moorehead, *The Fatal Impact*, Harmondsworth, Penguin, 1968.

31 Friedrich Nietzsche, *Untimely Meditations*, transl. R. J. Hollingdale, Cambridge, Cambridge University Press, 1983, p. 68.

32 Peter Campbell, *London Review of Books*, 4 March 1999, p. 8.

33 E. H. Gombrich, *The Story of Art*, London, Phaidon, 1960, p. 302.

34 Quoted by Erich Heller, *The Artist's Journey into the Interior, and Other Essays*, London, Secker and Warburg, 1966, p. 91.

35 Virginia Woolf, 'The New Biography', an essay from 1927, quoted by Judith H. Anderson, *Biographical Truth: The Representation of Historical Persons in Tudor–Stuart Writing*, New Haven and London, Yale University Press, 1984, p. 70.

36 Edward, Lord Herbert of Cherbury, *The Life and Raigne of King Henry the Eighth* (London, 1643), p. 1, quoted by Anderson, *Biographical Truth*, p. 172.

37 The Venerable Bede, *The Life and Miracles of St Cuthbert*, Preface, published with *The Ecclesiastical History of the English Nation, etc.*, London, J. M. Dent, 1958, p. 287.

38 J. A. Froude, 'Representative Men', in *Short Studies on Great Subjects*, 5 vols, London, Longmans, Green, 1907, 2, 283.

39 See Friedrich Nietzsche, *The Gay Science*, transl. Walter Kaufmann, New York, Vintage, 1974, pp. 181–2.

40 David Harlan, quoted by Keith Jenkins, *Why History?*, London, Routledge, 1999, p. 199. See further, ch. 7 below.

3

History and psychology

Identity – memory and forgetting; meaning and purpose

Introduction

History's interactions with psychology are central to our current question of why we should bother with the past and its representations. Those interactions take place at a number of levels, but the most obviously relevant here are those that derive from a common interest in identity (whether personal or national), and in identity's relationship with memory and forgetting, meaning and purpose. It's clear that those main points of contact are closely inter-connected, but in this chapter I'll try to disentangle some threads and consider them in turn. Together they contribute an important dimension to my argument concerning history's own importance.

First, though, we should notice that the central psychological concept of identity has always puzzled historians in their 'professional' (as well as personal) capacity. For those who like to deal with concrete, empirical facts, identity must always prove highly unsatisfactory, as being frustratingly indeterminate – even something of a 'will-o'-the-wisp', which always just evades our grasp. As such, it has often been distorted – by which I mean that (as we noted in relation to biography) people have been described in such a way as to make them appear as much more complete, coherent, consistent entities than any human actually is; or the problematic nature of the subject has seemed inappropriate for discussion in proper 'scientific' history, and such 'psychological' issues as identity have been relegated to the domain of (mere) fiction. It is, of course, for these reasons that 'fictional' representations of the past and of past characters have sometimes seemed to their readers to be more 'authentic' than those presented in supposedly more 'factual' histories.

More recently, further complications have arisen. Deriving their theoretical stance from the work of Michel Foucault, whose seminal *History of Sexuality* was published in English from 1979,[1] some historians (especially of gender and sexuality) have promoted a 'constructionist' theory of selfhood, in terms of which personal identity is seen as very much (if not entirely) the product of social and political forces. So in the context of historical study, there is considered to be no such thing as a fixed 'human being' that exists autonomously through time. Even such seemingly fundamental categories as 'male' and 'female' are contingent; which is to say that they are differently determined and defined at different periods of history. 'There *aren't any* "women"', proclaims one feminist, to make the point that '"women" is historically variable, constituted differently in different social formations';[2] and the existence of an enduring individual human 'ego' can be similarly challenged.

In other words, according to 'constructionists', the most basic constituents of the 'self' are not simply *given*, but are *constructed* within the impositional constraints of a specific historical context. Rather than being a comparatively fixed entity (the human ego) which positively responds to and interacts with its environment, the *essence* of personality dissolves into something far less stable, something passive, a sum of responses to environmental stimuli, and something therefore malleable and subject to the prevailing power structures which surround it.

Foucault himself was concerned to show that concepts such as 'insanity' or 'homosexuality' did not express essential, timeless 'realities', but derived their meanings from specific contexts; and those meanings were somehow imposed by the prevailing powers – not necessarily by external physical constraints, but as often as not by internal mental pressures. For members of any society are bound within the rules of that society: consciously or unconsciously, they conform to expectations; and they accept the definitions, of human characteristics no less than of material objects, that are conventionally accepted in their time and place.

Foucault's own work, then, serves to confirm what we have come to expect: that terms such as madness, criminality and perversion, are

applied differently at different times, and need to be understood historically. They are not absolutes, referring to unchanging human attributes,
but are relative to specific contexts, and derive their meaning and their
force accordingly. Once that contingency is understood and accepted, it
becomes clear that things could have been otherwise: different definitions and connotations could have prevailed – and could prevail in the
future. So the result is one of empowerment. Recognising the power
encapsulated in language, we are enabled to resist it; and another answer
is provided for why we should bother with history: we are liberated from
the imposition of other people's definitions, and left free to create our
own identities. In Foucault's own words: 'From the idea that the self is
not given to us, I think that there is only one practical consequence: we
have to create ourselves as a work of art.'[3]

That sounds like the very reverse of the deterministic theories of
constructionists, who have extended Foucault's arguments about some
human characteristics to cover the whole of human identity. Their reduc-
tion of the self to nothing more than a social 'construct', would seem to
deprive individuals of any ability to act discordantly from their own
historical situations – to proceed out of step with their contemporaries,
or to act (in Nietzsche's phrase) *'against* history'; and that seems to be
patently wrong. There are, after all, numerous examples of people who
have so acted, retaining a sense of their own autonomy against all the
odds, and resisting any external or internal pressures to conform.

One such example is provided by Nancy Partner, in a characteristically
witty critique of constructionist theory, where she cites the case of a
young girl in twelfth-century England. That girl defied every social convention of her time, and every historical expectation subsequently, by
resisting all attempts to force her to conform and give up her adulterous
affair. Not only did she refuse to leave her lover, but she publicly spat in
her husband's face when he tried to re-claim her. And she compounded
her sins by performing that act of defiance in church, near the altar
and in the presence of her would-be counsellor, the bishop. That story,
as Nancy Partner indicates, illustrates how a mediaeval young girl
could defy the powerful authorities of her own time, as well as those
twentieth-century theorists who would seek to reduce her to a much
more passive being than she obviously was. She didn't just reflect her

environment, but in important respects determined it. She was able to set her interior 'self', her autonomous and demanding ego, in diametric opposition to the exterior expectations and forces by which she was confronted; and she succeeded in resolving the inevitable conflict that resulted in her own very personal way.[4]

My own arguments in this chapter, though, do not depend on any one particular theory of selfhood. Whether socially constructed or innate (or in whatever proportion of these), identity depends importantly on what we remember and forget; and our historical past (both personal and public) is necessary to provide some meaning and purpose to our lives and selves.

Identity and memory

Everyone needs his memories. They keep the wolf of insignificance from the door.[5]

History is a manifestation of memory[6] – a laying out, a disclosing of the past; a way of ordering, recording and retaining that past; and so it serves to underpin our identities at both a personal and public level. It's difficult, as Saul Bellow's hero intimates in the quotation above, to see how we could retain any sense of a significant identity without our memories. Proust writes of how, when sleeping in a strange bedroom, he might wake up and lack all the usual reference points to enable him to know where, or even (at least initially) *who* he was. 'But then the memory . . . would come like a rope let down from heaven to draw me up out of the abyss of not-being, from which I could never have escaped by myself.' Many of us will have shared Proust's experience of memory coming to save him in that way, by restoring his sense of identity and gradually piecing 'together the original components of my ego'.[7]

Some of those components, as Proust indicates, can be forgotten and then retrieved – not always deliberately or to order, but often triggered off by something else. One sight or smell or sound can bring back to us (or bring us back to) a whole past experience. The classic example of this in literature is that of Proust's own madeleine, or little cake, the taste of which re-awakened in him long-lost memories – at first of the similar madeleines he used to be given by his aunt on Sunday mornings, but then of their whole surrounding environment, which included the house and town and countryside and people that he had known as a child years previously.[8]

Other component memories, as Freud has taught, can be repressed in our unconscious; and they may need an analyst to provide the rope to draw them up again, for therapeutic re-incorporation into our psychic narratives. These can be memories of experiences that we would have preferred not to have – that we have been unable to cope with at a con-scious level. Well-publicised cases of alleged child abuse, and counter-claims of false memory syndrome have recently highlighted some of the attendant problems, which inevitably impinge on questions relating to the reliability of historical evidence.

Yet other memories remain persistently with us, whether we want them to or not; and these refuse to let us separate too rigidly the present from the past. The novelist William Makepeace Thackeray presents a character named Henry Esmond (in the novel of that name) who illus-trates their practical (or psychological) inseparability. He describes how Esmond's great passion for Beatrix may be long since dead, and firmly relegated to the past, but 'such a past is always present . . . ; such a passion once felt forms a part of his whole being, and cannot be separ-ated from it'.[9]

At whatever level of consciousness, then, memories remain crucial to our own sense of personal significance, so we shouldn't be surprised that one of Dr Oliver Sacks's patients, who had lost his memory for many years, is recorded as having felt his sense of personal identity so threatened that he came to doubt his own sanity. Lacking a memory of anything that had happened to him for several decades, this man was aghast when he looked in the mirror and was confronted by the image, not of the young man he had been, but of the much older man he had become. Without any memory of the intervening years, he couldn't make any sense of what he saw. 'Christ!', he exclaimed, 'What's going on? What's happened to me? Is this a nightmare? Am I crazy?'[10]

This, then, already provides another answer to our question of why we should bother with history: the memories of the past that make up history constitute an absolutely crucial part of what we presently are.

Without some autobiographical narrative, the ingredients of which are provided by memory, our identities literally disintegrate: they fall apart into unrelated fragments, and we are indeed in a nightmare situation, where anything might have happened and anything might; and that's enough to drive us crazy. For the sake of our sanity and our sense of significance, we take those straws from the past which history provides, and we can then utilise those straws to fashion bricks, which are needed to build the edifice that confronts us in the mirror.

That dependence of our selves – our personal identities – on memory has been recognised by philosophers for centuries, but the classic treatment of the subject appears in David Hume. Having concluded that, as individuals, we consist simply of 'a bundle or collection of different perceptions' – perceptions that are inevitably in a constant state of flux – Hume needs some glue to hold those transitory perceptions together; for, after all, most of us still believe that, despite their constant flux, we do in fact enjoy some continuing identity, or, as he puts it, 'an invariable and uninterrupted existence'. The glue he cites is memory: it is that that enables us to relate one perception to another, to establish causal connections between them, and so to postulate an identity which continues through time. 'Had we no memory, we never should have any notion of causation, nor consequently of that chain of causes and effects, which constitute our self or person.'[11]

Memory, though, is not something that we just passively receive. Obviously, as Hume goes on to point out, we don't remember everything: we don't, for example, recall 'our thoughts and actions on the first of January . . . the eleventh of March . . . and the third of August . . .' That would be the equivalent of a simple *chronicle*, in which everything is assumed (albeit wrongly) to be of equal importance. So memory seems to be something that, at least to some extent, we personally *choose*. As in acts of perception more generally, phenomena are not simply apprehended: they are filtered through our sense-organs – through our eyes and ears and nose and sense of touch – in such a way that we can understand and use them. Our identity depends on their coherence, and we apply our memory in such a way as to provide that.

Coherence, however, is not always so easy to achieve, for there's a continuing fluidity in the interplay between identity and memory, causes and effects. That point is interestingly pondered by a character in Aldous Huxley's novel, *Eyeless in Gaza*. Anthony realises how (like Proust with his madeleine) a present sight or smell or sound can transport one back into the past – a past that can then become 'importunate', asserting itself even against our own wishes, precipitating us into other times and places, and destabilising our present experiences and selves. Memories are not fixed essences, and nor are they naturally strung together in a coherent causal and narrative structure: indeed, the significance of events some-times becomes clear to us (or is attributed by us) only long after they have taken place. So it's as if the reason for something happening was 'not before the event, but after it, in what had been the future'. And memories then appear like 'a pack of snapshots', shuffled and dealt out at random by a lunatic, who takes no account of chronological succes-sion, and who remembers 'no distinction between before and after'. Our insanely shuffled memories recur to us in a seemingly quite arbitrary order; and the chaotic nature of the whole enterprise – the enterprise of our lives, that is – is re-emphasised by the realisation that only some few parts of our past have been retained anyway. And 'who decided which snapshots were to be kept, which thrown away?'[12]

For those of us who are not 'constructionists', then, there is a constant 'negotiation' going on between our indeterminate selves and the outside world – a negotiation in which we, by definition, are each at the centre, at our own centre. Normality implies a successful outcome to such negoti-ation: we contrive, on the whole, to assimilate the external to the internal, to make sense of what we experience in terms of what we already know and are. But where there is an inability to conclude such an agreement – where some anomaly remains, some incomprehension, some failure to make sense – there some sort of breakdown occurs: an abnormality.

Abnormalities in relation to memory (and not only its loss) have been described in further fascinating studies by Oliver Sacks. For example, the memory system in the brain of one his patients, named Greg, had been destroyed as the result of a tumour. As a consequence, Greg had virtually no memory of anything after 1970: he was effectively stuck in the 1960s, marooned there, and 'unable to move on'. Mentally unchanged from that time, and still unchanging, he effectively constituted a relic from that earlier time: he was 'a fossil, the last hippie'.[13]

That fossilised man can help us further with our answer to the question of why we should bother with history, for he was a man who, at a very personal level, was forcibly deprived of any continuing history. For Greg, there was no longer any flow of time: he was caught in what to others was the past, but to him that past remained forever the present. Effectively, he was confined to a single time, which necessarily remained uninformed by any apprehension of a past or future. That generally accepted continuity of time – of past and present and future – which we all take as 'normal', was lost to Greg; and the result was that he lacked any sense of continuity or coherence in his own identity. Without any conception of a personal history, he was deprived of any sense of self.

Greg's case exemplifies at a personal, psychological level what happens as a result of losing history – of losing the ability to see oneself in a flow of time. Instead of making continual adjustments and adaptations to the present, in the light of what he remembered from the past and aspired to in the future, he remained 'immured . . . in a motionless, timeless moment'. His present was given no meaning from the past, no potential or tension from the future; and, although his enforced 'living-in-the-moment' could be (and was by some followers of Hare Krishna) viewed as an achievement of higher consciousness, the practical effect was less inspiring. He seems to have lived in a flat, one-dimensional world, rather like a robot. Without memory, he not only lacked any sense of his own continuing identity, but he was equally unable to retain any sense of other people's personal identities through time. So if he saw the same person on two different occasions, he assumed that he was confronting two different people; and he couldn't register any absence or loss of their presence, or even retain the knowledge of his father's death. It is clear, in other words, that Greg's lack of memory and any sense of history had seriously disabling effects on his own identity, his apprehension of others and his ability to live a purposeful, meaningful life.

The importance of what Greg lacked (any apprehension of the passing of time) has long been recognised in very practical terms by captors and captives. When placed in solitary confinement, prisoners know that, in order to retain any sense of self-identity, they need to mark the passage of time; and numerous accounts have indicated how, when denied any other contact with the outside world, or even awareness of the passing of days and nights, they have tried to keep some record of time – by making a mark on their cell walls, for example, whenever they think that another twenty-fours hours have passed. They need, at the very least, to maintain an awareness of themselves in relation to the passing of time; and their captors, conversely, know that deprivation of that chronological awareness will quickly lead to disorientation and their own ability to manipulate.

To re-emphasise that point, and hammer home our argument of history's supreme importance in this context, we can take another interesting example from Oliver Sacks. He records the case of Franco Magnani, another man whose memory functioned far from normally. In one respect like Greg, a significant part of Franco's mind was somehow trapped in the past. But his case differs – and throws a slightly different light on our question of history's use – inasmuch as he was completely obsessed with memories of his childhood past. Most of us at times recall our childhood – the places where we lived and played, the houses and church and streets of our home town. But with Franco such memories took over – completely dominating him, as it were, and so rendering him incapable of living satisfactorily in the present. 'He is not at liberty to mis-remember, nor is he at liberty to stop remembering. There beats down on him, night and day, whether he likes it or not, a reminiscence of almost intolerable power and exactness.'[14]

The practical effect of that condition is that Franco devotes his life to reproducing his past in paintings: in meticulous detail, he paints his childhood environment as he remembers it – his house, and other buildings and views of the Tuscan hill-town of Pontito. What justifies his description as a 'memory artist' is the fact that he apparently records these scenes in such minute and accurate detail; he has somehow been able to retain and recall the visual experiences he had as a child, and then reproduce them. His obsessive focus on that past is linked with a compulsion to preserve it – or at least preserve the physical environment of Pontito – exactly as it was, before he moved away; so he paints almost ceaselessly, no sooner finishing one work than starting on another. 'I shall create it again for you', he apparently promised his mother; and that is what he seems determined to do. In some twenty-nine years, he completed literally thousands of paintings, and thousands more are planned.

Franco's psychological story again has lessons for the historian; for, as also with Proust and his extraordinarily detailed 'remembrance of things past', the desire to retrieve the past from memory, and then re-create it in his art, closely parallels the historian's aspiration. There can be, and often is, an obsession with the minutest of details, on the assumption that the sum of those details must constitute the sum of reality, and that their reconstitution enables the restoration of that reality – the truth of the past as it was. But of course there can never be an end to that potential labour: those details are literally infinite in number, so that neither the painter's nor the writer's (nor historian's) task can ever be completed.

And for the historian, more specifically, there are attendant difficulties and dangers. One difficulty arises from historians' reliance on evidence which (as we have just seen) is necessarily incomplete; and the manner, as well as the scale, of the incompleteness will depend on earlier witnesses – the (psychological and physical) viewpoint that they chanced to have, and their estimate of who and what mattered, of where significance and importance lay. Even in the case of supposedly reliable eyewitnesses, there are problems: as one witness with personal experience of the holocaust has noted, he saw what happened with a child's eye. Just as Franco painted Pontito as he had seen it as a child – with external physical objects relatively larger, for instance – so survivors from Auschwitz must necessarily report from their own (by this date, probably childhood) perspectives. And our memories may or may not be (and in Franco's case were not) informed or influenced by subsequent experience.

A related danger is that by focusing too much on the past, we may jeopardise our present: we can stand dazzled, transfixed and paralysed, not only in the headlights of what is approaching, but also in the rearlights of what has already passed. We may even find that comforting, as a way of evading present problems, and historical study has sometimes been seen as just such an escape-route. Rather than confront, or live in, the present, we choose to take up residence in an excavated, or remembered, or imagined, past. 'My own age', writes the Renaissance poet Petrarch, 'has always repelled me . . . In order to forget my own time, I have continually striven to place myself in spirit in other ages.'[15] And, in a similar way, both Franco and Proust withdrew from their present worlds, and retreated to a past that they were determined to retrieve and hang on to. Proust has been described as having been 'ready to renounce all that people usually consider an active life, to renounce activity, enjoyment of the present moment...'; and, in relation to Franco, Dr Sacks has reported on 'a certain impoverishment and depreciation of the here and now', and of his 'half existence' in the 'human void' that lies at the centre of his potentially infinite enumeration and recording of externals.[16]

That highlights again the point that history, like memory and identity, is something malleable – not fixed in tablets of stone or concrete, but more like a flexible construction that needs to be constantly modified, to enable us to bridge the distances and seeming discontinuities between the past and present and constantly evolving future. Sometimes, like St Augustine,[17] we seem able to select from our 'storehouse' of memory those images which we wish to remember – brushing some aside, and allowing others to emerge into clear remembrance. But at other times, we seem to have little control over such activities: some aspects of our past intrude, despite our best defences; and we ask, with T. S. Eliot, 'Why... out of all that we have heard, seen, felt... do certain images recur, charged with emotion, rather than others?'[18] At such times, our memories seem to have a life of their own, and we remain in a state of continual negotiation with them, in the formation of our own identities.

Identity and forgetting

There ought to be some way of getting rid of one's superfluous memories.[19]

The words quoted above, from Aldous Huxley's previously cited hero, will resonate for many. 'Lest we forget', inscribed on numberless memorials, may remind us of our human propensity to forget those aspects of the past which distress or disturb us, or which no longer seem to concern us; but there can be a parallel problem of being unable to forget. It is, of course, impossible ever to know which (if any) of our memories will ultimately prove 'superfluous': the architecture of our identities is such that the once rejected memory can 'become the headstone of the corner'. But it can anyway sometimes seem that we are weighed down with too many remnants of our pasts, and that it is necessary, in the poetic words of Dante Gabriel Rossetti, to 'teach the unforgetful to forget'.[20]

That need arises in part because we can't possibly remember *everything* that is there in our past, any more than we can possibly see everything there is to see or hear everything there is to hear in our present. In matters of both perception and remembering, we'd be totally incapacitated from taking any action at all, if we didn't expend a lot of energy in selecting – selecting those few aspects of experience that contrive together to make some sense for us, that provide some sort of route through what would otherwise be an overwhelming chaos. Without selection, as Carlyle noted, 'an hour with its events, with its sensations and emotions, might be diffused to such expansion as should cover the whole field of memory, and push all else over the limits'; so memory needs to be counterbalanced by 'oblivion'.[21] That is, we need to forget.

In this context, Nietzsche contrasts the lot of animals with that of humans. Animals such as cows, he notes, look so happy (or at least content) as they gaze at us from their lives which consist solely of eating, digesting and resting, precisely because they lack any memory and so any sense of a continuing identity; lacking memory of any past, they are enabled to live purely in their present moment. Humans, on the other hand, are forever burdened by their past, entrammelled in it, unable to escape from it: 'however far and fast [they] may run, this chain runs with [them]'. Even some apparently quite unimportant and discrete moment in time can come to be seen as forming a link in that chain, and 'returns as a ghost and disturbs the peace of a later moment'. The past thus exerts its pressure – an ever greater pressure; and so long as we remain always conscious of the ceaseless flux and flow of time, we lose not only our facility for happiness in the present moment, but also our ability to act. 'Condemned to see everywhere a state of becoming', the man who cannot forget 'would in the end hardly dare to raise his finger . . . The past has to be forgotten, if it is not to become the gravedigger of the present . . . Forgetting is essential to action . . .' It is, in short, so Nietzsche insists, 'altogether impossible to *live* at all without forgetting'.[22]

Nietzsche's conclusion can be illustrated by a number of persuasive literary examples. From classical antiquity, Sophocles's tragic heroine Elektra shows how an obsessive memory can result in an inability to act, even when a long-awaited opportunity to do so is finally presented: so fixated is she on the past murder of her father Agamemnon, that she is incapacitated from later taking effective action to avenge his death. 'I shall weep *unending* tears', she insists; 'I am crushed with grief . . . *forever* sorrowing . . . my hope is gone, my strength destroyed.' The paralysing effect of her inability to extract herself from her memories is recognised by relatives and friends. 'What good does all your anger do?', asks her sister Chrysothemis; and the chorus of women agree: 'No tears or prayers will bring him back . . . You are eating your life away in a grief past bearing . . . Is it not time to give up this misery?' But, however much she might wish it, Elektra is unable to extricate herself from her memories, or re-assess them: all that is left to her is to 'lie down . . . and starve to death, alone . . . What use is my life to me? It is agony.'[23]

Elektra's insistence on retaining her memory intact, on refusing to release her hold on her past trauma, results in her being caught in a time-warp, unable to develop from that point, and so unable to take effective action to remedy the situation when an opportunity is finally offered. She exemplifies well some conclusions reached by psychologists and psychotherapists some two and a half millennia later. Norman Brown, for instance, helped to inspire the revolutionary generation of the 1960s with his confirming prescription of the need to loosen 'the grip of the dead hand of the past on life in the present'; and more recently Michael Jacobs has reiterated what has by now virtually become an article of common sense, that 'unfinished business and unresolved issues from the past can have a damaging effect on living in the present'.[24]

Another classic literary example of Elektra's malaise is, of course, shown in Shakespeare's *Hamlet*. Hamlet similarly mourns the death of a father at the hand of his mother's lover, and again, however understandably, his grief persists too long: 'To persevere/In obstinate condolement is a course/Of impious stubbornnesss', as the King hints (admittedly not without his own motives); and Hamlet's inability to extract himself from the past results in a destructively depressive attitude to the present. As with Elektra, the very point of life has been lost: 'I do not set my life at a pin's fee.'[25] In the interests of life, as Nietzsche and Rossetti saw, it is again sometimes necessary 'to teach the unforgetful to forget'.

At a seemingly more humorous level, Franz Kafka too recorded the debilitating effects of obsessive memory:

> I can swim like the others, only I have a better memory than the others. I have not forgotten my former inability to swim. But since I have not forgotten it, my ability to swim is of no avail, and I cannot swim after all.[26]

And for a final, and very practical, example of the destructive effects of a refusal to compromise with the past, we can turn to Bruno Bettelheim. He has recorded how Jews in Nazi Germany often owed their survival to an ability quickly to forget about the past and adapt to an altogether different present. Those who remained trapped within their traditional mode of thinking became in practical terms ineffectual. When, for example, they were deprived of the respect which they had previously enjoyed, they tried to regain and retain it, and to insist that they were treated appropriately. And that just made matters worse: they were further humiliated, and ultimately perished. Quite understandably, again, they too were caught in a time-warp: they were fixed in their past, and unable to adjust to their present; and so they lacked the resources to survive into any future. Their histories needed to be re-written more quickly than they were able to make the requisite revisions. They might well have needed subsequently to remember their previous lives, if only (like Primo Levi and others) to bear witness to what they experienced, but for the moment they needed to be taught to forget.[27]

And so, for very practical reasons, we all need to be taught. It was his 'hysteric patients' that Freud described as suffering 'mainly from reminiscences' – as being disabled by the excessive intrusiveness of their pasts. What, Freud asks, would we think of Londoners 'who paused today in deep melancholy before the memorial of Queen Eleanor's funeral', or 'who shed tears before the Monument' that commemorates the Great Fire of 1666 – instead of going about their (present) business? Such people are neurotic, still clinging emotionally to what has long since passed; 'they cannot get free of the past, and for its sake they neglect what is real and immediate'.[28] For the practical purposes of everyday life, such awareness and cultivation of the past can go too far, and be at the expense of the present; it can become a form of self-indulgence or incapacitating 'hysteria'. Sometimes, like the Roman dead described in the underworld by Virgil, we need to drink the waters of the river Lethe (the waters that give oblivion of our past) before we are fit for re-birth.

Sometimes, though, we just want to forget. When memories of what we've done in the past fail to cohere with the way we see ourselves in the present, or want to see ourselves in the future – and by implication want others to see us – we try to cut the causal connections on which our identities have previously depended, to interpose a gap in the narrative of our lives. 'I can't remember', we say of something 'best forgotten' – rather like we may claim to have been drunk at the time, in an attempt to avoid taking responsibility for something we don't like about our past. That, we like to think, was done by some other 'self' – an identity with which we don't want to be identified. As human beings, after all, we must be allowed to change, and that implies re-writing our histories.

And that changeableness of identity applies not only to individuals but to whole nations, and so affects public history as well as personal psychology. There can be parts of a nation's past which seem, again, best forgotten. Late twentieth-century German historians have been strug-gling endlessly with the problems of the holocaust – how to remember it, and how much of it, and how long to keep it at the forefront of memory; and discussions continue concerning the newly opened Japan-ese War Museum which has conveniently failed to provide any memory of the attack on Pearl Harbor or of military atrocities committed by Japanese troops in the Second World War. 'Forgetting' in such cases cannot simply mean *denial* (as becomes obvious in the example of the holocaust):[29] indeed, by deliberately excising disagreeable aspects of the past, we may (paradoxically) only increase the longevity of their negat-ive influence. Rather, it constitutes an integration, a fitting into place. And so (paradoxically again) by their very historical work, whereby they assimilate (and so normalise and even harmonise) what has previously been considered discordant and anomalous, historians themselves can contribute to the cathartic process of forgetting.

We can, then, see once again why we need to bother with history: historians, for better or worse, manipulate the past (our memories and forgettings), and thereby our personal and national identities. And that manipulation can necessitate in turn some adaptations to the identities

of others, for we define ourselves in relation to those others. (
Cook's biographers (as noted in chapter 2) characterise their ~~~,~~
as worthy or wicked, in relation to the indigenous inhabitants of his
landing-places. Cook appears as a hero and a 'saviour', if those inhabitants are defined as barbaric and 'backward'; whereas their re-definition
as more 'natural' and so culturally superior, results in his relegation to
the status of an illegitimate intruder and invader. As one view of the
past, or one set of memories, is presented, so are others generally (though
perhaps not necessarily – if we retain a more fluid and multi-faceted
concept of identity) excluded and forgotten.

In these ways, then, historians are again confronted with enormous
moral responsibilities. They are indeed god-like, as Nietzsche's madman
required. Or, as Samuel Butler thought, they are actually more powerful
than God himself; for 'it has been said that though God cannot alter the
past, historians can'.[30]

Meaning and purpose

Historians are the professional custodians of pattern. – Nancy Partner

Why bother with history? Why bother with anything? Here today and
gone tomorrow: in the longer term, there sometimes seems little point.
Those with religious faith can still inject, or rather detect, some point – a
meaning and purpose that is inherent in life, already there, imposed
from without. But those for whom God is dead have, in some respects,
a harder time; for, rather than discovering their purpose, they have to
invent it; they have to find some reason for getting up in the morning;
they have to find some rationale for going on living. Purposelessness (as
we saw in chapter 1) may have been Lord Acton's (unrealisable) goal
for an ideal history, but it makes an unlikely aspiration for anyone in
real life. Humankind, as T. S. Eliot noted, can't bear much reality, and
we devise various stratagems for avoiding confrontation by existential
meaninglessness.

That applies to our histories too, both personal and public: uncomfortable with the chaos of a purposeless past, we impose a meaningful
structure upon it, a narrative thread – either one that we believe has

been left for us to follow, or one that we have laid out for ourselves. Whatever the thread's origins, it has at any rate the great advantage of appearing to be going somewhere and of leading us out of the labyrinth. It may sometimes strike us, as it struck the historian H. A. L. Fisher, that there is no rhyme or reason to what happened in the past – that there are no general laws to enable us to give causal explanations of events, no harmony or 'predetermined pattern', but 'only one emergency following upon another as wave follows upon wave'.[31] But even while recognising 'the play of the contingent and the unforeseen', we have to make some sense of them – to impose our own meaning (or meanings) on them; we have to find, or assume, our directing thread. It is in this way, as Nancy Partner indicates, that historical narratives present 'our primal defiance of the endless pointlessness of successive time', and historians become 'the professional custodians of pattern'.[32]

The terminus of historians' narrative thread, its final destination, is not what really matters to the non-religious: in personal terms, it's the one we are all destined to reach, and the one at which most of us welcome late arrival. But it's the journey itself (the 'pattern') that's more important, and the way that we describe it. For the story of the journey is the story of our lives, and constitutes our history. For some people, that story turns out to be a tragedy – a tale of how we could and should have experienced or done something better; for others, it proves a success-story, with an upward sweeping curve representing a success-fully negotiated career structure, or increasing wealth or power, or a pro-gressive share in whatever it is that ultimately matters to us; for yet others, of a more ironic turn of mind, the whole may resemble a series of laughable interludes that together constitute a comedy or farce. But, however we may characterise the history of a life, the act of writing it necessitates the imposition of some literary form, some pattern.

The nature of that form and pattern is influenced, too, by whether we see its central thread as a single unitary strand, running like a motorway remorselessly onwards, regardless of the surrounding terrain; or see it rather as a plaited rope made up of many strands, or like a stream of water, periodically branching out in several directions, as it follows the natural contours of the land. In the last case, what might be called the will-to-integrity requires that the streams come to be viewed as tributaries: instead of coming to their own dead-ends, they must ultimately be seen to contribute to the final reservoir of whatever it is that we leave.

However we come to see our pasts, we are all the time taking decisions on how to approach them – on how to write our histories and our lives; taking decisions on whether to rest content in the transitory present, or to retreat and 'live in the past'; taking decisions on whether to re-write that past, in order perhaps to live 'for the future'.

It can be instructive, in this context, to consider other people's own self-assessments of their pasts. In a recent survey, the Heads of Oxford colleges were asked what they were most proud of. Eminent men and women as they are, many predictably cited their professional achievements: they were proud of publishing a book, for example, or contributing to cancer research, or 'being the first home-grown Director-General of the British Council, with its 6,500 staff, turnover of £420 million, and operations in 110 countries'. Others, though, looked to more personal aspects of their lives: they were proud of their families, of bringing up their children, or simply of 'surviving'. And yet others chose fields quite outside what they might normally have been associated with: scoring a try at school, 'walking the Pennine Way', or (most enviably) 'learning how to gybe without capsizing'.[33] The point is that what it is that we are proud of, or want to be thought to be proud of, really matters little: what matters is that there is something which, looking back, gives our life some point – that there is something which serves, at least in part, to confirm our sense of a personal and purposeful identity.

The need for that foundation of a meaningful past has led to some bizarre constructions. Mark Twain has, not entirely frivolously, written of how 'Once I could remember anything,whether it happened or not. Now I can remember only those things that didn't happen';[34] and more recently (as noted above), 'false memories' have been widely reported. Sometimes with the encouragement of counsellors, people have allegedly dredged up a supposed past which justifies their present situations and selves; and in particular some trauma as a child has been invented, where it cannot be genuinely retrieved, to serve some psychological purpose. An illusory past might, for instance, help to explain (or excuse) a perceived problem of personality, or underwrite a seemingly more significant identity than the one we're currently ashamed of.

Such retrieval or manufacture of 'false' memories, for the sake of a more meaningful identity, is well illustrated for historians by the case of Bruno Grosjean, whose supposed memoirs were published in England as *Fragments: Memories of a Childhood, 1939–1948* in 1996. The adopted child of a wealthy Swiss couple from Zurich, Grosjean assumed for himself an entirely new past, as a holocaust survivor. Adopting the name of Binjamin Wilkomirski, he described how he had been brutally separated from his family in Riga, and went on to endure and somehow survive the rigours of a Polish death camp. Then, at the end of the war, he was supposedly rescued from an orphanage by a couple, who insisted on his repressing the memories of his former life. The intrusive fragments of his childhood memories were what he finally claimed to have published, and his hoax was only revealed after his book had been widely acclaimed as a moving contribution to holocaust studies. Elena Lappin, who researched and helped to expose the deception, described Grosjean as 'someone who has invented an identity for himself out of other people's heritage'.[35] She reports that he genuinely wanted to believe that he was a survivor of the holocaust, and somehow convinced himself of the authenticity of his newly assumed identity; but his retrieval, or assumption, of false memories to underpin that wished-for self, relates again to our central question of why we should bother with history, and raises some moral issues which we shall need to address in our concluding chapter.

The story of our lives, though, is not always in our own hands: others play their part in defining us; and they can of course remember us in different ways – and not always as we'd like. Making his own point about our individual responsibility for assuming an identity and defining our selves, Jean-Paul Sartre recorded how the French writer Jean Genet as a child overheard adults referring to him as a thief, and thereafter lived up or down to that imposed identification; Freud was apparently long affected by hearing his father angrily proclaim that 'the boy will come to nothing', after obeying 'the calls of nature' in his parent's bedroom;[36] and many will recall the burden of other people's (positive or negative) expectations. But despite the dangers in such presumptuous identifications and impositions of meaning, historians are bound to make their assessments – bound to constrain the objects of their study within certain parameters. Even (or especially) loose cannon need to be spiked, and integrated for the sake of coherent and meaningful written history.

Imposed reintegration lies at the very core of the writing of obituaries, which necessarily present personal narratives of very recent history. As a form of potted biography, they have to be produced, or at least finalised, at short notice, following what is sometimes an unexpected death. Designed concisely to encapsulate the essence of its subject, an obituary often starts with what is perceived as being a key episode in its subject's life – an outstanding achievement, perhaps, or a particularly brave action, which somehow gives coherence to the whole and makes it seem worthwhile. The headlines which summarise obituaries in the *Daily Telegraph* often neatly encapsulate a typically British ideal of heroic or worthy activity linked with eccentricity and a light-hearted and ironic detachment. Thus, for example, we read of an 'Officer, rocket engineer and restaurateur who served snails he bred in a disused swimming pool'; an 'Englishman who fought with the Foreign Legion in Algeria and once spoke to a legionnaire's ghost'; and a 'Labour MP who sought economies through the greater standardisation of municipal sanitary ware'. Such one-liners give the appearance of a coherent narrative (a meaningful and purposeful life) to what (some days before) might have seemed to the actual obituary subject to be a far less well organised plot. Unfortunately, an end is a prerequisite for the imposition of such meaning, and for the detection of any 'pattern'. As the inscription on an unsuccessful scriptwriter's tomb-stone in Los Angeles reportedly reads: 'At last – a plot!'[37]

Conclusion

The psychological answers to the question of why we should be bothered with history may seem too obvious to labour. After all, it has become a platitude of history's defenders that the subject is needed as an essential part of education to provide a sense of national identity; and, at the personal level, we are all well enough aware that we have memories (or constructions of our pasts) that have something to do with who we are, and where we are, and even where we hope to go.

But, if only because they seem so obvious, these answers can easily be taken for granted, and it's only when we are deprived of our pasts (whether personal or public) that we realise their importance – if not our actual dependence on them. That is why the examples of deprivation and abnormality recorded by Oliver Sacks and others are so instructive. From them we can see that a malfunctioning memory, or a complete loss of memory, has crucial implications for our sense of personal identity and therefore our ability to live in society with other people. Our personal histories provide support for our selves and our sanity. And similarly with more public histories: we can't in practice do without them; so any temporary vacuum will always soon be filled. And that is why it's of the utmost importance to be aware of who is filling it, with what, and why.

That links the psychological with the political, to which we'll turn in the next chapter. But before doing so, I want to re-emphasise one point: whether on a personal or public level, I am not suggesting that our identities and meanings are *determined* by our pasts. Identities and meanings are not fixed entities. Like human relationships, they constantly evolve, in a state of flux resulting from a never concluded 'negotiation' between our pasts and presents and prospective futures. That is why we must not, as Nietzsche insists, 'let the dead bury the living'[38] (or of course vice versa) through our own lack of historiographical and psychological awareness.

Notes

1 Michel Foucault's *The History of Sexuality* was originally published in English in three volumes, in 1979, 1986 and 1988.
2 Christina Crosby, *The Ends of History*, London, Routledge, 1991, pp. 156–7, quoting Denise Riley.
3 Michel Foucault, quoted in Alec McHoul and Wendy Grace, *A Foucault Primer: Discourse, Power and the Subject*, London, UCL Press, 1995, p. 124.
4 Nancy F. Partner, 'No Sex, No Gender', in Brian Fay, Philip Pomper, and Richard T. Vann (eds), *History and Theory: Contemporary Readings*, Oxford, Blackwell, 1998, p. 278. See also in relation to the case of Héloïse and Abelard.
5 Saul Bellow, *Mr Sammler's Planet*, Harmondsworth, Penguin, 1977, p. 190.
6 Cf. Michael Bentley, who has claimed on the contrary that 'history is precisely non-memory, a systematic discipline which seeks to rely on mechanisms and controls quite different from those which memory triggers and often intended to give memory the lie'. *Modern Historiography: An Introduction*, London, Routledge, 1999, p. 155. But, although historical research may give the lie to one individual's aberrant memory, it's hard to see how that research itself does not depend on memory: all records (both literary and oral) are surely expressions of someone's memory.

7 Marcel Proust, *Remembrance of Things Past*, vol. 1, Harmondsworth, Penguin, 1983, pp. 5–6.
8 Proust, *Remembrance*, pp. 48–51.
9 Thackeray's *The History of Henry Esmond*, published in 1852, is discussed and quoted by Crosby, *Ends of History*, ch. 2.
10 Oliver Sacks, *The Man Who Mistook His Wife for a Hat*, London, Duckworth, 1985, p. 22.
11 David Hume, *A Treatise of Human Nature* (1739), Book 1, part 4, section 6.
12 Aldous Huxley, *Eyeless in Gaza*, Harmondsworth, Penguin, 1955, pp. 18–19.
13 Oliver Sacks, *An Anthropologist on Mars*, London, Picador, 1995, p. 45. The later quotation in this section is from p. 46.
14 Sacks, *Anthropologist,* p. 160. Later quotations in this section are from pp. 177, 163, 157.
15 Quoted by D. R. Kelley, 'The Theory of History', in C. B. Schmitt, Q. Skinner and E. Kessler (eds), *The Cambridge History of Renaissance Philosophy*, Cambridge, Cambridge University Press, 1988, pp. 747–8.
16 Ernest Schachtel on Proust, quoted by Sacks, *Anthropologist,* p. 157.
17 See Augustine, *Confessions*, transl. R. S. Pine-Coffin, Harmondsworth, Penguin, 1961, X.8.
18 T. S. Eliot, *The Use of Poetry and the Use of Criticism*, London, Faber & Faber, 1933, p. 148.
19 Huxley, *Eyeless*, p. 9.
20 Memorials are indebted to Rudyard Kipling, 'Recessionals'; builders to Psalms 118. 22; the unforgetful to Dante Gabriel Rossetti, 'The House of Life', pt. II. ci.
21 Thomas Carlyle, 'On History Again' (1833), in *English and other Critical Essays*, London, J. M. Dent 1915, pp. 95–6.
22 Friedrich Nietzsche, *Untimely Meditations*, transl. R. J. Hollingdale, Cambridge, Cambridge University Press, 1983, pp. 61–2.
23 Sophocles, *Electra*, transl. Kenneth McLeish, Cambridge, Cambridge University Press, 1979, pp. 8–10 (my emphases), 14, 29.
24 Norman O. Brown, *Life Against Death: The Psychoanalytical Meaning of History*, London, Routledge & Kegan Paul, 1959, p. 19; Michael Jacobs, *The Presenting Past*, Milton Keynes, Open University Press, 1985, p. 5.
25 William Shakespeare, *Hamlet*, Act I, sc. 2, ll. 92–4, 129; Act I, sc. 4, l. 65.
26 Quoted by Adam Phillips, *London Review of Books*, 20 June 1996, p. 12.
27 Bruno Bettelheim, *Surviving and Other Essays*, London, Thames & Hudson, 1979, pp. 253ff.
28 See Sigmund Freud, *Studies in Hysteria* (1895) and *Five Lectures on Psycho-Analysis* (1910), quoted by Michael S. Roth, *The Ironist's Cage: Memory, Trauma, and the Construction of History*, New York, Columbia University Press, 1995, pp. 186, 188.
29 See further ch. 4, esp. pp. 72f.
30 'It is', Butler concludes, 'perhaps because they can be useful to Him in this regard that He tolerates their existence.' Samuel Butler, *Erewhon Revisited*, quoted by Lewis W. Spitz, 'The Historian and the Ancient of Days', in *The Reformation: Education and History*, Aldershot, Variorum, 1997, p. 149.
31 H. A. L. Fisher, *A History of Europe*, London, Edward Arnold, 1936, Preface.
32 Nancy Partner, 'Making Up Lost Time: Writing on the Writing of History', in Fay *et al.* (eds), *History and Theory*, pp. 70, 72.
33 *Oxford Today*, vol. 11, no. 2 (1999), pp. 52–3.

34 Quoted by Spitz, *Reformation*, pp. 153–4.

35 Elena Lappin's work, published in *Granta*, was reported by Rebecca Abrams, who was herself duped into writing the story of a supposedly (but fraudulent) HIV positive girl, in *The Sunday Telegraph*, 4 July 1999. Grosjean's book (extravagantly described on the cover as a 'beautifully written, unselfconscious and powerful . . . masterpiece') has now been withdrawn from bookshops by its German publisher: *Jewish Chronicle*, 22 October 1999.

36 See Roth, *Ironist's Cage*, p. 190.

37 Inscription in Pacific Palisades Cemetery, quoted as Nigel Havers's favourite saying of the millennium, *Sunday Telegraph*, 19 December 1999.

38 Nietzsche, *Untimely Meditations*, p. 72.

4

History, politics and power

If history have no professorship, if all universities be closed, she will always have a hospitable reception in palaces and in the innermost chambers of kings and princes. – Daniel Heinsius, c. 1613[1]

Introduction

The close links between history, politics and power, have been recognised for centuries. Even the earliest historians of antiquity realised the political implications of their subject, for, in Nietzsche's words, 'Knowledge of the past has at all times been desired only in the service of the future and the present'.[2] 'To gain or maintain political power', then, was one of the very first answers to the question of why we should bother with history; and in our own time history's inevitable entanglement with politics and power has again been made abundantly clear, and exemplified on numerous occasions. So, as the early seventeenth-century historian Daniel Heinsius noted in the quotation above, even if the subject were to cease to exist as an 'academic' study, history would continue to perform a very practical political function, and would be utilised in the corridors of power accordingly.

In this chapter, then, I look at the way history has been and is used as an extension of politics, and at the way new political régimes have required history's revision or even abolition. I also consider some of the ways in which history has been used to subvert exisiting power structures, and conclude that no history can ever be proof against some political involvement.

History as politics

Every wise History [is] full, and as it were impregnate with Politicall Precepts and Counsils. – Francis Bacon[3]

Francis Bacon, as a man who had been actively involved in politics as well as in philosophy, was far from advocating in the quotation above that history should be seen as politics. On the contrary, elsewhere in the same passage he clarifies that it is wrong for the aspiring historian to intrude his own political reflexions into his narrative: if it is inevitable that history incorporates, or is 'impregnate with' such matters, then he is clear that 'the Writer himselfe should be his own Midwife at the delivery'. History itself may incorporate political lessons, but the historian should not be involved. Indeed, he insists, 'History of all writings . . . holdeth least of the author, and most of the things themselves.'

In that description of, or aspiration for, history, it's clear that Bacon is following again in the well-trodden footsteps of Lucian, and stands as an early-modern forerunner of many subsequent historians who would be shocked by any imputations of ideological involvement. But there has also been a long succession of historians who have been well aware of political dimensions (whether explicit or implicit) in their work, and we'll first consider some aspects of that on-going entanglement.

Political history

History is but past politics and . . . politics are but present history.[4]

That much-quoted aphorism, taken from E. A. Freeman's inaugural lecture as Regius Professor of Modern History in Oxford (though often attributed to Sir John Seeley), may seem to encapsulate a ludicrously narrow interpretation of what historical study is about, and to emphasise what is now only one minor aspect of the subject. But as an indication of the symbiotic relationship between history and politics it serves as a useful reminder that history – by which I mean here historical writing – has very often had political purposes and political effects.

Indeed, it might sometimes seem that historians are politicians manqués – people who would, perhaps, have liked to be politicians and who resorted to history as a substitute for more active and direct political involvement; and it's certainly the case that some politicians adopt the role of historian after withdrawal from a more active life. The Greek historian Thucydides made his record of the Peloponnesian War, only after being deprived of his position as a military actor in that war. At the time of the Italian Renaissance, both Guicciardini and Machiavelli took up writing history after being excluded from their roles as active politicians; and they hoped by so doing to continue having some influence on people and events. And in the twentieth century it has become quite common for retired politicians to spend their new-found leisure writing (or re-writing) history – with Winston Churchill as one of many obvious examples.

Polybius, then, was no doubt justified in suggesting that historians themselves often view their own subject as being 'the truest education and training for political life'.[5] That claim may sound presumptuous, but it has suited historians' vanity and purses to believe that it is only by studying how people have acted in the past, and assessing the aims and methods of those who have failed and succeeded in the political arena, that aspiring politicians can hope to learn their craft. It was, for instance, with just such a belief that Sir Walter Raleigh wrote his *History of the World* in the early seventeenth century. Another example of a man compelled to take premature retirement from his active political life, Raleigh was actually incarcerated in the Tower of London; and thus excluded from direct participation in public events, he composed a work that might have sounded purely theoretical. But in fact his *History* was designed as a manual of instruction for King James's son and heir. The prospective recipient, Prince Henry, in the event died before he could succeed to the throne and benefit from Raleigh's advice. But the courtier's didactic work of history was nevertheless far from wasted: its political message may have needed some adjustment, but it came to serve, in the words of one biographer, as 'a mainspring of revolutionary thought' in mid-seventeenth-century England.[6]

Raleigh's optimistic belief in a moral order, imposed by God through the ages, enabled him to present his history as a morality tale for any would-be political leader. Essentially it shows us how good rulers have been rewarded, and bad ones punished – 'how kings and kingdoms have flourished and fallen, and for what virtue and piety God made prosperous, and for what vice and deformity he made wretched both the one and the other';[7] so the political lesson is clear, that success depends on submission to a God-given moral order which will ultimately prevail. In the end, we are all – whatever our rank on earth – subject to the law of heaven; and that divine law has one unavoidable and ultimate sanction – death. 'O eloquent and mighty Death! Whom none could advise, thou hast persuaded. What none hath dared, thou hast done. And whom all the world hath flattered, thou only hast cast out of the world and despised.'[8]

So long, then, as we all remain subject to death, justice will ultimately prevail; and that remains the case even when tyrannical rulers seem to gain the upper hand. So while Raleigh avoided explicitly promoting any one particular form of government, his message came through clearly enough to his contemporaries: the glory of Queen Elizabeth's reign was a direct reward for her undoubted virtue and for her professed love for her people; and that was to be contrasted with the many problems faced, and no doubt deserved, by the early Stuarts. As Raleigh clarified in his Preface, kings who ruled tyrannically invariably came to grief; and grief, by implication, was what awaited King James, as he struggled with parliament and his own increasing unpopularity.

The clarity of Raleigh's political message in his supposedly historical work is demonstrated by the fact that the *History* was soon deemed to warrant censorship by the political authorities. It was seized some nine months after its publication in March 1614, and remained under royal prohibition for two more years. But, as so often happens in such cases, censorship proved counter-productive: the work soon became an inspiration to the mid-century parliamentarians, giving a theoretical justification for their struggle against the perceived tyranny of yet another king. In addition to accolades from such outspoken revolutionaries as John Lilburne and John Milton, Oliver Cromwell himself confirmed its political credentials by proposing it as recommended reading for his son.

History, though, can work both ways, even for discredited monarchs; and James found some comfort in the support to his political agenda afforded by William Camden. How self-consciously political Camden's motives were, is not clear; but his first major historical work, published in 1586, has been assessed by at least one modern historian as having had considerable practical importance. As the title *Britannia* implies, the history was designed to give a coherent account of the development of 'Britain' as a whole, and it thus encouraged interest in that political entity which had been declared by King James after the union with Scotland in 1603. It's noteworthy that by the time James proclaimed himself King of Great Britain in 1604, Camden's history had already run to five Latin editions; and English versions appeared not much later, in 1610 and 1625. With such evident popularity, it does seem possible, as Denys Hay suggests, that 'Camden did more to unite Britain in the long run than did King James'.[9]

King James himself was very well aware of history's political importance. Though naturally pleased with Camden's work, he had been enraged by another historian's account of recent events in his northern territory: George Buchanan's *History of Scotland* was unashamedly republican in tone, and had portrayed James's own mother, Mary Queen of Scots, in a most unfavourable light – as a profligate, murderous idolator and tyrant who 'so demeaned her self . . . as if she had forgot not only the Dignity of a Queen, but even the Modesty of a Matron'. Buchanan's position was the more provocative for his having emphatically claimed to be presenting what was 'truly a *History*, and not a *Romance*, wherein the Author representeth Things *as they were*';[10] and unsurprisingly his work was banned by James to the best of his ability. Unfortunately for the king, his sphere of influence did not extend to continental Europe where, in its Latin version, Buchanan's representation proved persuasive, and was used in particular by the French historian Jacques-Auguste de Thou in his own *History of his Times*. King James actually tried to persuade de Thou – a historian whom he had previously praised for impartiality – to change his draft, and certainly de Thou was aware of James's attitude towards the source that he had used: 'I hear', he wrote, 'that his royal pupil is angry with him [i.e. Buchanan] . . . However, facts are facts, and an honest man cannot conceal them.'[11] Brave words – and ones that historians, working as they inevitably do within a political context, have often been urged to bear in mind. But, in the event, de Thou himself – harassed as he was, not only by James, but also from the Catholic authorities in Rome who consigned his *History* to the Index of prohibited books – refrained from having the later sections of his work published until, through death, he had removed himself from any potential danger.

That same route, too, was later taken by Camden. Despite his previous favour, he was forced by James to show him the manuscript of his next projected work, *The Annals*, and was distressed to see a copy that had suffered badly at the royal censor's hand. It was, he lamented, 'full of mutilations and gaps and certain words . . . effaced'. His practical solution was to arrange to have the offending sections of his work published posthumously in Leiden, when he dedicated his work, pointedly, not to the king, but 'to God, my country and posterity, at the altar of Truth'.

King James, then, obviously saw good reason to be bothered with history, and the political function of such early-modern works as those of Camden and de Thou both was and is very clear. Later, nineteenth-century historians too had their own political messages to put over to their readers, but readership, message and motivation had changed. By then history was becoming more popular – not only in the sense of appealing to more people as a literary subject, but also of being itself more concerned with more 'ordinary' people. It wasn't, as William Morris pointed out, Henry III who built Westminster Abbey, nor the emperor Justinian who built St Sophia in Constantinople, but rather, nameless craftsmen, 'men like you and me'.[12] So historians often take on a more 'social' role, with the result that political history is increasingly supplemented by social history. But the latter nonetheless remains (as we shall now go on to see) highly politicised.

Politicised history

History into inconsequent nonsense? – William Morris, 1894

When William Morris was asked how he had become a socialist, he explained that it was his study of history (together with his practice of art) that had 'forced me into a hatred of the civilisation which, if things were to stop as they are, would turn history into inconsequent nonsense'. Looking back at the past, from his vantage point in the later nineteenth century, he concluded that 'the struggles of mankind for many ages had produced nothing but . . . sordid, aimless, ugly confusion':

Think of it! Was it all to end in a counting-house on the top of a cinder-heap, with . . . a Whig committee dealing out champagne to the rich and margarine to the poor in such convenient proportions as would make all men contented together . . .'[13]

Unlike some of our own contemporaries who see our age as the culminating 'end of history', Morris couldn't believe that civilisation was to end in the industrialised wasteland, with all its associated human evils and injustices, that he saw everywhere around him. So the course of history had to be changed: the ideal of socialism – by which he meant 'a condition of society in which there should be neither rich nor poor' and in which equality would prevail – had to be actively pursued; and that left historians themselves with a purpose.

William Morris's idealistic politics derived, then, not least from his 'passion for the history of the past', which taught him that his own time, by comparison with that (no doubt idealised) past, left much to be desired; and other would-be reformers, too, appealed to history in other ways for their own political purposes. By the middle of the century, the negative effects of industrialisation were inspiring not only novelists such as Charles Dickens with a social conscience, but also historians including Henry Mayhew. The inspiration for both those writers becomes social reform, and they both engage in a politicised form of what we would call contemporary history. No longer interested in teaching kings how to rule morally, they nevertheless retain their political involvement and try to use their writings to practical effect, Dickens' descriptions of the social conditions of his day (well known as a part of his crusading mission for reform) being paralleled by Mayhew's graphic reports on the London poor.

Claiming to present 'the first real History of the People that has ever been attempted in any country whatsoever', and 'the first attempt to publish the history of a people, from the lips of the people themselves', Mayhew published the results of his personal researches during the 1840s and 1850s, first as essays in the *Morning Chronicle* newspaper and later in his best known compendium entitled *London Labour and the London Poor* (finally published in four volumes in 1861–2). Working self-consciously as an early 'social scientist', he deliberately derived his methodology from the physical sciences, of which he had some previous personal experience. So he describes how:

> I made up my mind to deal with human nature as a natural philosopher or a chemist deals with any material object; and . . . to apply the laws of the induct-ive philosophy for the first time, I believe, in the world to the abstract ques-tions of political economy.[14]

But that scientific approach to his material did not preclude political motivation. Indeed, his socio-political message was well served by his presentational techniques. Juxtaposing economic factors with their so-cial effects, and showing for instance how exploitative employers were effectively forcing women into prostitution, Mayhew's work has been described as akin to melodrama – not least in its successful engagement of his reader's emotions.[15] The results of his investigations are presented virtually as transcripts of his conversations – like the presentation of tape-recorded material by oral historians today; and, as often happens in such cases, the appearance of such supposed 'objectivity' only adds to their emotional effect. No less than the characters in a novel by Dickens, the characters who are enabled or encouraged to reveal themselves in Mayhew's 'real History of the People' inspire remedial action. By talking in the first person, they engage the reader's emotions, and encourage identification with their situation; and so they perform their political, as well as historical, function.

Mayhew's work provoked others to adopt similar socio-political mis-sions. Charles Kingsley effectively plundered Mayhew's articles in the *Morning Chronicle* for his novel *Alton Locke* (1850); and other journalists and parsons amplified his work in other ways. An anonymous self-styled 'River-side Visitor', for example, recorded his 'sketches of life and charac-ter in a Thames-side district' as *The Great Army of London Poor*; and that contribution to what again we might term contemporary history was (as with Mayhew) published with the avowed political aim, 'that it may be so far blessed as to become a means, however humble, of strengthening or spreading a feeling of active good-will towards the Great Army'.[16]

Similar battles were fought by historically conscious reformers in the United States. Dorothea Dix undertook to illustrate 'the history and present condition of American prisons' in her campaign for penal reform;[17] and

Robert Wiles Hunter presented vivid descriptions of his own experience (contemporary history again) in his classic work on *Poverty* (1904). At the centre of Progressive thought, Hunter was concerned to extend the vision of his contemporaries and, like his European counterparts, to offer socialist ideals as an alternative to what he saw as 'the selfish interests of capitalists and landowners'. His avowed aim was 'to show the grievous need of certain social measures calculated to prevent the ruin and degradation of those working people who are on the verge of poverty', and his method was to approach his subject as 'scientifically' as possible, by defining and analysing the problem, quantifying where practicable, and presenting the conclusions of his own empirical research. Having defined 'poverty' and calculated that at least ten million (and possibly as many as twenty million) Americans lived in destitution, he sought his readers' sympathy by such accounts as the following:

> I shall never forget a 'flop-house' which I inspected a few years ago in Chicago . . . I made a thorough search for a place to sleep, but, not being successful in finding an unoccupied spot, I decided not to remain for the night. The air made me faint and weak, and I hardly had strength to pick my way out of the room . . . The animalism and despicable foulness and filth made one almost despair of mankind.

With descriptions worthy of Mayhew, Hunter presented another politicised form of contemporary history that has been fairly described by his modern editor as 'principally intended as a call to arms'.[18]

Three years later, another American, Walter Rauschenbusch reaffirmed the political purpose of historical study in his enormously (if unexpectedly) influential book *Christianity and the Social Crisis*. As a theologian and priest who had worked in a poverty-stricken parish in New York in the depressed 1890s, Rauschenbusch came to believe in the regenerative power of a reformed Christianity: what was needed, he insisted, was a reversion to much earlier but forgotten ideals. Whereas, then, for William Morris the mediaeval grass had been greener, Rauschenbusch's model lay much further back, in the very origins of Christianity. A critical understanding of the past, he believed, would reveal that the words and deeds of Christ himself, though long obscured, were of continuing social relevance. Without such historical understanding, people would continue simply to take their own situation as natural and normal, and they would lack any vision of possible alternatives: 'Without . . . a conception of the evolution of social institutions, any larger idea of social regeneration could hardly enter into the minds of men.'[19] So once again history takes on a highly politicised purpose.

That overt socio-political role for history has been continued through the twentieth century, and again often quite explicitly, with the growth of interest in 'history from below' resulting in a succession of works devoted to the retrieval of previously unrepresented or under-represented groups. E. P. Thompson, for instance, openly aimed to consolidate a class identity in his study of *The Making of the English Working Class*; more recently feminist historians have rescued women from their previous historical 'exile'; and now a whole series of writers from various minority groups has turned the academic spotlight on those who have hitherto been in the shadows of, or totally excluded from, mainstream histories. All these have a clear political motivation: by putting those previously at the periphery (or even totally outside) into the centre, historians deliberately seek some re-alignment and re-focusing, and seek to answer William Morris's implied question of whether we should permit history to culminate in a perception of 'inconsequent nonsense'.

History, then, though greatly changed from Francis Bacon's time, continues to be full of 'political precepts and counsels', and in many cases has become explicitly politicised. These continuing (and arguably inevitable) political connotations of historical study ensure – as we shall now go on to see – that new political agendas in turn require new histories.

New politics, new history

Blair offers Adams choice of history. – The Times, 12 December 1997

Postmodernism came of age in England when the Prime Minister established his intellectual credentials by offering nothing less than a *choice* of history to the Irish negotiator Gerry Adams. To some that may have sounded like the concept of 'consumer choice' being carried to some surreal ultimate, and to others it must have sounded like a hubristic repudiation of academic values. (Was Tony Blair god[20], to be in a position to offer a choice of historical truth?) But it was only an explicit recognition of what politicians have always known (if not publicly admitted), that, just as individuals sometimes need to construct new narratives of their past in order to validate a newly projected self-image in the present[21], so, on a public level, new politics requires new history.

Enoch Powell once suggested that 'the greatest task of the statesman . . . is to offer his people good myths'[22]; and he could have cited many examples of such political generosity. Pericles in the fifth century BC mixed history with myth and propaganda in the idealised account of Athenian culture with which he aimed to inspire his fellow citizens in their war against the Spartans. In Anglo-Saxon times, a mythical English past was deliberately designed by King Alfred, to justify his own position and provide the foundation for a unified identity for his newly conquered territories.[23] Shakespeare's representation of Henry V on the eve of the battle of Agincourt has assumed the dimensions of a myth, to be utilised for patriotic purposes whenever the English are thought to be in need of a further injection of nationalism. And in a not dissimilar way, thirteenth-century crusading Teutonic Knights provided mythical inspiration and underpinning for twentieth-century German militarism. Whether Enoch Powell would have described such myths as 'good' is another matter, but they would all qualify as providing an effective past for present political purposes.

And it was for that sort of provision that Tony Blair was searching in December 1997. Whether 'myth' or 'history', a new past was needed for a new politics. On the day before his preferred choice, he had had an 'historic' meeting with Gerry Adams, in their ongoing negotiations to secure peace in Northern Ireland; and Blair's point was, then, that Adams did have a choice. That choice involved not only the future, but also and necessarily the past, since any future depended on the past, grew out of the past; or rather it would derive from historical interpretations of that past. So either Gerry Adams could continue to accept the conventional historical narrative of confrontation, a history of 'violence and despair'; or he could break out of that seemingly inexorable cycle, revise his perceptions of what had gone before, and his response to it – and make a fresh start. And that latter route, with its alternative historical narrative, could, it was suggested, lead to 'peace and progress'.

In other words, Gerry Adams's ability to choose a political future derived from his freedom to choose a political past. He did actually have a chance to review the historical record, to re-assess conventional narratives of what had happened, and to put a different spin on it all. He could replace his previously negative perceptions with alternatives that might provide the basis for something more constructive. Was the future to consist of continuing conflict, or compromise and peace? If the latter, then the new politics would require the choice of a new history.

A similar requirement has been noted in relation to the history taught in schools. Supposedly riddled with guilt about Britain's imperial past, and about history's previous male orientation, many 'extremely left-wing' teachers, according to a reporter in the *Daily Mail*, 'want to smash this country's past, and that is what they are doing'. An example was cited in the headline: 'Winnie, you're history'. It introduced a patriotic lament, highlighted by pictures of a cigar-smoking, V-signing Winston Churchill, a spear-bearing but rather willowy Boadicea and a smugly determined Henry VIII. The journalese vernacular on this occasion paradoxically concealed the real cause of concern: that new proposals actually entailed 'Winnie's' (and his companions') removal from history, or at least from the history of the national curriculum. It was the turn of such 'landmark figures in British history' to 'face the [very] axe' that they had all so heroically wielded against their enemies. They were to be consigned (using the word in another sense) to history.

Their historical demise, through this truncation of history, derived from new political emphases; or so it was alleged. These were explained by Chris McGovern, director of the History Curriculum Association: the deprivation of their natural historical 'birthright' was intended to undermine children's sense of British identity, and so facilitate their submergence into a European super-state; for 'If you want to see the United Kingdom as part of a federal European state, then history gets in the way.'[24] Or at least it has to be revised and renewed in such a way as to indicate that Britain is not after all an isolated entity.

One attempt has already been made to produce a new history of Europe in the light of new European politics: simultaneously published in eight languages, it aimed to produce a history 'seen in overall European as opposed to national perspective'. Strangely denying on the one hand that there can be any such thing as 'committed history', while conceding on the other hand that in the attempt to justify a united Europe 'what we have produced is inevitably political', the work was not a great success.[25] But it clarified once again our main point here that new politics requires new history, and in a constantly evolving political situation it's impossible not to be bothered with the past and its representation.

It is not, of course, only in Britain or Europe that history is adjusted to take account of changing political situations: Japan's past too (or part of it) was reported as being deliberately smashed in 1999. In a newly opened war museum, officials tactfully refrained from making any mention of what, to the west, was the defining moment of recent Japanese military history – the attack on Pearl Harbor in 1941; nor was any reference made to the well-documented atrocities committed by Japanese soldiers in the Second World War (an account of which had already been removed from school textbooks by order of the Japanese Ministry of Education, in 1989[26]). In these cases, too, the 'smashing' of, or excising from, the national past has been the subject of controversy and criticism. '"It's yet another whitewashing of history", said Shigenori Nishikawa [as reported in another newspaper] who is leading a campaign to make the museum face the facts.'[27] But it is, perhaps, more like yet another illustration of how 'the facts' can be suppressed, hidden and manipulated, and how history can be washed in white or any colour at all, as politics require.

Nearly four hundred years ago, Francis Bacon recommended to his king that histories might emphasise past political upheavals, in order to show by contrast the 'future Stability' under James I himself and his successors. In the late eighteenth century a new German nationalism was perceived by Johann Gottfried Herder to require a new historical underpinning, and in 1821 the *Monumenta Germaniae Historica* was set up as a national resource which would (and does) bring together all the various records of Germany's past to consolidate a sense of national identity.[28] Currently, history continues to be written and re-written for similar political purposes. India's anti-British 'mutinies' are recognised as 'wars of independence'; statues of Stalin are unceremoniously removed from previously communist states; street names in South African towns are changed, in order further to eradicate the still surviving traces of Englishness and apartheid (still, in 1999, respectively represented by such names as Smith and Broad, Malan and Verwoerd).[29] New political presents require new pasts and new histories – or, as we shall go on to see, no histories at all.

New politics, no history

The struggle of man against power is the struggle of memory against forgetting.
Milan Kundera[30]

When the Roman emperor Domitian died on 18 September AD 96, the Senators sent for ladders, and 'had his images and the votive shields engraved with his likeness brought smashing down; and ended by decreeing that all inscriptions referring to him must be effaced, and all records of his reign obliterated'.[31] The so-called *Damnatio Memoriae* (condemnation of memory) was a standard measure used against those considered traitors: it implied that the condemned person's name could not be used, and that all physical traces in inscriptions or written records would be removed; such people in short were to be officially eliminated from memory and from history.

Kundera in the quotation above refers to a modern equivalent. His observation comes after a description in one of his books of how a previously powerful Czech politician, later executed, had been 'air-brushed out of history'. Only his hat survived in the historical record: having lent it to a colleague, it could be seen, on someone else's head, in the photograph of a group of dignitaries of which he had been a member. His own image had been deliberately erased: he was destined not to be remembered; he would be forgotten, and so powerless. Under the new political dispensation, his history was superfluous to requirements, and so had to be rendered non-existent.

Removing an unwanted past – eliminating history – in this way is a well-tried formula for revolutionaries in many fields. In the early-modern intellectual revolution, the new philosophers were often concerned, in their efforts to establish their own credibility, to distance themselves from any predecessors and from any past. Francis Bacon claimed to be presenting something 'quite new, totally new', in his ambitious attempt to 'commence a total reconstruction of sciences, arts, and all human knowledge';[32] and his rhetoric proved sufficiently persuasive to provoke

Goethe's complaint some hundred years later that he had dared 'to wipe out, as if with a sponge, everything that had been inscribed upon the tables of mankind'.[33] Descartes, similarly, became so depressed by his review of earlier philosophies that he came to believe in the need for a completely fresh start: 'Regarding the opinions to which I had hitherto given credence, I thought that I could not do better than undertake to get rid of them, all at one go, in order to replace them afterwards with better ones.'[34] Other luminaries of the time, such as Galileo, Hobbes and Boyle, took care to emphasise their liberation from the past, and to assert their total repudiation of what had gone before: the pristine image of their own theories (whether in physics, political philosophy or chemistry) was not to be tarnished or contaminated by any contact with the past. They were, as one critical commentator at the time put it, 'fiercely set to disgrace and cry down whatsoever former ages have most esteemed and reverenced'.[35]

In the visual arts, similarly, novelty is often emphasised at the expense of any historical tradition. The self-styled 'Futurists', in the early twentieth century, set about removing the dull old past in order to make way for their wonderful, vibrant future. 'We want no part of it, the past', their manifesto proclaimed; 'we are the young and strong *Futurists*! So let them come, the gay incendiaries . . . Set fire to the library shelves! . . . flood the museums! . . . Take up your pickaxes, your axes and hammers, and wreck . . . !'[36]

Arson and destruction are common components of political revolutions too, and so is the attempted elimination of the past. One commentator on the French Revolution noted that France's history had been effectively guillotined, so that the sovereign people would be 'uncontrolled by the past': after 1789, 'it was no longer France, but some unknown country to which the nation was transported'.[37] In China similarly, at the time of the Cultural Revolution in the late 1960s, the mission of the Red Guards was announced as being 'to rid the country of the "Four Olds" – old culture, old customs, old habits and old ways of thinking'. Many street names were changed to suit the new dispensation, books were burnt, historic temples and antiquities deliberately smashed. Nien Cheng, who wrote an account of that time and of her own six and a half years imprisonment, recorded how the Red Guards, in their frenzied determination 'to destroy the old culture', trashed her house and stamped on her exquisite seventeenth-century porcelain figures. Any vestiges of the past had to 'be swept away onto the rubbish heap of history'.[38]

Parts of that rubbish heap, however, may prove convenient for sub- sequent recycling, so that even revolutionaries can sometimes be selective about their disposals. The immediate past may be jettisoned, simply in order to re-write a narrative from some earlier historical point, as if the intervening years had not existed. So the Red Guards denounced one Chinese man for having worked for a foreign imperialist company that had been guilty of aggression against the country over a hundred years earlier. The prosecutor, notes Nien Cheng, 'was talking about the opium war of 1845 as if it had taken place only the year before'; and other accused people 'were judged not by their own deeds but by the acreage of land once possessed by their ancestors'.[39] Such manipulation of chrono- logy is a well-used political tool: the Jews return to their ancient homeland of Palestine, the Germans to their pre-Nazi past, and the Poles to their pre-Communist traditions. For all of them, the intervening years are to be seen as an unfortunate break in a much longer history. The Swiss historian, Walter Hofer, wrote in 1954 of the need for Germans to rehab- ilitate those pre-war writers, who had 'warned that the wrong path had been taken'. They had been temporarily 'forced aside by the main stream of development', but should now be re-adopted in the attempt 'to direct the German spirit back to its true historic mission'.[40] Similarly, proposing new directions for his liberated country in 1991, the Polish Prime Minis- ter suggested that 'Poland's communist past is but a 40-year aberration in a history that stretches over a thousand years . . . a short-lived, insane experiment'.[41] Other insane experiments, from Nazism to Little Red Books, have similarly come to be seen as temporary 'aberrations'; and mobility towards a preferable future can often be improved by jettisoning the weight of any constraining traditions that shackle people to the immedi- ate past. That immediate past has to be removed from history.

The most notorious late twentieth-century example of this is some historians' denial of the holocaust. That negation raises with particular force our central question of why we should bother with history – bother in this case both with the past itself and with its representation (or not).

We have already noticed (in chapter 3) that on a personal level we all have aspects of our pasts that we might prefer to forget – especially those aspects that give us cause to feel such uncomfortable emotions as guilt or remorse which, in the manner of the ancient Greek Erinyes, pursue us and prevent us from getting on with our lives until expiation is extracted. On a public level too, it can be seen that it might be preferable to have the past forgotten, and holocaust-denying historians presumably have some such motivations for denying a part of the past which has often been described as the defining event of the century. Just as it would have been better for Elektra to come to terms with the (for her) defining event of her father's murder, and to forget it in the sense of emotionally 'getting over' it, so (it has been argued) it is better for the future health of Germany to erase the trauma of the holocaust from memory and history.[42]

The problem of holocaust denial is exacerbated by claims that such denial has been facilitated (if not actually entailed) by postmodern theorising. In particular, it has been alleged that, if 'history' is relegated to being solely 'textual' (a 'discourse' that lacks any necessary referent), any 'actuality' may become so elusive as to escape, not only historical representation, but any attribution of 'reality' at all. In other words, if historical representation is nothing more than a linguistic enterprise (a matter of making an aesthetically pleasing composition of words, like any other literary work), then it becomes easier to say that something in the past didn't 'really' happen.

Since therefore I have advocated in some cases a 'forgetting' of a past that enables one to get on with life in the present, and since I believe that historical reconstructions are indeed 'literary', I need (without adding further to what is already a massive literature on the subject) to clarify that my recommended 'forgetting' does not by any means constitute a *denial*, but rather a coming-to-terms, which enables assimilation of the past and thence further development. And likewise the literary nature of historical representations does not (to my mind) by any means entail a denial that something actually happened in the past – that some events took place.

So (to repeat the obvious) the holocaust remains as a well-documented event to which numerous survivors have borne personal and moving witness. Its representation is inevitably problematic, if not actually impossible. But that is not to say that we don't need to be bothered with it – it as the past event itself, or it as (inevitably inadequate) historical description. So here we just need to note that it has become another example of a new political situation leading to a denial of past history, or to its diminution by relativisation and comparison (in this case treating the holocaust as but one example of many similarly horrific episodes).

Indeed, even where history is not entirely erased for political purposes, its content can be effectively rendered into what is non-history. By that, I don't just mean that historical accounts can be deliberately replaced with lies, but that history can be made to seem so anodyne and unimportant that it's not worth bothering about anyway. That danger has become more pressing since the prescient Nietzsche noticed it over a hundred years ago. In words that must resonate for many later readers, he wrote of how the past is *tamed* – reduced to easily digestible morsels, for quick and easy consumption, and providing instant gratification and entertainment. Thus, for example, 'The war is not even over before it is transformed into a hundred thousand printed pages, and set before the tired palates of the history-hungry as the latest delicacy.' An 'instant' historian of that kind, concerned 'to adapt the past to contemporary triviality . . . spins his web over the past and subdues it'.[43]

That is one danger of comparisons, which somehow 'normalise'; and another such web-spinning spider was the subject of newspaper reports in May 1999. A Lithuanian entrepreneur, in his attempts to capitalise on communism's collapse, was succeeding incidentally in trivialising the not long distant past. He was said to be collecting all the discarded statues he could find of Marx, Lenin and Stalin, and planning – in defiance of the local population who had suffered deportations and other horrors under the Russian occupation – to open a museum and theme park. Amongst other attractions, visitors would be able to sit in a train and enjoy a 'deportation experience'. Such instant taming of the past as a delicacy for 'the tired palates of the history-hungry' is in danger of being no less a negation and destruction of history than was the airbrushing perpetrated by Kundera's revisionist.

The projected destruction of the past in one way or another seems, by the end of the twentieth century, to be increasingly practicable, and more than ever possible of attainment. It's not only that 'picks and shovels' have been superseded by far more efficient means of destruction, but that the fabric of history itself – by which I mean here the *presentation* of the past – is often becoming less 'material'. Electronic means of presenting and preserving information make the instant *destruction* of that information infinitely easier.

To give but one example, it has been noted that the histories of great corporations – those powerful, multi-national companies of which we hear so much – are now routinely published on web sites. And the material on those web sites can be instantly, and irrevocably, removed at the stroke of a delete button. 'Executives who resign, products that flop, strategies that are later reversed, reorganisations that turn out to be a mess – all can be wiped out.' Personnel can have their records instantly adjusted, to suit their changing circumstances; and that includes the possibility of their total erasure where that seems convenient. And once removed, such records, or even whole archives, become irretrievable. 'Companies can now, in effect, rewrite their corporate histories' – or eliminate them (or parts of them) at a whim.[44] The implications for the wider, political stage are obvious: airbrushing a photograph, or removing a statue, are the primitive equivalents of picks and shovels.

Secret histories and subversion

To tell the whole unvarnished truth.[45]

The historical record has sometimes consisted of more than officialdom would have wished, for since classical antiquity it has included a whole alternative tradition of what has been described as 'secret history'. Public figures today may resent so-called intrusions into their personal lives and the exposure of their foibles, but not even Roman emperors were immune to such treatment. Suetonius, as the second-century biographer of the first twelve Caesars, set out, like some investigative journalist today, to describe his subjects 'warts and all'; and the Greek historian Procopius later (*c.* AD 550) provided an influential model, with his *Anecdota* or *Secret History* (which supplemented his more conventional account of the wars of Justinian) for those minded like him (in his editor's words) 'to tell the whole unvarnished truth' – or at least a truth that had not been officially and artificially glossed.

Suetonius himself, having been in public service until his dismissal, could claim with some justification to have first-hand knowledge of at least some of his subjects; and he certainly succeeded in revealing some of their less savoury characteristics. He showed Nero, for example, as an incestuous megalomaniac: he described the young emperor as murdering indiscriminately for his own material gain, and as living a life of debauchery, taking his own mother as his lover before having her bludgeoned to death. Domitian similarly is shown as having had his 'cruel streak', witnessed allegedly by the historian himself: 'As a boy, I remember attending a crowded Court where [he] had a ninety-year-old man stripped to establish whether or not he had been circumcised.' Like Nero, too, Domitian eliminated any enemies, and put 'many senators to death on the most trivial charges'.[46]

That scandalous behaviour of Roman emperors was, then, deliberately made public by Suetonius, and for that very reason he was later held up as a positive model for historians. When a tradition of 'secret histories' really took off in early modern England, Suetonius was explicitly applauded as a model by John Phillips, one of the nephews of the revolutionary poet John Milton. The Roman historian, explains Phillips, 'made Publick to the World, the Vices and Miscarriages of the Twelve Caesars, with the same freedom with which they were by them Committed'; and through revealing that other side of political leaders' characters, he had provoked a proper scepticism about official, more sanitised historical records. In his own accounts of the later seventeenth century, Phillips himself was determined to apply that same method to his treatment of contemporary royalty – the reigns of Charles II and James II; so, like Suetonius, he set about revealing the devious plots and sexual misdemeanors in which his subjects had been involved.

John Phillips was but one sceptical critic engaged in exposing another, darker side of political life at that time. In a fascinating recent work (from which the quotation in the previous paragraph is taken[47]), Annabel Patterson has revealed a whole alternative tradition of historical writing, which she sees as one of the essential building-blocks of modern liberalism. Our own belief in the essential equality of human beings, and of their equal individual rights to education, speech, the law and the validity of their own consciences, did not simply arise by chance. It emerged in the context of an essentially authoritarian government, and so it had to be positively fought for. And an important weapon in the struggle to foster such ideas was a written record of past dissent. Then as now, such records could provide encouragement, by giving examples from the past: at moments of crisis and decision, it is consoling to think that we are a part of an ongoing tradition. We need not then feel utterly alone.

Such consolation and confirmation was provided not least in the context of early-modern treason trials, where unofficial transcripts were surreptitiously published and came to constitute a recognised canon of dissent. In such cases the government, by definition, was reacting to some perceived challenge to its own authority, and individuals were arraigned against the whole power of the state in an inevitably unequal struggle. Defendants were often held, like the victims in some Kafka novel, without any specific charges laid against them, and without any chance of gaining legal help; and when cases did come to court, the proceedings could easily be tilted in favour of the prosecution.

After the restoration of the monarchy in 1660, for example, Sir Henry Vane was charged with treason, and accused of having made war against the king. Having played an important part in the impeachment (and consequent execution) of Charles I's minister Thomas Wentworth, he assumed that the king in question was Charles I, and he prepared his defence accordingly. But then to his amazement, he learnt at his actual trial, at the very last minute, that the charge against him was intended to relate to Charles II, who had just been restored to the throne. All his legal preparations and arguments were rendered utterly irrelevant.

The dice were loaded in other ways too, for jurors at treason trials could often be pressurised by the powers that be. When Sir Nicholas Throckmorton successfully defended himself at his trial in 1553, the members of the acquitting jury were themselves summoned to appear before the judges of Star Chamber. Some were easily persuaded to confess the error of their ways, and to reverse their original verdict. But the more resolute continued to resist official pressures, so themselves suffered imprisonment and heavy fines.

As Annabel Patterson has shown, the 'secret histories', or illicitly published records of such events, became key documents in the development of a liberal tradition that opposed government authoritarianism. That tradition emphasised the need for individual independence and for resolute resistance to the pressures of authority; and its strength, again, was enhanced by the use of historical examples, and by keeping alive the memory of those who had previously suffered. A century after the Throckmorton case, the jurors who held out against authority were cited as models by the Leveller William Walwyn: they had, he recalled with approval, 'valued their consciences above their lives'.

Keeping alive the record of such people became, then, a politically motivated activity: 'alternative' historians worked self-consciously for what they believed would be a better society – a society in which ordinary people would be properly informed and so able to act in ways that they thought were appropriate (rather than simply following orders). Alternative or secret histories furnished ordinary people with information that was useful in at least two ways. First, by giving a fuller picture of those in authority, it enabled them to see their supposed 'superiors' as fallible human beings – not as divinities or divinely authorised, but as people rather like themselves. Second, by showing alternative options taken by a few in the past, it enabled them to make more informed choices and decisions about how to act in the present. It's not surprising that it is to this subversive tradition that the New England historian John Wingate Thornton drew his readers' attention in 1860 when considering historical roots for American nationalism.[48]

Such politically inspired histories might seem to stand in stark contrast to conventional academic history even today, yet much history in the twentieth century has been written with the professed motivation of giving a voice to the hitherto voiceless and at least applying to the whole a different coat of varnish. 'Ordinary' people, women, racial minorities, the previously colonised and the prematurely killed – all these have, to a greater or lesser extent, had their voices restored to them in a multi-vocal cacophony or harmony of postcolonial, feminist, postmodernist historiography. Nevertheless (as I shall argue in my concluding chapters), much history continues to be, however unconsciously, highly conformist and conservative.

Conclusion

History is . . . never history, but history-for. – Claude Lévi-Srauss[49]

Writing in the 1960s, Claude Lévi-Strauss's point is now widely accepted: that there cannot ever be such thing as a simple, true, factual, unbiased, purposeless history of the sort envisaged by Lucian, Leopold von Ranke, Lord Acton and a few of their surviving followers; but that history must always be written from, and therefore *for*, some or other point of view. History, in short, is inevitably in some sense political.

The inevitability of its partiality in one sense derives from its inevitable partiality in another. As Lévi-Strauss went on to argue in *The Savage Mind*, history cannot possibly embrace the whole of the past, the totality of what happened: 'a truly total history would confront them [historians] with chaos'. So it's necessary for them to 'choose, sever, and carve . . . up' the past in such a way as to make it coherent and manageable, and that means leaving some things out. Even statistics, it has been noted, *'especially* statistics, are concepts saturated with politics, classifying what is visible and what counts' (what is to be included and what left out).[50] History thus 'inevitably remains partial – that is, incomplete'; and that in turn results in partiality in the other sense of being 'biased'.[51]

The only question then is as to the *nature* of our bias, the standpoint from which we make our selections and impose our coherence on the potential chaos. We have to have some reason for acting as we do; we have to have some rationale, some motivation, and therefore some agenda. We must always have something in mind when we write our histories: our histories are always written *for* some purpose, and in that sense are always, and inevitably, 'political'.

In personal terms, as we have seen, we compose our histories to underwrite the identities with which we wish, or need, to be associated. Forgetting things that don't fit in, we dissociate ourselves from those aspects of our past which no longer seem consistent with our present selves and future aspirations for ourselves. Our memories from the past are monitored, filtered, selected and de-selected for our present purposes; and so our identities are constructed and confirmed on the foundations of a history-*for* us as we want to be.

And similarly with more public histories. We shall see in the next chapter how religions have sought confirmation of their validity through the acquisition and promulgation of appropriate historical foundations. Those histories have been borrowed, or retrieved, or composed, *for* the sake of an agenda, just as have more overtly political histories provided the bases for nations and their national identities. We don't celebrate Christmas, or Thanksgiving, or Bastille-Day, for nothing; nor is it for nothing that Irish Protestants continue to insist on joining Orange Order marches, and that the celebrations of Britain's Empire Day have long been discontinued. These aspects of our history are never 'value-free': they have a purpose, and are inevitably (whether in their maintenance or in their repudiation and forgetting) political.

That is why Samuel Gott, writing amidst the political upheavals of mid-seventeenth-century England, reminded historians of their need for 'foresight': 'the sensible historian does not content himself with a mere recital of things; he rather considers how history may be of present use'.[52] The only qualification needed to that advice, is that we can now see that any 'mere recital of things' is actually impossible; and that makes it even more imperative to consider 'how history may be of present use' – or to consider, again, why we are bothering with it at all.

To deny that need, finally, itself constitutes a 'political' position. Historians who persist in arguing that, in their professional lives at least, they should take no thought for the morrow, seem by implication to be expressing their satisfaction with what they have today: they want the future to resemble the present, which indicates, not that they do not have a vision for the future, but that they think things will be just fine if they go on as they are. Professing impartiality in this case means professing partiality for what now is: in political terms, no change is needed or desirable; the best prospect for the future is more of the same. Such conservatism may sound an unlikely ideal in the present condition of the world, but that is not the point: the point is that, whatever approach historians adopt, even where that is a refusal self-consciously to adopt any approach, it must inevitably have political connotations. Political motivations of one sort or another lurk behind our reasons for bothering with some things and ignoring others, and that applies to the past as

much as anything. History and politics and power constitute an indis-
soluble trinity, or three-in-one.

Notes

1 Daniel Heinsius, *The Value of History*, transl. G. W. Robinson, Cambridge, Mass., privately printed, 1943, p. 14.
2 Friedrich Nietzsche, *Untimely Meditations*, transl. R. J. Hollingdale, Cambridge, Cambridge University Press, 1983, p. 77.
3 Francis Bacon, *Of the Advancement and Proficience of Learning*, Oxford, Robert Young and Edward Forrest, 1640, p. 100.
4 E. A. Freeman, *The Office of the Historical Professor*, London, Macmillan, 1884, p. 13. *The Oxford Dictionary of Quotations'* attribution to Seeley is from a work dated 1895.
5 Polybius, quoted in A. J. Toynbee, *Greek Historical Thought*, London, J. M. Dent, 1924, p. 23.
6 Robert Lacey, *Sir Walter Ralegh*, London, Weidenfeld & Nicolson, 1973, p. 326. Lacey confirms: '*The History of the World* came to be the backbone of anti-authoritarian thought through the years leading up to and following the Civil War, for it provided the average member of the English gentry with the context in which his revolt against the king could be justified, and it held the positive proof that the Protestant God was on his side' (p. 325).
7 Sir Walter Raleigh, *The History of the World*, London, W. Burre, 1614, Preface.
8 Raleigh, *History*, Peroration, quoted by Lacey, *Ralegh*, pp. 328–9.
9 Denys Hay, *Annalists and Historians: Western Historiography from the Eighth to the Eighteenth Centuries*, London, Methuen, 1977, p. 151.
10 George Buchanan, *The History of Scotland*, London, A. Churchil, 1690, p. 184, and 'To the Reader'.
11 Quoted by Hugh Trevor-Roper, *Queen Elizabeth's First Historian. William Camden and the Beginnings of English 'Civil History'*, London, Jonathan Cape, 1971, p. 13. I am indebted to Trevor-Roper's work for this section, including the following quotations, from pp. 16, 18.
12 William Morris, 'The Lesser Arts', in Asa Briggs (ed.), *William Morris: Selected Writings and Designs*, Harmondsworth, Penguin, 1962, p. 87.
13 William Morris, 'How I became a Socialist', in *Justice*, 16 June 1894, reprinted in Christopher Harvie *et al.* (eds), *Industrialisation and Culture, 1830–1914*, London, Macmillan, 1970, pp. 191–5. For a selection of Morris's historical writings, see Nicholas Salmon (ed.), *William Morris on History*, Sheffield, Sheffield Academic Press, 1996.
14 Quotations from Christina Crosby, *The Ends of History*, London, Routledge, 1991, pp. 97, 100, and from John L. Bradley (ed.), *Selections from London Labour and the London Poor*, London, Oxford University Press, 1965, p. xxxiv.
15 See Crosby, *Ends*, ch. 3.
16 Anon, *The Great Army of London Poor*, London, Charles H. Kelly, n.d., p. vi.
17 Dorothea Lynde Dix, *Remarks on Prisons and Prison Discipline in the United States* (2nd edn 1845), ed. Leonard D. Savitz, Montclair, New Jersey, Patterson Smith, 1967, p. 5. My thanks to Alun Munslow for referring me to this and the following two works.

18 Robert Wiles Hunter, *Poverty* (1904), ed. Peter d'A. Jones, New York, Harper & Row, 1965, pp. 333, xxviii, 117, 119, xxii.

19 Walter Rauschenbusch, *Christianity and the Social Crisis* (1907), ed. Robert D. Cross, New York, Harper & Row, 1964, p. 195.

20 Since writing this, the identification has been made: see Press reports, *c.* 25 October 1999.

21 Those narratives may, of course, be mythological: for the fabrication of bogus genealogies 'to dignify family lines with spurious longevity', see Adam Fox, 'Remembering the Past in Early Modern England: Oral and Written Tradition', *Transactions of the Royal Historical Society*, Sixth Series, 9, 1999, p. 243. And more generally see Eric Hobsbawm & Terry Ranger (eds), *The Invention of Tradition*, Cambridge, Cambridge University Press, 1983.

22 Quoted by Frank Füredi, *Mythical Past, Elusive Future*, London, Pluto, 1992, p. 103.

23 See Sarah Foot, 'Remembering, Forgetting and Inventing: Attitudes to the Past in England at the End of the First Viking Age', *Transactions of the Royal Historical Society*, Sixth Series, 9 1999, pp. 185–200. Cf. Norman Davies's allegations of historians' politically motivated construction of 'Britain' in *The Isles: A History* (1999), reviewed *London Review of Books*, 6 January 2000.

24 For the report, see *Daily Mail*, 29 March 1999, p. 17, where it is conceded that the criticised proposals are contained in a draft produced for consultation by the Qualification and Curriculum Authority.

25 Jean-Baptiste Duroselle, *Europe: A History of its Peoples*, transl. Richard Mayne, London, Penguin, 1990, pp. 21, 411. For an impressive attempt to provide a new one-volume history of Europe, see Norman Davies, *Europe: A History*, London, Pimlico, 1997.

26 Cited by Füredi, *Mythical Past*, p. 3.

27 *The Daily Telegraph*, 1 April 1999, p. 24.

28 See Michael Bentley, *Modern Historiography: An Introduction*, London, Routledge, 1999, p. 19.

29 See report in *The Daily Telegraph*, 31 March 1999.

30 Milan Kundera, *The Book of Laughter and Forgetting*, London, Faber & Faber, 1983, p. 3.

31 Suetonius, *The Twelve Caesars*, transl. Robert Graves, Harmondsworth, Penguin, 1957, p. 309. Christian authorities maintained a similar tradition: the Synod of Reisbach in AD 798 decreed of an excommunicated man, that 'after his death let nothing be written in his memory'. See Jacques Le Goff, *History and Memory*, New York, Columbia University Press, 1992, p. 73.

32 Francis Bacon, *The New Organon* (1620), ed. F. H. Anderson, Indianapolis, Bobbs-Merrill, 1960, Proem, Epistle Dedicatory.

33 Goethe, quoted by Erich Heller, *The Disinherited Mind*, Harmondsworth, Penguin, 1961, p. 24. Cf. Goethe's poem 'On Originality', against the claims of those who would deny historical influence: 'Somebody says: "Of no school I am part,/Never to living master lost my heart;/Nor any more can I be said/To have learned anything from the dead."/That statement – subject to appeal – /Means: "I'm a self-made imbecile".' Stephen Spender (ed.), *Great Writings of Goethe*, New York, Mentor, 1958, p. 45.

34 Descartes, *Discourse on the Method* (1637); in *The Philosophical Writings*, transl. John Cottingham, Robert Stoothoff and Dugald Murdoch, 2 vols; Cambridge, Cambridge University Press, 1985, I.117.

35 Méric Casaubon, *To J.S. (the Author of Sure-Footing) his Letter, lately Published . . .*, London, Timothy Garthwait, 1665, p. 22.

36 Emilio Filippo Tommaso Marinetti, 'The Founding and Manifesto of Futurism' (1909), reprinted in Lawrence Cahoone (ed.), *From Modernism to Postmodernism: An Anthology*, Oxford, Blackwell, 1996, p. 189.

37 Quoted by Füredi, *Mythical Past*, p. 71.

38 Nien Cheng, *Life and Death in Shanghai*, London, Flamingo, 1995, pp. 56, 68, 89.

39 *Shanghai*, pp. 13, 116.

40 Quoted by R. V. Sampson, *Progress in the Age of Reason*, London, Heinemann, 1956, p. 160.

41 Quoted by Füredi, *Mythical Past*, p. 201. The same ploy can be used at the micro-political level. Erich Heller recorded how a conservative Master of a Cambridge College responded to a young Fellow's claim to be following, in his apparently innovatory proposal, a three-hundred year old precedent, with the question: 'But wouldn't you agree that the last three hundred years have been . . . rather exceptional?' *The Artist's Journey into the Interior*, London, Secker & Warburg, 1966, p. 3.

42 On holocaust denial, see esp. Deborah E. Lipstadt, *Denying the Holocaust: The Growing Assault on Truth and Memory*, Harmondsworth, Penguin, 1994; and on the highly problematic and controversial nature of the subject, including the holocaust's belated historical 'discovery' (in 1967), subsequent 'sacralisation', and associated political ramifications, see Peter Novick, *The Holocaust in American Life* (published in 1999, too late for further consideration here).

43 Nietzsche, *Untimely Meditations*, pp. 83, 91–2.

44 Louise Kehoe, report in *Financial Times*, 19 May 1999.

45 Procopius's editor (1935), quoted by Annabel Patterson, *Early Modern Liberalism*, Cambridge, Cambridge University Press, 1997, p. 156 – a fascinating work to which I am particularly indebted for this section on secret histories.

46 Suetonius, *The Twelve Caesars*, transl. Robert Graves, Harmondsworth, Penguin, 1957, pp. 210f; 301–4.

47 John Phillips, quoted by Patterson, *Liberalism*, p. 194.

48 See Patterson, *Liberalism*, pp. 11–12.

49 Claude Lévi-Strauss, *The Savage Mind*, London, Weidenfeld & Nicolson, 1966, p. 257.

50 Crosby, *Ends*, p. 151.

51 Lévi-Strauss, *Savage Mind*, pp. 257–8.

52 Samuel Gott, *Nova Solyma, the Ideal City: or, Jerusalem Regained*, London, John Legat, 1648, p. 252.

5

History and religion

Introduction

It's not only the disposition of material (political) forces that needs historical justification: that of spiritual (religious) forces too needs rational (historical) underpinning and support. Theologians, no less than politicians, have always *used* history to provide foundations for their own beliefs – in order, that is, to validate their own intellectual and emotional constructions. They have had their own reasons for bothering with history (and sometimes, using the word slightly differently, for being bothered by it).

Religion's need for history has been recognised from the earliest times, or at least from the time when humans started to ask fundamental questions about who they are, and how on earth they've ended up where and how they are. For answers to such questions must lie in the past: starting from some original creation, we've either simply stayed the same, or declined or progressed to what we are today; and in any case, we need some historical narrative to provide an explanation of what's happened.

Recognising that need, one of the earliest Greek poets, Hesiod, resorts to an historical explanation in his attempt to account for the deplorable state in which people of his own time found themselves – needing to work for their living, and constantly falling sick, and going to yet another war. The world, he concludes, started off well enough, but thereafter, throughout the course of history, there has been a continual decline. From an original Golden Age, a steady deterioration, through ages of silver and metals of steadily decreasing value, have led to the iron present. A historical narrative thus serves, for Hesiod and early religious thinkers, to answer the fundamental question of how we have come to be like we are.

And in a Christian context, too, history is soon summoned to account for humans' present predicament. In particular their current sinfulness and imperfection have to be reconciled with a belief in the whole world's original creation by a perfect, loving God; for on the face of it, there seems to be a contradiction there – an inconsistency in the theological story. The problem is resolved through an historical account of what has happened: the bible describes, not only the creation, but also what subsequently happened – how the originally innocent delights of the Garden of Eden were forfeited through our own fault. A reasonable explanation for our sad condition is found in our past history, and that history incorporates (as histories do) a moral tale – in this case of how disobedience is punished.

Another historical narrative was required for the theological purpose of validating Christianity itself. Jesus Christ, it had to be shown, was not some upstart who suddenly appeared in the present: his arrival had long been foretold and prepared for in the past, with his coming prophesied in much earlier writings. An established historical tradition, that is, served immediately to confirm his authority. And that Old Testament tradition was then continued in the writing of the gospels, which provided, not only an historical record, but also a legitimation for the then new religion.

The historical record in the scriptures of the New Testament, however, became the subject of as much contention as any other form of history – which is one point at which theologians became particularly concerned with the subject. Following the Protestant Reformation, especially, the validity of biblical history was endlessly debated, with Protestants putting their reliance on the scriptures alone to link them with their Christianity's beginnings; while Catholics, on the other hand, substituted oral tradition as an alternative form of historical justification for their faith. Either way, the debates of that time provide a clear illustration of how history has been used by religion – of why theologians were much concerned with (and sometimes by) history – and we'll consider this further below (pp. 102f.).

First, though, it's worth noting that history itself has sometimes virtually taken on the role of a religion. The quest for truth has often been seen as common to both subjects: in that respect both can be seen as aspiring to the same goal; and even in a secular age there is a quasi-religious aspect of history, which will be the subject of the following section.

And our central section will be concerned with two main ways in which religious belief has been manifested in much historical writing – first in the representation of supposedly miraculous events, and second in the assumption of an over-riding providence and moral order. Religion in these cases has been actually *in* history; or, to look at it another way, religion (and I refer here mainly, though not exclusively to Christianity) has again *used* history to confirm some of its most central tenets.

History as religion

However one conceives divinity, he will look for it in history. – Meinecke

The eminent German historian Friedrich Meinecke (1862–1954) noted how his predecessor and mentor, Leopold von Ranke, for all his talk of 'scientific' history, linked an 'exposition of *value* to causal enquiry', and thus, 'in the last analysis . . . sought God in history'. And he himself insists on similar connections. Distinguishing between two separate historical traditions, respectively emphasising the search for causal connections and for moral values, he assimilates the two, claiming the theoretical and practical impossibility of pursuing one without the other. 'The "essential" in history', he affirms, 'involves not only causalities but values'; and spiritual values are inevitably revealed within even natural causal complexes. History becomes, then, 'divine service in the broadest sense'. One may replace a conventional 'divinity' with a secularised quest for 'truth as such', but the search still brings us back to history. It remains the case that, 'however one conceives divinity, he will look for it in history'.[1]

For historians trained to see their subject as modelled on some idealised conception of twentieth-century science, that will sound like a strange confusion. Modern science, after all, has been virtually defined by its *exclusion* of any considerations of 'value'; or at least that has been the theory. The practice, however, has always been less clear-cut, and many scientists from the seventeenth century to the present have been motivated by their belief that their unravelling of the secrets of nature has served to reveal the wonders of a divine creation; so that their work has brought them nearer to God. 'Thanks be unto you, my Lord Creator', writes the astronomer Johannes Kepler, 'for granting me the delight of beholding your creation . . . To those men who will read my demonstrations, I have revealed the glory of your creation.' Robert Boyle wrote a whole treatise to show 'that, by being addicted to experimental philosophy [i.e. science], a man is rather assisted than indisposed to be a good Christian'; and Isaac Newton agreed that 'this most beautiful system of the sun, planets, and comets [as revealed by the new science], could only proceed from the counsel and dominion of an intelligent and powerful Being'.[2] If later, in the twentieth century, Einstein still refused to believe that God played dice with the universe, the implication was a continuing belief in a divinely ordered system of nature, the underlying laws of which science was finally revealing to their author's greater glory.

To many eminent scientists, then, Meinecke's conception of historical study as being (even when it strove for 'scientific' status) an essentially religious activity, would not have sounded strange at all. Indeed, Joseph Priestley, as the late eighteenth-century 'father of modern chemistry', explicitly and typically links the religious aspects of both science and history:

> Both methods are equally attempts to trace out the perfections and providence of God, by means of different footsteps which he has left us of them, differing only in this, that the one is much more distinct than the other.[3]

For self-confessed romantics and for those historians who repudiated the model of science for their subject anyway, such quasi-theological aspirations become a commonplace. Meinecke's near contemporary in England, the novelist George Eliot, has been described as 'making history take the place of God'. Much influenced by the work of Hegel and his view of history as the process of Spirit's self-actualisation, George Eliot refers to historical forces as the 'Invisible Power', and uses her novels to teach the need to submit to that power.[4] Matthew Arnold likewise emphasises the function of history as being ultimately to reveal the orderly laws that lie behind what initially seems chaotic; an understanding of those laws is what restores man's sense of meaning, so the search for them derives again from a quasi-religious aspiration.[5] And in similar vein, and rather later, the social historian G. M. Trevelyan had no compunction about calling the past, not just an ordinary foreign country where things were differently done, but 'that land of mystery'[6] – implying once more an almost mystical conception with which historians were necessarily concerned.

Francis Bacon had earlier written of historians working diligently to 'recover and save somewhat from the Deluge of Time'. That work of recovering some surviving traces from the inundated past was difficult and even 'painefull', and as in the case of scientific research, it needed, so Bacon believed, to be 'attended with a kind of Reverence'.[7] That religious analogy may again sound odd in our own more secular age. But even though the conventional concept of a Christian God may be dead for many historians, the closely related idea of 'Truth' lives on – perhaps as a substitute. The search for historical truth is still undertaken by some, as Bacon would have wished, 'with a kind of reverence', and can sometimes come to resemble nothing short of a revived quest for the Holy Grail: Felipe Fernández-Armesto has recently (1997) written of how 'historians today are priests of a cult of truth, called to the service of a god . . .'[8]

The twentieth-century muse of History, then, still had its parallels with earlier conceptions of a personified image of Nature. In the context of natural philosophy, or science, some nineteenth-century depictions of Nature show a woman, still clothed, but waiting to remove her drapery and expose herself – not promiscuously or indiscriminately, but specifically to the scientist who had located the methodological key which would unlock her chaste secrets. Even so, one can picture history, Historia, lying like some princess or Wagnerian Brünnhilde – in this case a 'past' that has been shrouded and dormant for centuries, but is only waiting to be aroused by the kiss of a suitor, who had fought his way with superhuman persistence through the surrounding ring of fire to reach her. Hazards and dangers, deliberately planted along the way, were designed to ensure that her virtue would remain intact, and that only the right man would reach her – a heroic, single-minded, truth-seeking suitor. And if that all sounds too fanciful, we must remember that Ranke actually described historians' primary material, those archival documents which correspond to the scientist's 'nature', as 'so many princesses, possibly beautiful, all under a curse, and needing to be saved'.[9]

Continuing the analogy with personal relationships, one educationist, Paddy Walsh, has recently written of an actual 'love of the past'. Such a love constitutes for him a form of 'piety' – a piety that implies a respect for the past in its own right. Just as one would, through respect, refrain from violating or taking advantage of another individual person, so, he argues, one should respect the essential 'otherness' of the past and treat it accordingly. For that past was, of course, the present for human beings in the past, just as the present seems to be our own; and just as we wouldn't want ourselves to suffer what seems to us to be misrepresentation, so we owe it to others (not only in the present, but also in the past) not deliberately to misuse or misrepresent them.

Deliberate falsification (or denial) of the past does, as Walsh suggests, clearly seem to be unethical, but he goes beyond that simple moral point when he concludes that, 'only those who love the past for itself can be trusted to mediate it to the present, to draw the *right* lessons from it and indicate its *proper* relevance'.[10] The central difficulty here pertains to the postulation (and presupposition) of a separate individuated 'past', which is out there (like personified nineteenth-century Nature), and existing independently of historians themselves. We are back with Lucian and Lord Acton, and their assumed ideal of a 'purposeless' response to an objectified entity – 'the past in itself'. But, paradoxically, here we have, as an additional ingredient, the inclusion of a specifically moral purpose: historians' motivation is to draw the 'right' lessons from the past, and show its 'proper' relevance. In other words, for Walsh, the past, when approached morally, itself intrinsically contains moral lessons, and it is only when 'the past is explored for its own sake, [that] its more profound relevance to the present may be realised'. But while agreeing that in the choice of subject and the treatment of that subject ('in historical selection and construction'), 'values are always involved',[11] I would argue that those values emanate, not from the past itself (however envisaged), but rather from historians.

Paddy Walsh's approach nevertheless brings us back to the idea of history as religion. For as moral mediators between past and present, historians again appear as saviours; and to qualify as saviours, they need to cultivate saintliness. They need, indeed (and as we have seen before), to be trained to become something literally super-human – able to rise above human frailty. They must be able, in R. H. Tawney's words, to 'become impersonal', like any other scientist, and 'suppress [their] own fancies and predilections'.[12] 'Modernist history', we are reminded by a modernist historian, 'is an exacting discipline, requiring a great exercise of self-restraint, even self-sacrifice.'[13]

The religious connotations of such suppression and self-sacrifice had previously been noted by Nietzsche. Writing deprecatingly about 'the religion of the power of history', he invites us to 'regard the priests of the mythology of the idea and their battered knees':

> Is it too much to say that all the virtues now attend on this new faith? Or is it not selflessness when the historical man lets himself be emptied until he is no more than an objective sheet of plate glass? Is it not magnanimity when, by worshipping in every force the force itself, one renounces all force of one's own in Heaven and upon earth.

The very language used by Nietzsche here – his use of such words as 'faith' and 'priests', 'selflessness' and 'worshipping', re-emphasises the religious-sounding aspirations of the then new historians – their attempted detachment and their ascetic emptying of 'self' in their quest for 'objectivity'. That 'sort of mysticism', Nietzsche sees as one response to the nihilism with which the death of God confronts us: it is for him a way of avoiding serious thought. So he writes elsewhere of 'Art for Art's sake, Truth for Truth's sake, as a narcotic against self-disgust'; habits, routines and fanaticism are adopted as escape-routes. And historians' readiness to fall down on their knees before their new god, Nietzsche believes, reveals an aspect of religion that has always had sinister political overtones: 'What a decorum is such a way of contemplating history! To take everything objectively, to grow angry at nothing, to love nothing, to understand everything, how soft and pliable that makes one . . .'[14]

We shall be considering such aspirations, and their implications, further in chapter 6, but we need to note here the religious-sounding language in which the historical agenda is set. Historians are required to sacrifice their selves, to stifle their individual personalities in the service of a greater good. Writing about the great Victorian historian Samuel Gardiner, John Hale (in 1967) explained how he qualified as 'the first English historian to write in the modern manner' through 'his sacrifice of nearly every device whereby a historian writes himself into his history'. Modernist historians continue to emulate that ideal, sacrificial depersonalisation, aiming to become (with Lucian again) reflective mirrors and mediums, who transmit without personal input; and they resemble thereby nothing so much as priests and priestesses. History has become a religious avocation – and, for many, that must be more than reason enough to be bothered with it.

Religion in history

Religion has actually been manifest *in* historical writing in a number of ways, and these indicate further motivations that theologians might have had (and might still have) to take an interest in historical study. Two most obvious theological intrusions have come in the form of concepts that are 'religious' by virtue of the fact that, by definition, they defy naturalistic explanations: these are 'miracles' and 'providence', and I'll briefly consider each of these in turn, in relation to our overall theme.

Miracles

So long, I presume, will the accounts of miracles and prodigies be found in all history, sacred and profane. – David Hume[15]

There are obvious motives for including accounts of miracles in history, the main ones being (a) to invest the performer of the miracle with some sort of divine authority and power, and (b) to enhance the standing of the religion under whose auspices the miracle has been performed. The utility of history's record for such purposes is so great, that Hume, while personally rejecting their validity, concluded that accounts of 'miracles' and 'prodigies' would continue to be included in histories 'as long as the world endures'.

In the western tradition, we may tend to assume that historical accounts of miracles are specifically Christian, and it's certainly the case that Christian histories include more than their fair share of such phenomena. But Hume himself reminds us that the highly sophisticated Roman historian Tacitus, a man he greatly admires as 'the greatest and most penetrating genius, perhaps, of all antiquity',[16] recorded miracles that had supposedly been performed by the pagan emperor Vespasian – a man who was himself destined for posthumous divinisation.

By the first century, and following the successful early examples of Julius Caesar and Augustus, it had become customary for Roman emperors to be divinised, or promoted to god-like status – if not during their lifetime, then at least after death had removed any empirical evidence to the contrary. Their divinity was claimed with the obvious intention of enhancing political authority and power, and we read in Suetonius's biography that Vespasian, in the early days of his reign, felt a lack of such authority 'and of what might be called the divine spark'. To rectify matters, a miracle is summoned up, or as Tacitus describes, 'Many wonders occurred which seemed to point him out as the object of the favour of heaven and of the partiality of the Gods.' Somewhat to his own surprise, Vespasian succeeded in healing one man's blindness with his spittle, and another man's disability (lameness in Suetonius, a bad hand in Tacitus) with the touch of his foot. Significantly, these miracles are recorded as having taken place 'in the presence of a large audience, too'; so that reports were considered by both Tacitus and Suetonius (notwithstanding the inconsistency of their respective diagnoses) to have been sufficiently authenticated to merit inclusion in their histories.[17]

Their accounts of Vespasian's successful intervention indicate, as Hume reminds us, 'one of the best attested miracles in all profane history', and their wide acceptance must have encouraged the emperor (as we are assured by his biographer) to joke on his death-bed, that he 'must be turning into a god'.[18] He had previously received intimations of his god-given powers, through his military successes against the Jews. At that time, he himself, according to the Jewish historian Josephus, came to believe that his good fortune derived from 'divine Providence', and 'that a righteous kind of fate had brought the empire under his power'. And as his recent adversary and captive, it was tactful for Josephus to agree. He therefore advises his readers that an 'ambiguous oracle' had been wrongly taken by the Jews as prophesying their own dominion of the world; but in fact, it 'certainly denoted the government of Vespasian'.[19] Both in his personally conducted miracles, then, and in his more public military campaigns, Vespasian could be seen as fulfilling a religious function and carrying out the will of god.

However, the identity of that god could still be disputed and, while it suited the pragmatic Josephus to identify Vespasian with the ancient Jewish oracle, the Christian writer Eusebius approached the matter from another perspective. In his history of the early church, Eusebius naturally puts more emphasis on the Christian God, and on the aspirations of his own religion. So, with regard again to the oracle's prophecy, he counterclaims against Josephus, that in fact Vespasian 'did not reign over the entire world, but only the part under Roman rule': the *universal* dominion referred to was actually to be enjoyed by Jesus Christ.[20]

That ambitious claim for Christianity is typical of Christian historians, who record such extravagant miracles (and, as we shall see in the following section, providential interventions) as put Roman imperial examples in the shade. In particular, the accounts of miracles performed by Jesus play an enormously important part in the early histories of the Christian church. They are, of course, designed to validate the divinity ascribed to their church's founding figure: Jesus was to be represented as not only Christ-like, but as the very incarnation of God himself; and as such, he was naturally able to transcend the laws of nature.

There is, then, no doubt about why the authors of the gospels – Matthew, Mark, Luke, and John – were bothered with history: they were writing it specifically to provide foundations for their embryonic church, and they included their accounts of miracles with the express intention of validating the authority of Jesus Christ himself. On a much wider scale than that subsequently assigned to Vespasian, Jesus is recorded as having healed the sick, fed the multitude, turned water into wine, calmed storms, and even raised the dead. Writing within about thirty years of Jesus' death, the gospel writers showed little hesitation in making their claims and, as in the case of Vespasian, the miracles are often described as having taken place in public – in the presence, not just of a few initiates, but of multitudes of ordinary people. The number of potential witnesses served persuasively to authenticate the historical record.

And those biblical and early Christian accounts of miracles were widely accepted through the Middle Ages. Historians such as the Venerable Bede re-affirmed their own faith with records of further supernatural activities, including miracles performed by holy men and saints. Those miracles, it seems, were sometimes appropriated by Christians from their pagan predecessors: late twentieth-century archaeological excavations have indicated that even the supposedly first English martyr (later Saint) Alban may well have been assigned a narrative derived from an earlier pagan head cult. It would have suited the Church in the fourth century to promote Alban's martyrdom and miraculous powers, and they may well have sought to enhance his authority (and the appeal of his shrine) by attributing to him the earlier drama of a decapitated hero.[21]

However historically questionable, Alban's story was but one of many recounted by Bede in his *Ecclesiastical History of the English Nation*. Bede also records, for example, how Bishop Germanus restored a blind girl's sight, healed a lame youth, diverted a raging fire from the house where he was staying, 'quelled the raging waves' of a storm at sea, and enabled the Britons to gain an unexpected military victory 'without the aid of human force'; while the good King Oswald's death initiated a number of similar miracles – with pillars of light appearing over his remains, a boy cured of an ague at his tomb, and his bones enabling a Scottish man on the point of death, and fearing instant relegation of his soul to hell, to be restored to life and so given a second chance to avoid vice and redeem himself.[22]

Already by the sixteenth century, Bede was criticised for having 'set down certain miracles vulgarly reported and credited'; in other words, for having been too credulous in his capacity of historian. 'The Criticks of our Age', explained the Spanish theologian Melchior Cano, 'will believe [such accounts] to be uncertain', or unreliable; and, as early modern biblical criticism inreasingly challenged unquestioning accept-ance of earlier religious authorities, many others started publicly to express more sceptical attitudes. The seventeenth-century English Catholic writer, Thomas White, for example, discussed the whole question of miracles in the more general context of historiography. 'History', he is clear, 'can testifie nothing but what men can witness, nor men witness more than they can hear or see.' So accounts of miracles and revelations are bound to prove problematic. In some cases, the experience is so personal that corroborating witnesses are inevitably lacking; and in other cases, even if reporters believe that they are telling the truth they can never guarantee that they haven't been deceived by others, or even that they haven't suffered from self-deception.[23]

Those are precisely the sorts of problem highlighted by David Hume, when he comes, as he hopes, finally (at least on an intellectual level) to dispose of the matter of 'miracles and prodigies'. So far as Hume is concerned, the only sort of historical evidence that is permissible is (as it had been for White) empirical – the evidence that we get from our senses. Historians obviously can't see everything for themselves: where they lack direct personal experience, they have to rely on eye-witness reports from others. Such reports at second hand have to be assessed for their reliability; and, while on the whole we tend to believe people, we do well to retain a sceptical approach. So we should be suspicious, for example, when witnesses contradict each other; when they are only few in number, or are of doubtful character; when they are not disinterested; when they are unduly hesitant, or unduly assertive about what they have seen; and when their reports seem inherently unlikely as contradicting our own understanding of what is actually possible. The trouble with reported miracles is that they usually fail to live up to such proper historiographical criteria; and they should, therefore, not be given credit. But nevertheless – and this is the main point here – one can see *why* they have become included in the historical record, and why (despite scepticism and all contrary evidence) they might well continue, as Hume feared, to be included in the future 'as long as the world endures'.

Providence

First that we may learne thereby to acknowledge the providence of God, whereby all things are governed and directed. – Thomas Blundeville, 1574[24]

When Blundeville considered the question with which we are concerned here – why bother with history? – he came up with three answers that, by his time in the sixteenth century, had become virtually stock responses. He asserts the traditional optimistic belief that we can learn from examples of past wise actions to act wisely ourselves, and he repeats once more the moral injunction about good and evil examples; but he puts first the most important justification for history, as quoted above, that it forces recognition of God's overall direction and control.

That last has been the answer to our question which has been most frequently given, by religious-minded historians (and, in the western tradition, especially by Christians). For them, the function of history has been the revealing of past developments as the unfolding of god's will, or providence, and their reason for writing history has been, above all, to make that clear. Even in the pre-Christian Homeric epics, earthly affairs unfolded in ways that had previously been planned in the councils of the gods: humans were pawns, in the hands of destiny; and no man, however strong and brave and heroic, could hope to escape the fate ordained for him by some offended goddess. The evidently arbitrary defeats and deaths, that were (and are) so often suffered by soldiers in battle, had to have some sense imposed upon them; or their sense-lessness had to be somehow rationalised. That could best be done by explaining everything, including what appeared to be misfortunes and injustices, in terms of the unfolding of god's will in the larger picture: events that seemed to mortals to be the result of random chance, were actually all a part of god's plan, and meaningful, and to be welcomed.

Later, in the Christian tradition more specifically, history became regu-larly used to demonstrate the all-inclusive nature of the Christian God. Being all-present and all-powerful, God is everywhere, and responsible for everything that happens; and history's function is to confirm that article of faith. It is, of course, a consoling doctrine, since it implies that, in the longer term (*sub specie aeternitatis*, or in the face of eternity), everything – including things that appear to be bad – happens for the best. Humans just need to view events from God's much wider perspect-ive. Then they will appreciate that ultimately the course of events through history is pervaded by a moral force, which ensures that good will be rewarded and evil will be correspondingly punished.

That the whole of history thus manifests God's will, and can be seen to serve his purpose, was accepted by such early Christian historians as Rufinus. In the fourth century, Rufinus contrived to make some moral sense of the great persecution suffered by Christians under the Roman emperor Diocletian. That persecution (like so many subsequently) must have seemed a huge injustice suffered by an innocent people; and as such it appeared to lack any moral justification or meaning. So as an historian Rufinus needed to make some moral sense of it, and the key was to blame what had happened on the Christians themselves and on the sinful condition of their own church. In that way, what had appeared to be an arbitrary affliction imposed by a wicked ruler became nothing but a justifiable punishment imposed by God; and that God furthermore was conveniently enabled to retain his reputation for benevolence. The human Diocletian was not so much the devil incarnate, as God's own agent, and the emperor's actions could be seen to be justified in terms of an over-arching moral plan.

Some two centuries later, the same approach is used by the earliest historian of Britain. Gildas, though, has an even clearer moral aim, with an eye to the future. His history is significantly entitled *The Ruin of Britain*, and his clear intention is to warn his contemporary readers of what to expect if they fail to mend their ways. The sins of the past had always been punished: that was what history showed. But the point about that – the reason we all needed to be bothered with the past – was that obvious implications could be drawn for the future: the evils of the present, proclaims Gildas, are no less liable to punishment and divine retribution.

In a gloomy assessment of his own time, then, he writes of how 'Britain has kings, but they are tyrants; she has judges, but they are wicked.' And worst of all, 'Britain has priests, but they are fools; very many ministers, but they are shameless; clerics, but they are treacherous grabbers.' This, he believes, can't be allowed to go on, and he adduces much confirmatory evidence from the Old and New Testaments to hammer that point home. Despite being recognised by Bede as the Britons' 'own historian', Gildas defied later constraining definitions of his subject by focusing upon the future; and he concludes his history with a resounding warning to his fellow-countrymen, which makes his underlying religious and moral purpose absolutely clear. You are, he accuses, with the priests particularly in mind, 'held bound so tight with iniquities in this world, that you cannot at all ascend to heaven, but must fall into the dreadful dungeons of hell, if you do not turn to the Lord in this life'.[25]

That dire warning about their souls' likely experience after death, indicates quite clearly why Gildas himself was bothering with history, and his lead was followed by many later historians of Britain through the Middle Ages. Thus, the Anglo-Saxon Chronicle provides one early example of what became a stock explanation for the success of the Norman invasion in 1066. The conquest may initially have seemed a national disaster, but with hindsight it was clear that the Britons were just being punished for their previous ungodly misdemeanors: 'the Frenchmen gained the field of battle, *as God granted them for the sins of the nation*'; or, in other words, providence was once again the director of operations at the Battle of Hastings. Nor, of course, did providential intervention stop there: some twelve years later, the victorious William's cruelty and excesses in turn brought about his own deserved downfall. Having become 'very harsh and severe', avaricious and unjust, he was actually shot by one of his own followers while hunting. That may have seemed like a human accident, but it was actually another manifestation of divine justice; and the very manner of William's death underlined the lesson. Not without a trace of vindictiveness, the chronicler notes how the king had become 'loathed by nearly all his people, and *odious to God, as his end testified*': his end in fact was so sudden and unexpected, that he was even denied any opportunity to repent and thereby improve his chances for his after-life.[26]

It is in this same tradition of providential history that, some centuries later, Martin Luther describes his own belief that:

> Histories are nothing else than a demonstration, recollection, and sign of divine action and judgment, how he upholds, rules, obstructs, prospers, punishes, and honours the world, and especially men, each according to his just desert, evil or good.

The telling of their providentially ordered moral tale is what makes historians 'the most useful people, and the best teachers'; and, no less than Gildas, Luther's own interpretation of the past carries clear implications and warnings for the future:

> God's guns are always loaded. He battered the Jews to pieces with the Romans, the Romans with the Vandals and the Goths, the Chaldeans with the Persians, the Greeks with the Turks . . . Perhaps there will also be a bullet for us Germans which will not miss us; for we have conducted ourselves outrageously, and still do.[27]

Luther's providentialist view of history served conveniently to justify his own activities as primary instigator of the Protestant Reformation. As with so many other leaders, he was, according to his own interpretation of events, himself to be seen as the very hand of Providence. And over two hundred years later, that is actually how he came to be perceived by the hero-worshipping historian, Thomas Carlyle. Believing (as we have seen in chapter 2) that the course of history was determined by a few great men, Carlyle selected Luther as one such 'Mighty Man'. He was 'a bringer-back of men to reality', a leader, whose stand at the Diet of Worms on 17 April 1521 had been 'the germ' of many subsequent historical highlights, including English Puritanism, the French Revolution and indeed virtually the whole of European history – or, as he put it, 'Europe and its work everywhere at present'. And, significantly for our present discussion, all this was 'doubtless wisely ordered . . . by the Providence presiding over him and us and all things'.[28]

That view of history's function, as being to demonstrate how nothing ever happens which is, in the words of one early eighteenth-century writer, 'not conformable to the Designs of the Creator',[29] was commonplace for centuries; and although it may now sound to some people like an outdated relic of a former age, it continues to fulfil a need for those who find it hard to accept that history, or human life, simply consists of 'one damned thing after another'. In the absence of any divine input, human history, as Jean Bodin put it, 'mostly flows from the will of mankind, which ever vacillates and has no objective'.[30] Constant vacillation and purposelessness are poor substitutes for providential ordering, and are still often found unacceptable in the context of historical explanation. So as recently as April 1999, the Emeritus Chief Rabbi, Lord Jakobovits, has been reported as attributing the sudden (and to many, shockingly inexplicable) death of Diana Princess of Wales to her own misdemeanors. There was, after all, some point to it: she had, quite simply, been punished for her own immorality. 'The People's Princess', Lord Jakobovits explained, 'would still be alive today, and so would her lover, if they had observed the laws on the sanctity of the marital bond.'[31] That little episode of history could still be seen to have its use 'for the Consolation of the minds of the Faithfull', as Francis Bacon put it, as well as 'for the Astonishment and Conviction of the Consciences of the Wicked'.[32]

History for religion

This I know, because I learn it from the Scriptures. – John Swan, 1635[33]

As Carlyle indicated, the Protestant Reformation had many profound historical effects, but not the least important was the effect it had on historical study itself; and some of the associated theological debates illuminate very clearly some further religious uses to which history has been put. No Christian theologian in the early modern period could have afforded *not* to be bothered with history, since appeals to history of one kind or another were made by spokesmen from both sides of those long running 'rule of faith' debates between Protestants and Catholics which were such a central part of early modern intellectual life.

The origins of those debates are recorded by Paolo Sarpi in his *History of the Council of Trent.* Sarpi reminds his readers that the Council (which dragged on from 1545 to 1563) had been intended to re-unite the church, but after many years it had succeeded only in reinforcing the schism it had been designed to heal. That very fact, that its outcome proved 'contrary altogether to the design of them that procured it', itself held a moral lesson: his history presented 'a clear instruction for us to refer our selves to God, and not to trust in the wisdom of man'.[34] But it also presented the germ of an historiographical debate which was to continue in England through the greater part of the seventeenth century, and which was to provide further motivations for theologians to concern themselves with historical study.

The debate centred on the basic theological issue of establishing a reliable 'rule of faith', or a dependable link with the origins of Christianity which could then serve as a foundation for belief. Protestant apologists insisted that the scriptures by themselves provided that link: following Luther's own original proclamation, that 'Scripture alone is the true overlord and master of all writings and doctrines on earth',[35] they repudiated the longstanding authority of the Pope and Church Councils, and put their whole trust in the historical account recorded in the bible. As John Swan confirmed in the quotation heading this section, Protestants remained adamant that the scriptures could indeed be relied on as an utterly reliable source of knowledge.

That was to put enormous emphasis on what was essentially a 'literary' or *written* history; but that scriptural record had of course for centuries been considered unimpeachable. The Old Testament histories, which purported to give a narrative of what had happened from the time of the creation of the world, were widely considered to be an absolutely reliable source as having been dictated to Moses, 'the Divine Historian', and other 'pen-men of the Holy Ghost', by God himself.[36] And the New Testament had been written by authorities who either had direct experience of their subject-matter, or had been in a position to benefit from reliable eye-witness reports from contemporaries. If, then, there were found to be any inconsistencies with other accounts by less privileged secular historians, the scriptural writings naturally took precedence: they were obviously much more credible, in Matthew Hale's words, 'than what the most do ordinarily allow to the History of Thucydides, Herodotus, Livy, Tacitus', and other human sources.[37]

The Protestant dependance on the bible put the Catholics in a difficult position. Determined as they were to undermine the authority of the upstart Reformers, they found themselves (in order to attack their grounds of faith) having to question the assumed validity of the bible's historical record. In this they were aided by a growing tradition of biblical criticism. Even Moses's history was proving to be not entirely unproblematic. His writings, as the Catholic philosopher and theologian Thomas White noted in 1626, may indeed originally have constituted nothing less than a transcription of 'god almighties word', but they had subsequently been rendered 'far more mortall' at the hands of human translators. Those translations furthermore (and this applied to all the scriptures) had been copied, sometimes by 'sacriligious hands', and then, with 'many errors committed', had been 'by print multiplied beyond number'. Any 'purity it [the bible] once had' was thus irretrievably lost,[38] so it certainly couldn't qualify (as the Protestants insisted) as a reliable basis for Christian faith.

Thomas White's early critique foreshadowed much questioning of the historical record of the scriptures. Biblical criticism has been traced back as early as the eleventh century, or even the fourth,[39] but it took off significantly in the seventeenth century, with the works of such scholars as Isaac La Peyrère, Thomas Hobbes, Benedict Spinoza and Richard Simon. Together these succeeded in undermining the authority of the bible as a reliable historical source – or at least as a source any more reliable than other humanly inscribed histories. Thus by 1677, the Anglican Edward Stillingfleet concedes to his Catholic opponents that the scriptures provide no more certainty than the historians of classical antiquity: 'All that I desire is that you will give an assent of the same Nature to the History of the Gospel, that you do to Caesar, or Livy, or Tacitus, or any other ancient Historian.'[40]

There was the historiographical problem in a nutshell: how could the Catholics undermine Protestantism without at the same time undermining the whole of historical study? They were by no means prepared to adopt a pragmatic or common-sense approach (ascribing relative degrees of probability, as seemed appropriate) to a matter as important as their souls' salvation, but the logic of their arguments led them inexorably to a general scepticism about the reliability of all historical writing. In a nice historiographical paradox, they were therefore seen as being responsible for promulgating, in relation to history, the most extreme form of scepticism: 'Pyrrho himself', complained their Anglican adversary John Tillotson, 'never advanced any Principle of Scepticism beyond this.'[41] In their search for absolute theological certainty, Catholics had contributed to the rise of that historiographical uncertainty which culminated by the century's end in 'historical pyrrhonism' – a sceptical approach to the validity of any history which, when carried to an extreme, can be seen as an antecedent of our own millennial postmodernism.[42]

But that, of course, is far from saying that the Catholics renounced any interest in history. On the contrary, no less than their adversaries, they needed historical support for their own position; they needed to re-establish their own direct links with Christ and the early Christians. Their problem was to find and utilise another form of history to do that. And so, having effectively invalidated the Protestant prop of *written* history, they resorted to what they called 'tradition' – or effectively a history that depended, not on literary, but on *oral* transmission.

Some justification for that emphasis is expressed by Dryden in his poem 'The Hind and the Panther', where he positions Christ's teaching in an initially oral tradition:

'Before the word was written', said the Hind,
'Our Saviour *preached* his faith to human kind . . .
Thus faith was ere [i.e. before] the *written* Word appeared,
And men believed, not what they read, but *heard*.'[43]

That priority of the oral over the literary was expressed, more prosaically perhaps but no less forcefully, by one of Thomas White's followers, who quoted the much earlier church historian Eusebius in describing a tradition 'not written with inke and on paper, but by the Spiritt in mens heartes'. That oral tradition, he emphasised, to which only Catholics could lay claim, had the great advantage of being 'more secure from errour and mistakes than writing'.[44]

That distinction between a literary and oral tradition (or history) is characterised by Catholics as a distinction between something dead and something living. No dead literary text (including the bible) can have any authority, unless backed up by a living oral tradition. As White's disciple John Sergeant repeatedly argued against his Anglican adversaries, 'No *Dead* Testimony or History has any Authority, but by virtue of *Living* Testimony or *Tradition*.'[45] And what that meant in practice is that orally transmitted history was passed from father to son, through the generations, and with the additional confirmation of related activities. Far from being just a matter of words, tradition implies 'a constant course of frequent and visible Actions conformable to those Words'; so there is a sense in which Catholics uniquely have access to an historical tradition which can be investigated and confirmed empirically, or with the senses.[46]

The sort of historical transmission proposed here is not restricted to Christianity. It can be seen also, for example, in the case of Alexander the Great. As with Jesus Christ, Alexander's memory is not preserved in written records alone, but in an alternative body of evidence derived from a continuing oral and practical tradition. We may not know anything definite about his more personal moments, but his military conquests were such extraordinary public events that they could hardly pass unremarked at the time. On the contrary, they were described by numberless eye-witnesses, who had been deeply affected by what they had seen. With 'their Hearts and Fancies full of it', they 'burst out into Expression of it', and so passed the story on into the next generation;

from which it passed successively on, right up until the present.[47] For Sergeant, the very number of witnesses rules out any likelihood of deceit, and his confidence in the oral tradition relating to Alexander was borne out by the presenter of a television series in 1998, who reported that misbehaving Iranian children are still warned that 'Alexander will get you!'

There is contemporary support, too, for another, much more recent, example cited by Sergeant in this context – the plot of Guy Fawkes and his Catholic colleagues to blow up the Houses of Parliament in 1605. Sergeant evidently resents the anti-Catholic feeling that was being kept alive by the annual commemoration of that event, and invites his reader to

> suppose the Anniversary of the Powder Plot should be kept on foot, by Ring-ing of Bells, Bonefires, Squibbs, and Spitefull Preaching against All Catholicks indifferently . . . I would know of him whether the Memory of it, tho' kept alive by this Practical Solemnity but one a year, would not be perpetuated for thousands of Generations, or how should it ever be forgot?[48]

Our continuing celebrations on 5 November, with their ritual burning of Guy Fawkes' effigy, confirm Sergeant's point; and we might similarly cite the commemorative marches by Protestants in Norther Ireland, as representing another historical tradition where memories of the past are kept alive by an oral transmission which is confirmed by practical ceremonies. These traditions can actually be empirically monitored by ordinary people, using their senses, and that (according to the Catholic disputants) is what gives them their reliability. And that same reliability can be attributed to the historical tradition – oral and ritual – linking Catholicism to its early Christian roots: a form of history had been found which could be reliably used in the service of religion.

The confidence placed by such Catholic spokesmen as White and Sergeant in an orally transmitted historical tradition may seem surpris-ing,[49] for as Dryden asked:

> If written words from time are not secured,
> How can we think have oral sounds endured?[50]

We are all aware of how often we mis-hear what others say, and party games have demonstrated how messages can get distorted as they pass from person to person. In the well-known pre-decimalisation example from the army, what starts as the military order, 'Send reinforcements: we're going to advance', becomes transmuted to the more attractive social prospect represented in 'Send three and fourpence: we're going to a dance.' The problem was recognised, not only by poets and soldiers, but by philosophers too. John Locke helped to undermine the Catholic position with his observation that the reliability of any report would inevitably decrease, the further it got from its source: 'any testimony, the farther off it is from the original truth, the less force and proof it has ... The more hands the tradition has successively passed through, the less strength and evidence does it receive from them.'[51] And Pierre Bayle concluded similarly that history (and so, presumably, religion too) was best served by records written immediately at the time of an event: oral history was far less reliable, and a properly wary person should always ask:

> if the Facts related were committed to writing at the time they were fresh; and if it is told him no, but the memory of them is preserved from Father to Son by word of Mouth, he knows well, that in such a case a wise Man will be a Sceptic.[52]

It was to scepticism, then, especially when applied more specifically to history as 'historical pyrrhonism', that early-modern theological debates paradoxically contributed. Both Catholics and Protestants needed history, and used it, in their attempts to demonstrate their own direct continuity with the early church, and accordingly to justify their own grounds of faith. Each, by seeking to undermine the other's position, contrived to undermine confidence in historical study itself. But that was far from being the outcome that either side desired, and so far as the argument of this book is concerned, the post-Reformation 'rule of faith' debates provide an important example of how theologians were much concerned with history, and attempted to use it once again, in its various forms and in their various ways, for the service of religion.

Conclusion

We shouldn't be surprised at the close relationship between history and religion, since, no less than politics, religion has much to do with power, and power needs somehow to be justified – justified ideally by reference to some long-established historical tradition. In an interesting article, Paul Antony Hayward has recently demonstrated this point by reference to some mediaeval monks.[53] Having arrived from France, these Cluniac monks took over the Anglo-Saxon church at Much Wenlock, together of course with all its material resources; and quite understandably they must have felt a need to justify their take-over. So, in 'a manipulative text' (surviving probably from the late eleventh century), they set about recording evidence for their own spiritual superiority. Their claim centred on the origins of the healing cult of Saint Mildburg. Her remains were found, supposedly through divine intervention, when some flooring in the church gave way beneath two skylarking boys, and her burial place was suddenly revealed. Her bones were then recovered, and as holy relics went on to achieve miraculous cures of leprosy and lesser disorders. In a re-written history of the episode, it was with this powerful tradition of healing that the new monks claimed to be associated.

One monk in particular was delegated to provide the corroborative history, and it's interesting to see how concerned he was to demonstrate the authenticity of his account. He re-emphasises the reliability of his own narrative by distinguishing it carefully from what are more questionable interpolations (such as a speech purporting to report what the floorboards would have said). He also takes care to distinguish between what he has personally observed, and what he has learnt only at second hand from witnesses; and he even presents the monks themselves as initially sceptical about the claimed cures of leprosy, and as having personally interrogated one girl who claimed to have been miraculously cured. Finally, and importantly again in the context of this book, the author claims his own moral superiority in his role as a truth-seeking historian: 'I transfix myself with my own sword if, condemning liars, I do not avoid the sin of lying.'

That mediaeval example of history's use (or abuse) for religious-cum-political-cum-economic purposes could be multiplied many times, with examples from both earlier and later periods; and there is little doubt that religion in its various guises will continue to be bothered with various sorts of history in the future.

Notes

1 Friedrich Meinecke, quoted in Fritz Stern (ed.), *The Varieties of History*, New York, Meridian, 1956, pp. 272, 274–5.

2 Johannes Kepler, *Harmonice Mundi* (1619), Bk. 5, ch. 9, quoted by Erich Heller, *The Artist's Journey into the Interior*, London, Secker & Warburg, 1966, p. 22; Robert Boyle, *The Christian Virtuoso*, London, John Taylor, 1690, subtitle; Isaac Newton, *Principia Mathematica* (1687), ed. Florian Cajori, 2 vols, Berkeley and Los Angeles, University of California Press, 1966, 2, 544.

3 Joseph Priestley, *Lectures on History and General Policy*, Birmingham, J. Johnson, 1788, p. 529.

4 Christina Crosby, *The Ends of History*, London, Routledge, 1991, pp. 33, 12. See esp. ch. 1 on *Daniel Deronda*, described as 'a lengthy demonstration of the effects of the impersonal invisible power of history' (p. 17).

5 See Matthew Arnold, *On the Classical Tradition*, cited by Crosby, *Ends*, p. 5.

6 Quoted in Keith Jenkins (ed.), *The Postmodern History Reader*, London, Routledge, 1997, p. 166.

7 Francis Bacon, *Of the Advancement and Proficience of Learning*, Oxford, Robert Young & Edward Forrest, 1640, p. 92.

8 Felipe Fernández-Armesto, *Truth: A History and a Guide for the Perplexed*, London, Bantam Press, 1997, p. 161.

9 Quoted by Ann Curthoys and John Docker, 'Metaphor in English Historiographical Writing', *Rethinking History* 1, 1997, p. 262.

10 Paddy Walsh, 'History and love of the past', *The Aims of School History*, London, Tufnell Press, 1993, pp. 36, 38 (emphasis in original).

11 Walsh, in *Aims*, pp. 41, 43.

12 R. H. Tawney, quoted by Joyce Appleby *et al.*, *Telling the Truth about History*, New York, W. W. Norton, 1994, p. 81.

13 Gertrude Himmelfarb, in Elizabeth Fox-Genovese and Elisabeth Lasch-Quinn (eds), *Reconstructing History*, London, Routledge, 1999, p. 72.

14 Nietzsche, *Untimely Meditations*, transl. R. J. Hollingdale, Cambridge, Cambridge University Press, 1983, p. 105; *Gesammelte Werke* XVIII, 24, quoted by Heller, *Artist's Journey*, p. 189.

15 David Hume, *Enquiries concerning Human Understanding and concerning the Principles of Morals*, ed. L. A. Selby-Bigge, revised by P. H. Nidditch, Oxford, Clarendon Press, 1985, p. 110.

16 Hume, *Enquiries*, p. 123.

17 Suetonius, *The Twelve Caesars*, transl. Robert Graves, Harmondsworth, Penguin, 1957, pp. 278, 279; Tacitus, *History*, 4.81, transl. A. J. Church and W. A. Broadribb, London, Macmillan, 1873, pp. 188–9.

18 Hume, *Enquiries*, p. 122; Suetonius, *Caesars*, p. 285.

19 Flavius Josephus, *The Wars of the Jews*, transl. William Whiston, London, J. M. Dent, 1906, pp. 319, 422; cf. p. 446.

20 Eusebius, *The History of the Church from Christ to Constantine*, transl. G. A. Williamson, Harmondsworth, Penguin, 1965, p. 120.

21 For a report of the scepticism-inducing excavations in St Albans, see *The Times*, 19 July 1999.

22 The Venerable Bede, *The Ecclesiastical History of the English Nation*, London, J. M. Dent, 1958, pp. 25, 27, 28–31, 120, 122–4. For further examples, see esp. Bede's *Life and Miracles of Saint Cuthbert*, appended to the *History*, pp. 286ff.

23 Thomas White cites Cano's criticism of Bede in his *Middle State of Souls*, London, 1659, p. 163; for White on Bede as an historian, and on historiography, see also *Devotion and Reason*, Paris, 1661, pp. 6, 55, 57, 60–1.

24 Thomas Blundeville, *The true order and Methode of wryting and reading Hystories . . .* , London, Willyam Seres, 1574, unpaginated.

25 Gildas, *The Ruin of Britain* (AD 540), ed. Michael Winterbottom, London, Phillimore, 1978, pp. 29, 52, 79. Bede cites Gildas in his *Ecclesiastical History*, Book 1, ch. 22.

26 *Anglo-Saxon Chronicle*, transl. James Ingram, London, J. M. Dent, 1912, pp. 149, 180–1 (my emphases).

27 Quoted by Lewis W. Spitz, 'Luther's view of history: a theological use of the past', in *The Reformation: Education and History*, Aldershot, Variorum, 1997, pp. 141, 142, 145.

28 Thomas Carlyle, *On Heroes and Hero-Worship*, London, Cassell, 1908, pp. 127–8, 122.

29 Richard Rawlinson, *A New Method of Studying History*, 2 vols, London, 1728, I.249.

30 Jean Bodin, *Method for the Easy Comprehension of History* (1566), transl. B. Reynolds, New York, Columbia University Press, 1945, p. 17.

31 *The Jewish Chronicle*, 2 April 1999, p. 48.

32 Bacon, *Advancement*, p. 103. In similar vein, following the discovery of dozens of large snakes on beaches in Southern California in winter 1995, the *Los Angeles Times* reassured its readers that 'as far as can be determined . . . [they] are not some Biblical curse visited on the region to punish the wicked and sybaritic'; but (according to the author of a book on ecology) 'native Californians might disagree'. Reported in *London Review of Books*, 19 August 1999, p. 16.

33 John Swan, *Speculum Mundi, or A Glass Representing the Face of the World*, 4th edn, London, W. Whitwood, 1698, p. 472.

34 Paolo Sarpi, *The History of the Council of Trent*, transl. Nathaniel Brent, London, Robert Barker & John Bill, 1620, p. 1. For the Tradition/Scripture debates, see pp. 142ff.

35 Luther, quoted by W. G. Kümmel, *The New Testament*, London, SCM Press, 1973, p. 20.

36 Matthew Hale, *The Primitive Origination of Mankind*, London, 1677, p. 315 and passim; Degory Wheare, *The Method and Order of Reading both Ecclesiastical and Civil Histories*, transl. Edmund Bohun, London, Charles Brome, 1685, p. 25.

37 Hale, *Primitive Origination*, p. 132. Cf. Sir Walter Raleigh: 'All histories must yeeld to Moses', *History*, quoted by D. R. Woolf, *The Idea of History in Early Stuart England*, London, University of Toronto Press, 1990, p. 46.

38 Thomas White, memorandum dated Rome, 7 November 1626, WA Stonyhurst Anglia A VIII, no. 33.

39 Richard Popkin cites the Spanish Rabbi Ibn Ezra as questioning Moses's authorship (*The History of Scepticism from Erasmus to Spinoza*, Berkeley and Los Angeles, University of California Press, 1979, p. 218); and N. W. Hitchin refers to St Jerome's correspondence with St Augustine concerning textual discrepancies in 'The Politics of English Bible Translation in Georgian Britain', *Transactions of the Royal Historical Society*, Sixth Series 9, 1999, p. 80, n. 57. Hitchin argues interestingly here for the *political* implications of biblical translations at a time when a new version was required to underpin Protestant British identity.

40 Edward Stillingfleet, *Letter to a Deist*, London, Richard Cumberland, 1677, p. 27.

41 John Tillotson, *The Rule of Faith*, London, 1666, p. 138.

42 See further Beverley C. Southgate, 'Blackloism and Tradition: from theological certainty to historiographical doubt', *Journal of the History of Ideas*, 61, 2000, 97–114.

43 John Dryden, 'The Hind and the Panther' (1687), part II, lines 305–6, 322–3 (my emphases).

44 Hugh Cressy, *Exomologesis*, Paris, 1647, pp. 174, 182.

45 John Sergeant, *The Method to Science*, London, W. Redmayne, 1696, p. 338.

46 John Sergeant, *Sure-Footing in Christianity*, London, 1665, p. 41.

47 Sergeant, *Sure-Footing*, pp. 217–20.

48 John Sergeant, *Fifth Catholick Letter*, London, 1688, p. 7.

49 It may well have seemed less surprising to their contemporaries in the seventeenth century, when there was still a strong tradition of orally transmitted history. For an interesting recent discussion, see Adam Fox, 'Remembering the Past in Early Modern England: Oral and Written Tradition', *Transactions of the Royal Historical Society*, Sixth Series 9, 1999, pp. 233–56. Fox cites evidence in the Middle Ages of 'unbroken oral transmission over at least seven centuries' (p. 254), and quotes Thomas Westcote's comment in the 1630s that 'some things seem more fabulous, interposed by some augmenting transcribers' than many others 'left unto us as tradition . . . from mouth to mouth' (p. 245).

50 John Dryden, 'Religio Laici' (1682), lines 270–1.

51 John Locke, *An Essay Concerning Humane Understanding*, London, Thomas Basset, 1690, IV, 16, 10.

52 Pierre Bayle, *An Historical and Critical Dictionary* (1697), English transl., 4 vols, London, C. Harper, 1710ff, II. 829.

53 Paul Antony Hayward, 'The *Miracula Inventionis Beate Mylburge Virginis* attributed to "the Lord Ato, Cardinal Bishop of Ostia"', *English Historical Review* 114, 1999, 543–73. I am indebted to this article for what follows (quotation from p. 556).

6

History and education

To be ignorant of what occurred before you were born is to remain always a child. – Cicero[1]

Introduction

In terms of education, history has not always received a good press. Advising his son in 1656, Francis Osborne was far from enthusiastic about the subject. His experience of hearing contradictory reports about the Civil Wars of his own time (contemporary history), led him to be sceptical about the reliability of records of less recent events. Such historical records, he concluded, were likely to present a 'false, or at best but a contingent beliefe';[2] and as such they hardly warranted serious study.

Osborne's anxiety about his son potentially wasting his time by studying history that is unreliable, implies an understanding of history as being ideally of a certain kind – the kind that yields certain, 'factual' knowledge about the past. Now, although that model was already under sceptical challenge in Osborne's day, it has persisted to some extent up to our own time, and has determined the content of many a syllabus involving 'spooned down doses of the past';[3] and it has in turn helped to promote a singularly unhelpful model of the ideal historian who might emerge from the educational process. Though possibly attractive to some other members of the profession, that model has proved less than universally enticing.

It was conveniently typified by Mr Casaubon in George Eliot's novel *Middlemarch* – a characterisation that appeared in the very decade (the 1870s) that Nietzsche and Herbert Spencer were registering similarly negative assessments of historical study in their time. The former complains of a degenerate brand of history that consists of little more than 'a restless raking together of everything that has ever existed', and is characterised by a 'habit of scholarliness [which] . . . rotates in egoistic self-satisfaction around its own axis';[4] while the educationist Herbert Spencer similarly repudiates *useless* history, which is concerned only with 'dead unmeaning events' – 'the births, deaths, and marriages of kings, and other like trivialities'.[5] Much more recently (1987), but similarly out of patience with the excessive specialisation and professionalisation of British history, Professor David Cannadine has claimed that 'the belief that history provides an education . . . has all but vanished'.[6]

These academic critiques of 'useless' history are, as it were, brought to life in George Eliot's portrayal of Casaubon. He is shown as a sad figure – a scholar duly dealing in dead unmeaning events. He meticulously burrows away in the archives for many years, but finds it hard ever to conclude his researches or show any practical justification for them. His initially laudable emphasis on the empirical aspects of his work – on the collection of data – serves in time to over-ride the more imaginative aspects, not only of his work, but also of his personality. So he is seen by the young romantic artist, Will Ladislaw, with whom he is contrasted, as a 'dried up pedant . . . [an] elaborator of small explanations about as important as the surplus stock of false antiquities kept in a vendor's back chamber'. And he is presented by George Eliot herself as 'a lifeless embalmment of knowledge', the sort of man who takes his younger bride, Dorothea, on a honeymoon to Rome, only to abandon her for days on end while he continues his essential research in the Vatican archives:

> 'And all your notes', said Dorothea . . . 'Will you not make up your mind what part of them you will use, and begin to write the book which will make your vast knowledge useful to the world?'

That challenge can be read by few writers without wincing, and many will sympathise with Casaubon's disturbed and angry response. But even he, in a rare moment of self revelation, realises his situation and confesses that, in his attempt 'mentally to construct [the world] as it used to be', 'I live too much with the dead'.[7]

Living too much with the dead is an occupational hazard for historians, and one that has to be confronted by educationists: there is always a danger that, by focusing attention on the past, historical study will promote an indifference to the future; the past can sometimes seem to provide a womb-like comfort, from which we may resent being ejected into what is necessarily uncertain and unknown. The famous nineteenth-century historical novelist, Walter Scott, was criticised by William Hazlitt for that sort of intellectual one-sidedness. His novels provided wonderfully vivid representations of the past, but only in their own terms, and at the cost of any thought for the present or future:

> If you take the universe, and divide it into two parts, he knows all that it *has been*; all that it *is to be* is nothing to him . . . The cells of his memory are vast, various, full even to bursting with life and motion; his speculative understanding is empty, flaccid, poor, and dead . . . Our historical novelist firmly thinks that nothing *is* but what *has been.*[8]

The temptation is, then, to ring-fence the past, and to avoid any possible contamination from the future. Overly concerned with an aesthetically pleasing and coherent account of what has been, historians, no less than historical novelists, can be in danger of deadening their speculative understanding of what might be; and their consequent appearance of irrelevance continues to be noticed. As recently as 1999, an American educationist published her warning that, even within her own profession, history is still (however unfairly) 'disparaged as nothing more than a bunch of names and dates about long ago events and dead people'.[9]

Despite such bad publicity from some quarters, and for a certain sort of approach to the subject, history has generally been regarded as an essential part of the school curriculum, and is still taught in most colleges and universities: why? Why should educationists and teachers, and their students, bother with the subject? In searching for answers to those questions, one is likely to come across a fair amount of general waffle about 'learning from the past', being able to set contemporary problems in their wider perspective, securing a stock of role-models for emulation or avoidance, and generally, as Cicero implies in our quotation heading this section, being enabled to grow up a bit without the pains of experiencing everything at first-hand.

Much of that seems to me to be wishful thinking, but I shall briefly discuss a few more possible answers of this kind, under the headings of 'Basic transferable skills' and 'Social skills', before going on, rather more provocatively perhaps, to consider some 'personal', or – more accurately – 'impersonal' skills, that are often seen as another potential by-product of historical study.

This chapter, then, by looking at some aspects of the past relationship of history and education, should prepare the way for our concluding consideration of why, in our postmodern era, we should (as teachers and students) still bother with history in the future.

Basic transferable skills

'History for its own sake' has often been an educational ideal, and we have already considered some exponents of that in chapter 1. There remains something alluring about an educational study which has its own intrinsic value, which is seen as an end in itself, and not as a means to help in the attainment of something else (presumably thought to be of higher value). But it seems hard now to justify the study of any academic subject without some reference to life outside the academy – that supposedly more 'real' life enjoyed by 'ordinary' people, whose life is not focused on schools and colleges and universities. With career-counselling currently being proposed for four year olds, we need to know why we're doing what we're doing, and our justification had better sound 'vocationally orientated'.

Fortunately for historians, there has always been readily available a list of so-called 'transferable skills' to which they could lay claim. Even in the bad old days, historical dates and 'facts' could vie with multiplica-tion tables, scientific formulae and chunks of poetry, as prospective fod-der for those intent on the training of young minds through rote-learning. Lists of the dates of the kings and queens of England could be commit-ted to memory, and the competence of pupils easily tested; and though not of any immediate benefit to the holder, such information might conceivably prove useful, if only for the solution of puzzles and other trivial pursuits. Above all, though, the mind had been 'trained', and the ability to memorise apparently useless data could be applied indefinitely in later life.

History, though, could do more than that – something which might give it the edge on chemistry or poetry: it could require an ability to assimilate and synthesise a great range of disparate material; it could inculcate an ability to make sense of – or to see a way through – a chaotic jumble of data (sometimes known as facts). And that, after all, was the essence of what many people had to do in their professional lives. The nature of the material with which they had to deal was irrelevant: what mattered was the technique of handling that material – of gathering it, putting it in some sort of coherent order, and presenting it. The skills of this kind, which are required in historical study, can be re-applied elsewhere; and so the subject can once more be justified in respectably vocational terms.

Above all, however, historians need to reach their conclusions in the knowledge that, with rather more data, they might have to change their minds: their conclusions are, and can be, only hypotheses provisionally expounded on the basis of a highly selective bank of evidence. As Graham Swift's history teacher in *Waterland* puts it: 'I taught you that by forever attempting to explain we may come, not to an Explanation, but to a knowledge of the limits of our power to explain.'[10] There can, then, be nothing definitive about historical writing or historical thought: another selection, or a new piece of evidence, or even a revised perception of evidence already available – any or all of these might indicate a need to adjust the argument and its conclusion. And what is, as a result of this deficiency of certitude, transferable is, firstly, an ability to formulate a judgement on the basis of admittedly defective data; and secondly, a humility derived from awareness of one's own limitations and constraints, and of the consequent provisionality of any conclusion in any historical or professional context.

The basic skills required for doing history, then, are readily transferable to any 'real' world situation; and that has given some minimal comfort to historians required to argue for their subject in an educational environment increasingly obsessed with 'vocationalism' and 'accountability'.

Social skills

An acquaintance with history is agreeable to us as sociable and conversable creatures. – Joseph Priestley, 1788[11]

The whole idea of 'social skills' has meanwhile been out of fashion for some decades, except inasmuch as these might relate to an ability to 'communicate'. Personnel managers and recruitment agents from corporations large and small have continued to pontificate about the need to 'communicate' in speech and writing, and to include that magic word in any list of their requirements; and historians, no less than their colleagues in other humanities disciplines, have been able to argue for the professional relevance of their personal teaching practices – their encouragement of oral communication in seminars, and of more literary skills through written work. But older ideas of 'social skills' encompass something more, and would no doubt nowadays provoke concerned accusations of élitism.

Earlier writers were less politically correct. In the early modern period, historical knowledge formed an important component of that liberal education which helped to make people socially acceptable. The Italian Renaissance writer Castiglione, whose enormously influential prescriptions for the education of the ideal courtier were translated into English and published in 1561, included some study of history, since he believed that it was not only intrinsically pleasurable, but also equipped one for the delightful task of conversing with women, who 'ordinarily love such matters'.[12] Early in the next century, Richard Braithwait not only stressed the moral benefits of history, but also advocated it as the best study to equip one for social life – 'to inable [i.e. fit] you for all Companies'.[13] John Locke later in the same century, although putting undue emphasis on the mechanical aspects of the subject as requiring 'little more than memory', still believed that history was the great moral and political teacher, 'the great mistress of prudence and civil knowledge'; and so it constituted a proper study not only for the 'man of business in the world' but also for 'a gentleman'[14] – a view implied some hundred years later by Joseph Priestley in the quotation heading this section. And in the later nineteenth century, Herbert Spencer could still observe how the absence of history in a curriculum – history of however fatuous a kind – would provoke 'unpleasant criticisms'.[15]

One advantage of history specifically in a supposedly liberal education was that it was not necessarily narrowly national. With some knowledge of European history more generally, young gentlemen from any country could set out on those Grand Tours, which formed an important part of their education, confident that they were equipped to converse politely with their own kind, even in initially alien surroundings. Guidebooks of the time, like our own today, also provided some essential historical information, in order not least to facilitate agreeable cosmopolitan conversation.[16]

This social motivation for the subject was considered too by Lord Bolingbroke. Though by no means his first consideration, he did note – not without some characteristic irony – that one reason for reading history was that it enabled people 'to shine in conversation'. Having contrived, as he puts it, to 'store their minds with crude unruminated facts and sentences', they can regurgitate these gems at dinner parties, and thus demonstrate their social competence.[17] This very practical consideration is repeated, without the irony, much nearer to our own time, by the well-known English historian A. L. Rowse. Writing at the end of the Second World War, Rowse concludes that 'History is an essential part of the mind of a cultivated man . . . As a subject of conversation, compared with the weather, or bridge or the dogs, it has greater variety and more intrinsic interest.'[18] And that this social aspect of historical education has not been entirely lost is indicated by an American professor, who describes liberal arts colleges where students 'pick up enough of subjects thought interesting in their circle and of the style of discussing them to permit agreeable and acceptable conversation'.[19]

Social skills, though, can imply more than simply sharing an interesting topic of conversation. They have to do with the old Socratic, or even earlier Delphic, aspiration to self-knowledge; for one has to know something of oneself before one can hope to be aware of other people and relate to them. In this far more difficult educational objective, too, history has been seen to make some contribution. The claim is well put by the eighteenth-century writer, Richard Rawlinson:

To study History, is to study the motives, opinions and passions of men, to be able to discover their engines, their windings, and inventions, finally to know all the delusions they put upon our intellects, and the surprises they seize our souls with: in one word, it is to learn to know oneself by others.[20]

This might properly remain as an aspiration for twenty-first-century educationists.

(Im)personal skills

It is somewhat difficult to be free from all emotion – a condition which we require . . . – Jean Bodin, 1566[21]

Jean Bodin, in the quotation above, is expressing a truism about what has conventionally been required of the historian. Any sign of 'emotion' has been enough to disqualify a writer from the respectability that is accorded to professionals in the field; emotion must be relegated to such lesser breeds as amateurs or poets, who cannot be taken seriously. So Thucydides, as an historian who aspired to scientific status, specifically distanced himself from the earlier approach of his predecessor Homer. As a mere poet, Homer might well have allowed his imagination and emotion to get the better of him; and he later, in fact, became demonised as the archetypal liar – the deceiving poet, from whom truth-seeking and truth-propounding historians had to be carefully distinguished. When the Elizabethan John Twyne wanted to insult Geoffrey of Monmouth, the twelfth-century historian of Britain, he derided him as 'the British Homer, the father of lies'[22]; and as the representative of new ideas in mid-seventeenth-century England, Joseph Glanvill can think of no worse insult to the old philosophy – distorted as that was by our mental deficiencies, deceiving senses, environmentally derived prejudices, and disordering passions – than to liken it to Homer's *Iliad*.[23]

From the time of classical antiquity, emotion has been seen as the diametric opposite of 'reason'; and in the context of history, as elsewhere, it is the specifically human, and higher, faculty of reason that makes feasible the adoption of a 'balanced', 'impartial' and 'objective' approach. In the western tradition, it is only reason that gives us any hope of reaching truth; emotion diverts us from the search, and carries us away from it. The Roman Tacitus has been but one of many to characterise history as being properly written with 'neither anger nor affection'; for, as Francis Bacon noted, histories are deservedly suspect, when 'written with passion or partiality'.[24] Many, then, have followed Paolo Sarpi in his claim to 'exactly follow the truth, not being possessed with any passion that may make me erre'.[25] As late as the 1960s, Geoffrey Elton felt justified in condemning his great predecessor Lord Acton as 'an amateur' – albeit 'a prince' of his kind – not least because he periodically and inappropriately displayed emotion, 'for ever expressing distress or surprise'.[26] And in the Foreword to the 1977 revised edition of his work on William Morris, E. P. Thompson confessed to the sin of having originally written 'in an embattled mood, from a position of strong political commitment'. Personally inspired by Morris's ability to liberate 'his mind from the categories of bourgeois thought', he had presented the Victorian as a socialist thinker whose ideas had continuing relevance. But he had come to realise of course that such displays of enthusiasm contravened professional norms; so 'it is not surprising', he concludes, 'that it [the first 1955 edition] dropped into academic silence'.[27] By displaying emotion, Thompson had, like Lord Acton, revealed himself as just another 'amateur'.

Nevertheless, in our opening quotation, Bodin is, of course, expressing an understatement of hilarious proportions when he writes of it being 'somewhat difficult to be free from all emotion'. Admittedly, there has been a longstanding aspiration on the part of some philosophers to liberate themselves in that way: the Roman Stoics in particular are renowned for their attempts to achieve complete invulnerability; and those attempts necessarily entailed the renunciation of emotion, since it is emotion that notoriously (and sometimes inconveniently) undermines our 'self-possession' (our ability to control ourselves). To achieve their freedom from emotion, the Stoics had to achieve complete self-sufficiency, and rise above such dangerous passions as fear and love and hate, and all those encumbrances which are often seen as the essential and defining attributes of human beings. To do that is indeed 'somewhat difficult'; and it is arguably highly undesirable too.

This brings us back to the question of what sort of people ideal historians might be, and returns us to some characters from chapter 1 – namely,

Lucian and Lord Acton. Their ideal of 'purposelessness' goes closely with the requirement to be 'free from all emotion', for emotions, by their very nature, impel us to take certain courses of action. But if we feel impelled to act, we are no longer purposeless: no wonder Bodin (and many subsequently) considered emotions to be inappropriate for a historian. I have already argued that purposelessness is a denial of what it means to be human; and, in the context of why educationists should bother with history, I shall go on to argue that Bodin's requirement of emotionlessness is no less inhuman, and so no less to be avoided even as an aim. If we're going to bother with history, it is for quite other reasons than to cultivate a denial or repression of emotion.

Back to Lucian's mirror, then – the idea that the historian is a passive reflector of events, not imposing any personal will or purpose on them, but simply receiving them for onward transmission to the lesser qualified. The point is that historians must remain detached from what they experience and then transmit. They must keep themselves tidily out of the way, not intruding their own personalities, or judgements; for any sort of personal intrusion would inevitably result in distortion of the pristine truth, and so it would disqualify the historian from any credibility. We have already seen how Francis Bacon believed that ideally 'History of all writings . . . holdeth least of the author, and most of the things themselves'; and the ideal has persisted of an 'objective' and depersonalised history, written in a plain and neutral, strictly unrhetorical style, giving every appearance of having been narrated by 'Nobody'.[28]

Thus, for example, the educationist John White, in a discussion pamphlet on the aims of history, has taken for granted a consensus concerning 'the historian's virtues of objectivity and impartiality': 'We can all agree, I take it, that the study of history depends on certain intellectual virtues – detachment and impartiality, and others . . .' And in the same pamphlet, Peter Lee confirms that history remains history by, in particular, meeting 'standards of detachment and impartiality'.[29] 'Detachment and impartiality' are quite simply taken to be history's (or historians') defining characteristics, and many (if not most) would agree with Richard Evans's recent reassertion of the traditional view that historians can attain 'objective historical knowledge' of a past that 'really is there entirely independently of the historian' – so long as they 'develop a *detached* mode of cognition'.[30]

So historians are trained to be dispassionate, detached, uninvolved; and herein lies, it is supposed, one of the great educational virtues of their subject – another invaluable transferable asset. Having been properly trained to remain 'detached' from their object of study, historians can amass their 'facts' without prejudice, reach their conclusions without any distortions from a personal input that might be unbalanced by emotion or imagination; and they can present their findings in an impersonal style which itself exemplifies their 'objectivity'. Such are the eminently transferable skills, by reference to which the discipline can best be sold to our paymasters and to our students' prospective employers. With those qualities, men and women should fit perfectly into any corporate machine; for, as in historical study, so too in professional life, facts need to be collected and collated, hypotheses drawn, evidence adduced and balanced recommendations made – all in an impartial, unprejudiced, objective manner, and without ever questioning the wider parameters within which the work is being done. There need be no fear of disloyalty or 'whistle-blowing' from graduates trained to study the past (or presumably anything else) 'in its own terms', for that, as one eminent practitioner has revealingly explained, 'does involve the subjection of the historian's self to the object of his study'.[31]

The 'subjection of . . . self to the object of . . . study' is related to the belief that, if the trained historian looks and listens hard enough, 'the facts will speak for themselves'. Determinedly avoiding the imposition of any 'subjective' input, the historian will realise that, 'confronted by his evidence, [he] has very little free will'. He will pose 'fundamental questions . . . to the evidence', but those questions will be 'independent of the concerns of the questioner'.[32]

Now, I may be overstating the case, but I suggest that this is not so very different in approach from that of some SS officers confronted by the problem of killing several hundred Russian prisoners during the Second World War. They are reported as having competed in proposing ingenious solutions to their problem. But 'only ways and means were debated; no one expressed any misgivings on the *principle* of preparing this slaughter'. In other words, the officers had been trained to give 'blinkered concentration on the prescribed task' – to focus on the evidence, confronted by which they would have 'very little free will'. As in the case of the atomic scientist who supposedly refused to let 'conscientious scruples' affect his evaluation of the Hiroshima bomb as 'superb physics', they were to remain professionally 'detached'; and the 'self' was to be differentiated from and subjected to 'the object of study'.[33]

To come both geographically and chronologically nearer home, one might cite a similar approach reportedly adopted (in 1994) by some researchers on nursing standards in Scottish teaching hospitals. So absorbed were they in their own 'object of study', that they are reported as having 'watched a woman dying of liver cancer struggle for four hours to reach a glass of water before they intervened', and to have 'monitored' for half an hour, but 'left unaided', a dying woman who begged for a drink.[34] To quote Albert Speer's attempted explanation of what transpired in Nazi Germany, 'Your conscience was quiet if you were educated to see things only in your own field; this was convenient for everybody.'[35] Researchers are not nurses after all: they have to remain detached from the object of their study. Potential disruptions from any personal input have to be avoided, where concern remains with 'the facts' of the situation as it is, and not with poetic or politically (or humanly) motivated alternatives of 'what might be'.

To question the traditional ideals of a detached and emotionless historical study is a sure way to provoke an emotional and far from detached response from contemporary practitioners. Such criticism itself, though, is nothing particularly new: Nietzsche, in particular, was quick to see the dangers of an approach that was gaining in fashion as historians aspired to scientific status for their significantly styled 'discipline' in the nineteenth century. He refers scathingly to the 'historically educated' as 'neuters' – 'neither man nor woman, nor even hermaphrodite, but always and only neuters or, to speak more cultivatedly, the eternally objective'. With such much applauded objectivity goes an 'ostentatious indifference', and an 'affectation of tranquillity'; and historians' repudiation of any emotion implies that 'he to whom the past *means nothing at all* is the proper man to describe it'. Such an historian is, for Nietzsche, nothing better than 'a passive sounding-board, whose reflected tones act upon other similar sounding-boards: until at last the whole air of an age is filled with the confused humming of these tender and kindred echoes'. And these academic echoes, of course, fail Nietzsche's first test for history – that it should have some practical effect. Critique provokes critique *ad nauseam*, but 'everything remains as it was: people have some new thing to chatter about for a while, and then something newer still, and in the meantime go on doing what they have always done'.[36] What is the point of bothering with that sort of history?

Historians' emphasis on the academic and literary, together with their subscription to the supposed ideals of detachment and objectivity, must conveniently serve to remove them from the responsibility of taking autonomous and effective political action; they are confined to the role of voyeur, or 'perpetual spectator'.[37] We have already noticed Nietzsche's warning about this, inasmuch as it related to historians' faith in their subject as virtually a new religion. But it's worth repeating his point here, that a training in acceptance of certain disciplinary constraints can have (what to him were) very negative effects. The traditional 'idolatry of the factual', for example, implying a requirement 'to accommodate oneself to the facts', may seem uncontentious enough; indeed, it seems to constitute the very essence of a virtuous historian's approach. But Nietzsche concludes more apprehensively:

> He who has once learned to bend his back and bow his head before the 'power of history' at last nods 'Yes' like a Chinese mechanical doll to every power, whether it be a government or public opinion or a numerical majority, and moves his limbs to the precise rhythm at which any 'power' whatever pulls the strings.[38]

A conventional historical training, in other words, can actually foster a conforming acceptance of the powers that be – however pernicious.

Nietzsche's concerns were reiterated by the founding-father of sociology, Max Weber. Writing in the 1920s, Weber indicated how the properly trained historian would make the ideal bureaucrat for, just as in the tradition of Tacitean history, so:

> bureaucracy . . . stands . . . under the principle of *sine ira et studio* [without anger or affection]. Its specific nature . . . develops the more perfectly the more the bureaucracy is 'dehumanised', the more completely it succeeds in eliminating from official business love, hatred, and all purely personal, irrational and

emotional elements . . . The more complicated and specialised modern culture becomes, the more its external supporting apparatus demands the personally *detached and strictly 'objective'* expert.[39]

The potential for dehumanisation is not, of course, confined to historians alone: it can afflict any whose disciplinary requirements include the much praised concept of detachment. The renowned photographer George Rodger became concerned about just such matters, of balancing 'professional' detachment with personally remaining human. Having photographed such war-time dramas as the London blitz, the Normandy landings and the liberation of Paris, he was confronted in 1945 by the horrors of Belsen. It was Rodger's job to photograph the corpses and the starved and emaciated prisoners, and so he tried, as any photographer (or reporter, or historian) would, to make some sense of it all, and compose his pictorial message. But then, as he later recalled:

> I said, 'My God, what's happened to me? This is the ultimate end, to be faced by this horror and to be putting the people who had suffered into nice compositions.' I thought, 'It's too much, something's affected me' . . . [And] I swore I'd never take another war picture. And I didn't. That was the end.[40]

George Rodger, then, like the news reporter Martin Bell, whom we cited in chapter 1, concluded that the professional ideal of detachment finally proved incompatible with his humanity, or with his vision of himself as a human being. Historians may come to feel similarly, and agree with John Slater in his discussion of school history, when he suggested that 'A balanced view of genocide would surely be impiety.'[41] Impartiality, detachment, balance – these words sound fine and virtuous: but what they can often imply is a cop-out – an acceptance of the prevailing order, of what is going on, however vicious.

Conclusion

In an essay 'Of the true Use of Retirement and Study', Lord Bolingbroke wrote:

> Men find it easy, and government makes it profitable, to concur in established systems of speculation and practice: and the whole turn of education prepares them to live upon credit all their lives. Much pains are taken, and time bestowed,

to teach us *what to think*; but little or none of either, to instruct us *how to think*. The magazine of the memory is stored and stuffed betimes; but the conduct of the understanding is all along neglected, and the free exercise of it is, in effect, forbid in all places.[42]

That short paragraph encapsulates a number of points discussed in this chapter, so may stand as an appropriate conclusion. Most importantly, it reminds us of the several pressures towards conformity – conformity in both our personal and our professional lives. Internally there are pressures, for we have a natural propensity to conform: it's simply 'easy'. And there are external pressures too: it's convenient for the prevailing power (whether in home, institution or nation), to have us all conform, so additional inducements will seek to confirm us in our ways, and (in various ways, no doubt) make conformity seem actually desirable, or profitable or virtuous. In furtherance of that, education conventionally encourages us to play a responsible part in society by conforming to established thoughts and actions. An enormous amount of time and effort is expended in telling us *what* to think, and our memories are stuffed full of ever increasing amounts of information. But as for learning *how* to think – that can be not only ignored, but actively discouraged and even, so far as possible, prevented.

Bolingbroke's eighteenth-century assessment may be thought by some to be no longer relevant, but for others it may resonate with contemporary concerns. Those others would certainly have included Nietzsche, had he ever read Lord Bolingbroke, for the German philosopher is scathing of the education in his own country in the 1870s. Indeed, he writes, 'education of the scholar is an extremely difficult problem, if his humanity is not to be sacrificed in the process'. For one thing, as for Bolingbroke, there is far too much emphasis on conformity. Students receive what is handed down to them through the generations, so are caught up in the conventionally correct attitudes of the time – what Nietzsche calls the 'unconscious canon of permitted sagacity', which we might translate as what is 'politically correct'. As a result, they engage in a 'sluggish promenading in borrowed fashions and appropriated opinions'; and thus 'fettered by the chains of fear and convention', they end up as mere 'pseudo-men, dominated by public opinion', and lacking any creative spontaneity of their own. And the problem is further exacerbated by the fashionable model of the sciences: that results in experience being reduced to over-intellectualised explanations, with students in danger of exhibiting 'the cold and contemptible neutrality of the so-called scientific man' – the sort of detached, non-judgmental impartiality that we've seen to characterise ideal historians in our own time.[43]

What is needed instead, proposes Nietzsche, is an encouragement to break free from such constraints. Education is to do with liberation: 'educators can be only your liberators' – liberators from the limitations and constraints of one's own time and place, making us, in the words of the early-modern historian Heinsius again, 'contemporary with the universe'.[44] And that liberation is achieved by the use of, not theoretical, but practical examples. Those examples must, for Nietzsche, be people who have refused to conform, who have rebelled against the conventions and pressures of their time, who have fought *'against history . . .* against the blind power of the actual', and have dared to stand alone. People need to be educated *against* their age: far from conforming with present pressures, they need to be taught to fight against them – to fail to fit, and positively to be *'untimely'*.[45]

And, if it's disturbing to be confronted by such radical thoughts and such unsettling examples, so much the better. As the ancient Greek philosopher Diogenes implied, one can't be great without disturbing people. To be educated, one has to be disturbed – to be provoked into recognition of one's own deficiencies. It's only then that there might be any hope of self-improvement. Could there be another reason here for being bothered with history?

Notes

1 Cicero, *De Oratore*, 34, quoted by Donald R. Kelley (ed.), *Versions of History from Antiquity to the Enlightenment*, New Haven and London, Yale University Press, 1991, p. 77.
2 Francis Osborne, *Advice to a Son*, Oxford, Thomas Robinson, 1656, pp. 10–11. This work ran to five editions within two years, and served to establish a wide reputation for its author (who lived from 1593 to 1659).
3 Graham Swift's characterisation in *Waterland*, London, Pan, 1992, p. 60.
4 Nietzsche, *Untimely Meditations*, transl. R. J. Hollingdale, Cambridge, Cambridge University Press, 1983, p. 75.
5 Herbert Spencer, *Education*, London, Williams & Norgate, 1910, pp. 4, 14. Carlyle had earlier written in similar vein in *Past and Present* (1834): 'Alas, what mountains

of dead ashes, wreck and burnt bones, does assiduous Pedantry dig up from the Past Time, and name it History . . .' London, Ward Lock, n.d., p. 36.

6 David Cannadine quoted by Norman Davies, *Europe: A History*, London, Pimlico, 1997, p. 32. For Professor Cannadine's more recent assessment, see his *Making History Now*, London, Institute of Historical Research, 1999, where he describes (p. 10) the preposterous 'superabundance of material [produced by historians] with all the frenzied energy of battery chickens on overtime, laying for their lives'.

7 George Eliot, *Middlemarch* (1871–2), London, Oxford University Press, 1947, pp. 218–19, 210, 213, 12.

8 William Hazlitt, *Lectures on the English Poets & The Spirit of the Age*, London, J. M. Dent, 1967, pp. 223–4. Cf. Goethe's Faust, who recognises his own duality: one part clings to the security of the known, while the other aspires to the unknown, however risky.

9 Diane Ravitch, 'The Controversy over National Standards', in Elizabeth Fox-Genovese and Elisabeth Lasch-Quinn (eds), *Reconstructing History*, London, Routledge, 1999, p. 242.

10 Swift, *Waterland*, p. 108.

11 Joseph Priestley, *Lectures on History*, Birmingham, J. Johnson, 1788, p. 2.

12 Count Baldassare Castiglione, *The Book of the Courtier*, transl. Sir Thomas Hoby (1561), London, J. M. Dent, 1928, p. 71.

13 Richard Braithwait, *A Survey of History*, London, Jasper Amery, 1638, p. 382.

14 John Locke, *Some Thoughts concerning Education* (1690), London, Sherwood, Neely & Jones, 1809, pp. 196, 217.

15 Spencer, *Education*, p. 15.

16 See Denys Hay, *Annalists and Historians*, London, Methuen, 1977, p. 134.

17 Henry St John, Lord Bolingbroke, *Letters on the Study and Use of History*, London, A. Millar, 1752, p. 5.

18 A. L. Rowse, *The Use of History*, London, Hodder & Stoughton, 1946, pp. 191, 204.

19 Donald Kagan, 'What is a Liberal Education?', in Fox-Genovese & Lasch-Quinn (eds), *Reconstructing*, p. 221.

20 Richard Rawlinson, *A New Method of Studying History*, 2 vols, London, W. Burton, 1728, 1. 25.

21 Jean Bodin, *Method for the Easy Comprehension of History* (1566), transl. B. Reynolds, New York, Columbia University Press, 1945, p. 44.

22 Degory Wheare (1635), quoted by J. H. M. Salmon, 'Precept, example, and truth: Degory Wheare and the "ars historica"', in D. R. Kelley and D. H. Sacks (eds), *The Historical Imagination in Early Modern England: history, rhetoric, and fiction, 1500–1800*, Cambridge, Cambridge University Press, 1997, p. 29.

23 Joseph Glanvill, *Scepsis Scientifica*, London, H. Eversden, 1665, pp. 6–7.

24 Tacitus, *The Annals of Imperial Rome*, transl. Michael Grant, Harmondsworth, Penguin, 1959, 1.1; Francis Bacon, *Of the Advancement and Proficience of Learning*, Oxford, Robert Young and Edward Forrest, 1640, p. 94.

25 Paolo Sarpi, *The History of the Council of Trent*, transl. Nathaniel Brent, London, Robert Barker and John Bill, 1620, p. 2.

26 G. E. R. Elton, *The Practice of History*, London, Fontana, 1969, p. 30.

27 E. P. Thompson, *William Morris: Romantic to Revolutionary*, London, Merlin, 1977, pp. ix, 28.

28 Francis Bacon, *De Augmentis*, quoted by Judith H. Anderson, *Biographical Truth*, New Haven and London, Yale University Press, 1984, p. 164. On 'the Narrator as

Nobody', see Elizabeth Deeds Ermarth, *Sequel to History*, Oxford, Princeton University Press, 1992, p. 27; *Realism and Consensus in the English Novel*, 2nd edn, Edinburgh, Edinburgh University Press, 1998, ch. 3.

29 Peter Lee *et al.*, *The Aims of School History*, London, Tufnell Press, 1993, pp. 14, 18, 26.

30 Richard Evans, *In Defence of History*, London, Granta, 1997, pp. 76, 252 (my emphasis).

31 G. E. R. Elton, *Return to Essentials*, Cambridge, 1991, p. 67.

32 Elton, *Essentials*, pp. 62, 55.

33 Henry V. Dicks, *Licensed Mass Murder: A Socio-Psychological Study of Some S. S. Killers*, London, Heinemann, 1972, pp. 102, 218 (my emphasis).

34 See report in *Independent on Sunday*, 11 December 1994.

35 Albert Speer, reported in *The Guardian*, 22 September 1970, quoted by G. E. M. de Ste Croix, *The Class Struggle in the Ancient Greek World*, London, Duckworth, 1981, p. xi. My old tutor Geoffrey de Ste Croix died, just before his ninetieth birthday, while I was writing this. I owe him much.

36 Nietzsche, *Untimely Meditations*, pp. 87–93.

37 See Ermarth, *Sequel*, pp. 38–9; and cf. the implied warning on p. 116, where Ermarth cites a character from Nabokov who becomes 'such a spectator that he ends up watching himself make love to his wife from an armchair in the next room'.

38 Nietzsche, *Untimely Meditations*, p. 105.

39 Max Weber, quoted by Lutz Niethammer, *Posthistoire: Has History Come to an End?*, London, Verso, 1992, pp. 31–2 (my emphases).

40 George Rodger, quoted in *The Sunday Telegraph*, 28 March 1999, p. 9.

41 Lee *et al.*, *Aims*, p. 52.

42 Lord Bolingbroke, 'Of the True Use of Retirement and Study', printed with *Letters*, p. 403 (my emphases).

43 Nietzsche, *Untimely Meditations*, pp. 132, 170, 127, 128, 153, 169.

44 Daniel Heinsius, *The Value of History* (*c.* 1613), transl. G. W. Robinson, Cambridge, Mass., 1943, p. 11.

45 Nietzsche, *Untimely Meditations*, pp. 129, 106, 133.

7

Postmodernism, history and values

History is not what it used to be. – Diane Elam[1]

Introduction

Following the postmodernist critiques of recent times, historical studies have changed, at least in some respects. Most obviously, historians are more hesitant about claiming to be 'objective', or to have have reached – or even to have tried to reach – any unitary historical 'truth' about the past. Many, forced to become aware of the historicity of their own subject, are now prepared to take as their starting-point the conclusion reached by Alun Munslow, that 'the idea of truth being rediscovered in the evidence is a nineteenth-century modernist conception . . . [which] has no place in contemporary writing about the past'.[2] There does, of course, remain some continuing nostalgia for the idealistic aspirations of Ranke and his followers, but Diane Elam is surely justified in her claim that, in theory at least, 'history is not what it used to be'.

What it used to be, derived from well-meaning attempts by historians to emulate procedures that were believed to characterise modern science: the ideal of the detached observer, who was expected to renounce any human characteristics in order to detect, measure and precisely (ideally, in that most precise language of mathematics) describe the supposedly mechanical operations of nature – this model, so fashionable from the seventeenth century on, was adopted by historians in their quest for truth in their own field. As 'scientists', it then seemed, historians could be – must be – insulated from any personal involvement in, or commitment to, the object of their study; for that would endanger their ability to remain impartial. As scientists, historians were denied any right, or ability, to take sides or to make evaluative judgements: their function, again, was not to reason *why*. Or that at least was the theory.

If that ideal of depersonalisation has now been exposed as a sham – as a meaningless aspiration in the sciences, let alone in the pseudo social sciences – we are still left with the question of whether historians have, or should have, any aspirations at all. In other words, we are left with this book's title: why bother with history? And I want to argue in these concluding chapters that there are indeed still reasons to be bothered with the subject, and that, even (or perhaps especially) in the face of postmodernist claims about the 'end of history', there is a sense in which the historian's task (though not the manner in which he or she performs it) may not in practice have changed so much at all. For, as it has been noted, 'Theory is good, but it doesn't prevent things from existing'[3] – and that includes the past.

In particular, I conclude that historians remain bound to express some values in relation to that persisting past. As I argued in chapter 4, historical study remains inextricably entangled with politics, and the inevitability of that has been increasingly recognised. But a further, though possibly more contentious, corollary is that historians bear the enormous responsibility of needing actually to commit themselves explicitly to some political – and therefore moral – values.

Postmodernism and the end of history

Perhaps we are now at a postmodern moment when we can forget history completely. – Keith Jenkins[4]

Keith Jenkins' radical (or ironical) proposal that we 'gather the strength to unburden ourselves of the historicised past', and simply 'wave good-bye to history', is unlikely to commend itself to many historians; nor is it of course (for many reasons, as it presently seems) a practical proposition. But, as a step in an intellectual argument, it can be seen to follow from the effective undermining by postmodernism of modernist history's most fundamental claims and assumptions. If we accept the inevitable disjunction between any historical (actual) past and the historicised (described) past, and so the contingency and arbitrary nature of any historical account; if we concede the relativism of all such terms as 'fact' and 'objectivity' and 'truth'; and if we conclude the practical impossibility of even distinguishing 'fact' from 'fiction' in historical narratives – then what possible point can there be in pursuing a study that has always been dependent on these now undermined foundations?

Postmodernists themselves, of course, may still claim to be doing something called 'history', but all that amounts to is the imposing on the past of a content and a form, a direction and a meaning, that happens to suit them at the moment. For that past is infinitely adaptable; it can be moulded to any shape we want; or, as Keith Jenkins more colourfully, or judgmentally, affirms, it 'is utterly promiscuous: it will go with anybody – Marxists, Whigs, racists, feminists, phenomenologists, structuralists, empiricists, Eltonians, Foucaldians, "postists" – anybody'.[5]

It is precisely for that reason that the poet Paul Valéry (writing after the First World War and long before 'postmodernism' was thought of) characterised history as 'the most dangerous product evolved from the chemistry of the intellect'; for containing everything it justifies anything, and has the capacity to provoke in any direction.[6] Historians, as we can all now see, of whatever intellectual (or emotional) persuasion, can (indeed, must) simply mould or manipulate the past for their own purposes. Their lopsided constructions may not deserve the accolade of reception as 'the truth', but they can all make something coherent out of the past. That's their job, and that's what gives them their enormous power; and it's also, as Valéry recognised, what makes their products so potentially dangerous.

It would, though, clearly be ludicrous to expect to learn any lessons (especially moral lessons) from such history – from something so fickle and so prone to prostitute itself to all and sundry. And with one of the most important of the previous justifications for the subject thus apparently eroded, why should we go on bothering with it at all? That question becomes even more insistent when, at Keith Jenkins' instigation, we remind ourselves that 'History' as a discipline is not, after all, some natural entity – something that exists out there in nature, independent and autonomous: on the contrary, it's as culturally conditioned as any other intellectual structure, with a form imposed upon it that has, at least since its professionalisation in the nineteenth century, been consistent with other components of modernity. That form itself therefore is contingent: it depends on us, and it could be quite different. And that means that 'history' could be constructed by us quite differently – or, as Jenkins concludes, *not at all.*[7]

That sort of prospect, of the 'end of history' – like the end of the novel, figurative painting, high-rise building and other elements of our culture – has been so often predicted, or even announced, by iconoclastic critics, that they may seem to be in some danger of having cried 'wolf!' once too often. Warned of imminent catastrophe so many times, we become blasé about our powers of survival, and may ignore the approach of real danger. In this case, paradoxically, our awareness of the past, our knowledge of history, may foster not so much alertness as complacency; and historians have been contemplating the demise of their subject, if not of themselves, for some considerable time.

There have been various reasons for (and various meanings of) the claim that history has, for good or ill, hit its terminal buffers. First there has been a recurring assumption that history has, as it were, gone far enough (if not too far already). Even the New Testament, with its prospect of our final judgement, has been seen as envisaging 'a culmination of history'; and certainly from the mid-nineteenth century there have been frequent assertions that historical development has come to its end. Thomas Arnold, for example, expressed his conviction that the then modern age bore 'marks of the fulness of time, as if there would be no future history beyond it'. Having nevertheless, for better or worse, survived into the next century, Oswald Spengler expressed the mood of post First World War pessimism with his diagnosis of the west's imminent decline and fall from the 1920s; and more recently, following the demise of communism in Eastern Europe in 1989 (and presumably with greater optimism), Francis Fukuyama has caught the popular imagination with his projection of 'the end of history', on the grounds that our own age of liberal capitalist democracy can be seen as the apogee and culmination of human development.[8]

The number of times that the 'end of history' in that sense has been announced, is itself a good indication that any such announcements are likely to be premature. Indeed, as *fin de siècle* angst gives way to millennial optimism, historical development seems rather to be at a new beginning. After all, judgement and resurrection in the Christian sense is far from necessarily implying an end (in the sense of conclusion); any Spenglerian style decline of the west seems increasingly likely to be offset by risings in the east; and the attainment of Fukuyama's political consensus remains as unlikely as it's undesirable on a parochial, let alone a global scale.

But it's another sense of the 'end of history' that we're concerned with here, which implies the end of history as a study of the past and its representations; and Keith Jenkins is not the first to sound apocalyptic in this respect. Some three hundred years ago an increasingly fashionable sceptical philosophy provoked some writers seriously to question the future of historical study. When carried to an extreme, it was realised, sceptical doubts could undermine any form of intellectual endeavour – whether philosophy itself, or theology, or science, or of course history. If one can't trust one's own senses or one's own powers of reasoning or memory, how much less reliance can one put on the evidence of those other people on whom historians inevitably depend as witnesses for any reports of what has happened? The whole of historical study becomes suspect, potentially no better than some scorned romance or fiction; and as both politician and historian, Lord Bolingbroke for one realises that the very best histories inevitably 'are defective'. Historians may postulate the most coherent and persuasive hypotheses about what has happened in the past, and they may possibly, or even probably, be right; but there's always the chance that they may still be wrong. 'Whole systems of lies get into history', Bolingbroke concludes, and 'there is no false-hood too gross to be imposed on any people.' And although person-ally rejecting extreme historical pyrrhonism, he does cite those early eighteenth-century proto-postmodernists, who are 'ready to insist that all history is fabulous, and that the very best is nothing better than a probable tale, artfully contrived, and plausibly told, wherein truth and falsehood are indistinguishably blended together'.[9]

Two centuries later, in the 1930s, Michael Oakeshott fires another broadside into the tottering historical hulk. He presents convincing arguments that effectively demolish the conventional belief in 'a fixed and finished past . . . , divorced from and uninfluenced by the present' – precisely that domain, supposedly pristine and isolated, which had long since been colonised by historians as their own. Oakeshott himself recognises how potentially damaging his critique must prove: he had effectively denied the previous existence of that very entity which historians claimed that they were resurrecting. So by implication, he'd taken away their very *raison d'être*. 'It is difficult', he concludes, 'to see how he [the historian] could go on, did he not believe his task to be the resurrection of what once had been alive.'[10] With their Lucian- and Acton-like claims invalidated, why on earth should historians go on bothering with their subject?

That question may be old and constantly recurring, but it has now become more insistent. Postmodernism has presented a challenge and a threat (or opportunity) that won't just go away: it is, as has been pointed out, a 'condition' that we're in rather than a fashionable and possibly transient 'philosophy' or 'modish blip'. As such it has been seen by traditional historians for some time as yet another manifestation of barbarism which indicates (or threatens to bring) yet another end to civilisation. In the face of increasing fears (or acknowledgements) that this time 'the study of history is under siege', a new Historical Society has recently (1999) been formed in the United States to shore up the defences. Unfortunately, while perversely ascribing 'a Manichaean view' to postmodernists, the new champions of the old adopt a Manichaean view themselves, casting themselves unsurprisingly as the good, while ascribing to postmodernism the diametrically opposed role of absolute evil. As a result they naturally feel justified in claiming 'the basic incompatibility of postmodernism [evil] and historical study [good]'.[11]

It's true that the somewhat extreme views of Keith Jenkins, with his inflammatory proposal for the (next) end of history, do need to be addressed, but it seems less than tolerant (one of the many supposed virtues of traditional historians) to cast him and his kind into outer darkness without first making some attempt to come to terms.

Keith Jenkins' suggestion that we are now in a position to abandon history altogether, to jettison any attempt to get to know the past (since it's anyway unknowable), will probably sound ludicrous to most people, alarming and even sinister to many others, and exciting to a few. The majority will reassert the need for history, if for nothing else, as a prerequisite for personal and national identity: for them, such a crucial constituent of our culture and our very being (or selfhood) is quite literally indispensable; and it has to be noted here that Jenkins' own argument is grounded in a modernist rationalism that undervalues its historic opposite – the emotional, which nonetheless continues to present its own demands. Others will suspect that Jenkins, like Plato and the Chinese cultural revolutionaries and many other advocates of a 'closed society', is intending to eliminate or manipulate the past for his own ideological purposes. And that may be true, which is why he himself and some few others may find the newly proposed prospect so alluring: it represents a liberation from the constraints of outdated modernist ways of thought and their 'restrictive cloyingness'. If postmodernism has already superseded conventional, modernist historical thought, and freed us from traditional ways of looking at the past and doing history, why (as Keith Jenkins goes on to ask) should we feel constrained to think up new ways of doing what amounts essentially to the same old thing? Why waste time agonising about the nature and purposes of postmodernist history, when that history is bound to turn out having a close resemblance to what we've just got rid of? Why bother to invent any replacement for something that's completely outmoded? The very fact that we feel constrained to do so indicates that we are still entrammelled in modernist intellectual bonds. But we don't have to be: rather, we can emulate Lyotard by *really thinking*, where 'really thinking' is defined as 'being prepared to receive what thought is not prepared to think'.[12] That, surely, is what would open the way to real emancipation . . .

Keith Jenkins's vision of 'a postmodern moment when we can forget history . . . altogether', and entertain 'new thoughts free of the shackles of history and ethics', presents (in his own words) 'an opportunity: the beginning of an exciting adventure'. Far from constituting a (negative) 'crisis' (as it is seen by its opponents), postmodernism offers the (positive) 'possibility of keeping emancipatory thought alive'.[13] What I want to go on to suggest is that that possibility is not inconsistent with denying the 'end of history'. In fact, rather the reverse: it is precisely the historian who is needed at this time to adopt the role of moralist in an imaginative 'poetic' way. That's why, now more than ever, we need to go on bothering with history.

The historian as moralist

History is not a value-free enterprise. – John Slater[14]

If the whole point of history is under question, it may seem perverse (or even presumptuous) to consider its potential moral role. Deprived of any meaningful narrative direction or purpose, robbed of any absolutist or essentialist pretensions, history may seem to have been left in a state of amoral relativism that would negate any claim to value. Yet paradoxically, postmodernist theorising has actually served to re-emphasise the importance of John Slater's claim that 'history is not a value-free enterprise', and by implication is inextricably bound up with morality; so that the postmodern historian becomes a moralist *malgré lui*.

That link between morality and history is not fortuitous since, for all their protestations, morality has always been at the core of historians' activities. They may (as we have seen in chapter 1) have often maintained the theoretical position that history should be 'purposeless', and should certainly be free of moral judgements. But in practice, historical work has always depended – and must always depend – on the acceptance (by which I mean imposition) of some moral order. That is not to say that there is some inherent morality or structure of values out there in the past or in the universe, awaiting the historian's discovery. 'In the world everything is as it is, and everything happens as it does happen: *in it no value exists – and if it did, it would have no value.*'[15] The past is a constituent part of 'the world', and Wittgenstein's words apply not least to history. But, although values don't simply exist there, they do have to be constructed and imposed – which is precisely what makes historians themselves so important.

The need for an imposed moral structure derives from the very nature of historians' work, for that work is essentially to do with people: it is about people, and it is done by people. Because it is about people, historians can't avoid becoming involved in making moral judgements – unless of course they turn themselves into something less than human, such as a Lucianesque mirror (supposedly) reflecting good and bad indiscriminately and purposelessly. Historians who retain their own humanity will inevitably respond to other humans, in the past just as in the present, in a human way; which is to say that they will respond to them as moral agents. To make some narrative sense out of their (essentially human) material, they will have to commit themselves and adopt some moral position; so they will perforce end up as moralists.

And that role is thrust upon them, too, by virtue of the fact that history is not only made, but also researched and written, by people. Historical work itself is a human activity, and collaborative; and historians depend on other people. In any such collaborative enterprise, trust is essential: people have to be able to rely on each other; at the most fundamental level, some values have to be shared. A mountaineer would be unlikely to join an expedition which included members who declined to take seriously their securing of a rope; the life of one person may literally hang on another, and that other had better be trustworthy. Mountaineering depends on morality, on the acceptance of shared values. And similarly – and certainly no less – with history. It's only by being able to depend on people's moral responsibility that history can get written; historians have to depend on other people's reports for their information about what has happened in the past, and they have to be able to rely on them.

But of course, they can't rely on them. The 'Donation of Constantine' (an eighth-century forgery purporting to authenticate papal claims to temporal authority), 'Piltdown Man' (an early twentieth-century fake), and 'Hitler's Diaries' (a more recent attempt at forgery) are just three well-known examples of historical evidence, initially accepted as reliable, but later found to dangle from untrustworthy anchor-men. Such frauds, whether pseudo-skulls or fabricated documents, can serve to make or break historical narratives, and sceptics have always questioned the dependability of such pieces of evidence from which history is constructed.

That problem of credibility has seemed particularly acute at times when sceptical philosophy has come to the forefront of fashion – in early-modern Europe, for example. At that time, theorists often discuss the criteria for credibility, whether of contemporary reports of scientific experiments, or past reports of events as recorded in the scriptures or elsewhere. And emphasis is invariably laid on the moral character of those involved. In science, that often means that we require our eye-witness reporters of scientific experiments to be 'gentlemen' – to share,

that is, the moral values of a certain social class. We can't trust everyone
– of course not. But on the whole, as Matthew Hale concluded when
he considered this matter in relation to history, 'we believe good and
credible persons'.

Those adjectives, 'good and credible', remind us of many earlier (and
later) decriptions of the ideal historian. As Hale and many others recognised, in our quest for reliable historical evidence, we ideally need as
many eye-witnesses of a past event as possible; and these should all
agree, providing mutual confirmation. But it's not only a question of
their numbers. Numerous reporters who are only 'light and inconsider-
able' are no use at all: what we need are witnesses who meet the description 'credible and authentick', and to qualify for that, they must at least
be seen to have no personal interest in the matter of their report, or in its
outcome: they must be, as we say, 'disinterested'. Preferably too, their
verbal reports will derive from personal experience, rather than being
second-hand from someone else's 'hearsay'; and ideally they will be
additionally corroborated by material evidence from archaeology or surviving architectural remains – 'the concurring testimony of real existing
monuments'.[16]

The essential point for Matthew Hale, though, is that we can only
believe in a history which has come to us from people we can trust –
from 'credible persons, and such as who could probably have no end to
deceive us'. Absolute certainty in such matters is an unrealisable goal,
but a fair degree of probability can be attained through the assurance of
the moral probity of our collaborators. As Hugo Grotius had written
earlier, it's reasonable for us to believe actual eyewitnesses, so long as
they are competent both intellectually and morally – 'defective neither
in judgment nor in honesty'.[17]

Those intellectual and moral qualifications can be used as bench-marks
in particular examples. Take, for instance, Moses. As 'the first Historian
that ever wrote', Moses has always enjoyed an enviable reputation as the
amanuensis of God himself. His account of the early history of the world
could be relied on for all sorts of reasons. In the first place, he had the
advantage of living geographically and chronologically nearer to the
events he described than other historians (who anyway customarily en-
dorse his version). Secondly, his words were not only originally dictated

by 'the special Providence of Almighty God', but were subsequently preserved with great care by that same power. Thirdly, it is relevant to note that he had been educated in Egypt, where people were good at those mathematical studies which are so important for historians; so his intellectual credentials were established. But highly important, too, in relation to his historical reliability, is his unblemished moral character: he is not boastful or ambitious; he voluntarily owns up to any faults he might have; and he avoids deceiving rhetoric, or 'any dissembling or alluring language, such as commonly colours over a lye'.[18]

Moses thus exemplifies the ideal historian, inasmuch as he is amply justified in trusting his own earlier sources, and is also absolutely trustworthy himself. As we saw in chapter 3, then, it was widely believed that, in the scriptural record for which he was responsible, there wasn't the slightest possibility of any deception or intention to deceive. Truth in short was guaranteed by the acceptance of a moral order shared by witnesses, authors, transcribers and readers.

That shared moral order underpinning historical study has been a function of a wider system of values enjoyed by society as a whole. When (as a contemporary of Hale) Edward Stillingfleet defended the scriptural record as the basis of Protestant faith, he found himself engaged in a defence of history more generally, but he was aware that some aspects of that defence impinged more widely, on moral and social order. If, for example, in the context of history, we accept sceptical arguments concerning witnesses – that friendly witnesses will show partiality on one side, and hostile witnesses distort the record on the other – then we are left with the conclusion that we can rely on no one, and that 'no History at all, ancient or modern, is to be believed'. But that is far from all: the lack of trust which removes our faith in history extends well beyond the confines of history itself. That demoralising tendency will, Stillingfleet believes, destroy not only all human faith, but also human society which depends upon that faith: 'it will destroy all Society among Men; which is built on the supposition of mutual trust and confidence that Men have in each other'.[19]

Stillingfleet's point might be illustrated by a parallel example of moral breakdown in the field of more personal relationships. Many of us will be able to relate to Proust's description of Monsieur Swann's descent into chaotic uncertainty, and his need for a total re-appraisal of his past relationship, following the discovery of a single untruth apparently perpetrated by his lover Odette. Long after the event, he came across a new piece of evidence about how she had previously behaved; and 'he could feel the insinuation of a possible undercurrent of falsehood which rendered ignoble all that had remained most precious to him'. One new piece of evidence undermined the trust on which all his previous perceptions had been based, and so cast doubt on the validity of his entire relationship. In Swann's case, the new information about his lover's deceit forced him to make a painful re-appraisal, after 'shattering stone by stone the whole edifice of his past'.[20]

It is the fear of having, not only intellectual but also moral, edifices shattered, with all the chaos that would then become apparent, that lies at the root of 'pomophobia', or fear of postmodernism; and the pomophobes do have a point. It's not for nothing that, in his latest book, Keith Jenkins is concerned with the end of both history *and* ethics: the two inevitably go together. But the result doesn't have to be negative: on the contrary.

And looking to that contrary, one positive approach has been indicated by Thomas Haskell, in an interesting (and often persuasive) attempt to rehabilitate 'objectivity', in large part by re-defining it in such a way as to make it compatible with political and moral commitment. He is particularly concerned to retain some moral standards (for the sake, again, not only of historical study but also of society more generally), in the face of a perceived Nietzschean tendency to 'blur all that distinguishes villainy from decency in everyday affairs'. That, he believes, is tantamount to 'defam[ing] the species', but is no doubt consistent with a species of postmodernism which he believes 'typically presupposes a self too vaporous to resist anything'.[21]

As an antidote, Haskell prescribes a dose of 'ascetic self-discipline', to enable historians to practise much as they have often preached: that is, for instance, to resist succumbing to, and being diverted by, wishful thinking; and to discard apparently supporting evidence which is known to be flawed. Above all, he recommends a 'detachment' that enables historians to suspend their own individualistic perceptions in order to enter sympathetically into other perspectives. Such detachment, he claims, is daily and practically shown in everyday life, when we decide what trust to put in other people, or when we reach conclusions in respect to various conflicting claims; and it is shown in academic life more particularly, when teachers contrive to assess essays impartially, or properly referee the work of their peers. That sort of detachment amounts to being fair and honest, and it implies that we succeed in developing a view of the world that does not have the self as the centre. *Neutrality* is not expected or required, but an openness to alternative and multiple perspectives.

Thomas Haskell's analysis is often persuasive, and I share some of his concerns. But I have already (in chapter 6) expressed my own reservations about 'detachment' (which admittedly I used in a different sense), and I believe that unfortunately his view of his peers may be optimistic (though this does not invalidate his overall position): one has only to look at some of their negative and denigrating reviews, and their personal, *ad hominem* attacks on dissenters from the orthodox, to recognise that historians often fail to live up to their own professed humanitarian ideals. The ability sympathetically to enter into another's perspective is not, it seems, easily acquired; but that is not to say that it shouldn't be aimed for. Multiple perspectives may not provide significantly higher levels of 'completeness' as Haskell suggests (for that implies the existence of a finite history to strive towards), but they have to be preferable to tunnel vision. And historians – whether modern or postmodern – who achieve those multiple perspectives surely do not have to renounce, or release, their own identities or selves to the extent of becoming 'vaporous' and universally amenable. On the contrary, they first need to be confident in themselves and in their own position, however provisional and improvable each may be: it is the insecure who feel vulnerable, and so close up and show aggression to alternatives.

So we come back again to the need for historians now to make their own existential, as well as historical, decisions – the need for them to become their own moralists. The fact that postmodernism leaves historians without any *foundationalist* structure of values (values that have been implanted in the world and/or ratified by some absolute religious or secular power) leaves them not only *free* but also actually *required* to make their own moral choices and decisions; and their histories will be constructed accordingly, in an enterprise that's far from 'value-free'.

The historian as poet

Poets are the unacknowledged legislators of the world. – Shelley[22]

Shelley's claim may sound extravagant now, or part of an unlikely bid for disciplinary recognition and additional funding, but it is to be understood in the context of a long tradition which emphasised the didactic, moral role of poetry. Aristotle's well-known distribution of intellectual property left poetry with the flighty moral function of proposing (legislating) what might be, in contrast with history's much meaner and earth-bound allocation of describing what already is. That territorial inheritance is still accepted with gratitude by those historians who prefer to avoid involvement in such dangerous activities as speculation or the formulation of value judgements; but, against any such affected disciplinary limitations, I have already argued in chapters 3 and 4 that historians are now effectively the world's (largely) 'unacknowledged legislators', inasmuch as it is they who provide the underpinning for our personal and national identities.

What that position implies, though, is that history has taken over a part of poetry's earlier role; and I would argue further that, having appropriated or assumed at least a part of poetry's legislative mantle, historians themselves now need to become more explicitly poetical. What does that in practice mean?

One of the achievements of poetry, and one of its sins in Francis Bacon's eyes, is that it is (apart from its formal stylistic constraints) 'extremely licensed' and ranges far too freely. In particular, since it is an imaginative rather than purely rational enterprise, it makes illegitimate distinctions and connections between things: 'being not tied to the laws of matter, [it] may at pleasure join that which nature hath severed, and sever that which nature hath joined; and so make unlawful matches and divorces of things'.[23]

History, on the other hand, has affected to be far too respectable to indulge in any such unlawful matches and divorces: despite Keith Jenkins' imputations of promiscuity cited above, history has had a long-time monogamous relationship with truth itself, so surely would never feel tempted to stray from the strait and narrow path of lawful factuality. But we might, suspiciously, still be justified in asking Bacon what constitutes an 'illegitimate' distinction or connection. Those distinctions and connections, after all, have been imposed by us, on a world where everything is interconnected (if only we could see). Aristotle may have carved up intellectual territory, and we may have similarly carved up the natural world into seemingly discrete atomic entities; and those carvings may have been confirmed (and even apparently as time goes by legitimised) by our language; and that in turn may have enabled us to apply labels to the universe's constituent parts (including history) as if they were entities defined by nature or by God's almighty direction. But in fact it has all been done at our own determination, to facilitate our own analyses and to suit our own convenience. The joining and severing has been done not by God or nature, but by us.

So poetry's function – and the arts' more generally – has been to re-assemble a world we've torn apart, to re-appropriate and reconstitute the wholeness of a world we've colonised, and then to re-arrange it in quite other ways. Poets have succeeded in jumping clear of our self-imposed boundaries; they have freed themselves from the trammels of convention; and so they have seen things differently and described them afresh. Having once recognised the contingency of our own dispensations, and realised that things could be ordered and described differently, they have (as Bacon saw) often linked together those parts which we have come to see as separate (and vice versa). That poetic linking and severing is not, then, 'illegitimate': it's just unexpected, unfamiliar. It comes as a surprise, because it defies convention; it's not what we've got used to; and it forces us to see things in another way, from an alternative perspective.

That is why Richard Rorty sees the poet as not only 'the maker of new words and the shaper of new languages', but as 'the vanguard of the species'[24] (and, one might add, the maker of new *worlds*). And that is just what I would wish for the historian. Emulating the procedures advocated by Bacon, scientists have classified the natural world, breaking it up into separate parts; and in the same way, we've divided up our knowledge (including our historical knowledge) and our ways of getting it and using it. But it may be time to pull the bits together again, and to see the bits – including history and poetry – as once more inter-related parts of a coherent (or even incoherent) whole, the boundaries of which are no longer fixed, but fluid.

For both history and poetry attempt to do the impossible – which is to express in static, finite form what is actually chaotically formless and in ever-changing flux. Each lays claim to some solidity, some security and certainty, in defiance of its practitioners' experience. Each imposes its markers, using language – words and punctuation points – to stamp a meaning and a structure on what is essentially inchoate, meaningless and structureless; and each represents a constantly re-negotiable interaction between the writer and the written-up event or experience. 'Poems', wrote the educationist William Walsh, 'are at once chronicles of events and reflections of self . . . They are activities which fashion what they comment on, which form and reform the image they reflect';[25] and with those words, written in 1959, he might have been describing postmodern histories.

The ever-changing balance between event and self, and the impossibility of any clear definition of either as they form and reform in what is a constantly evolving inter-relationship, requires that both historian and poet live with an element of uncertainty; it precludes the possibility – or at least the justifiability – of fixity and dogmatism. Dogmatism, of course, is a sin that few, if any, historians would in theory ever admit to; but the rhetoric of their trade, like that of politicians, does in practice require a measure of conviction. Historians do, in the end, have to come off the fence, and present their own case cogently; and they have to convince themselves before they can hope to convince others. So they may be less temperamentally suited to professional and personal uncertainty than they would readily concede. But that uncertainty is another characteristic that may need to be shared with poetry, or borrowed from it. For it was another Romantic poet who defined the quality of 'negative capability', that seems to suit the needs of the postmodern historian very well. In John Keats's words, it is manifested 'when a man is capable of being in uncertainties, mysteries, doubts, without any irritable reaching after fact and reason'.[26] In that respect too, then, we might hope to see the historian as poet.

And he or she would be in good intellectual company, for that seemingly most astringent of twentieth-century philosophers, Ludwig Wittgenstein, can also be found in his posthumous Arcadia aspiring to express himself in poetry. Wittgenstein too made his personal discovery, 'that the ground on which we stood, which appeared to be firm and reliable, was found to be boggy and unsafe'. He too perceived the need to enter into that boggy, unsafe territory, and 'to descend into primeval chaos, and feel at home there'; which is, perhaps, why he recognised that 'philosophy ought to be written only as a *poetic* composition'.[27] That did not imply that his philosophy would be presented as chaotic or formless: on the contary, much of it is structured in a singularly logical, even quasi-mathematical way. As with Immanuel Kant, who had earlier been a source of wonderment for his personal regularities while effecting an intellectual revolution, Wittgenstein challenged the existing structures of thought in what might seem to be a paradoxically disciplined way.

There is no paradox of course: poets of all writers are the most disciplined, inasmuch as their task is to present the infinite in strictly finite form; for them, as T. S. Eliot notes, 'organisation is necessary as well as inspiration'.[28] And so it must be for historians as the world's postmodern legislators.

Conclusion

Far from having reached the end of history – either the end of historical development or the end of historical study – we are at a new beginning for both. For the former, it must be as inconceivable for us as it was to William Morris that we have reached our *telos* or end: that would still be 'to turn history into inconsequent nonsense'. For the latter, it's equally inconceivable (to most) that we could manage without some memory and reconstruction (representation) of the past.

While it remains difficult to see what its new beginning might consist of, it seems clear that historical study cannot be and (in Diane Elam's words again) '*is not* what it used to be'; and I have chosen (in the sections above) two areas where there might emphatically (and beneficially) be rethinking – in relation to morality and poetry. These may sound to some like radical departures from traditional modernist history, but even in modernist terms each has respectable historical pedigrees. Poetry may have been firmly differentiated from history by some influential writers of classical antiquity, including notably the theoretician Aristotle and the practising Thucydides. But a more 'romantic' tradition has periodically resurfaced in the history of historiography, exemplified in Carlyle's 'creed that the only Poetry is History, could we tell it right'[29]; and it's time for historians to recover the didactic and legislative functions of their subject.

That links with history's moral function, or rather with the historian's function as a moralist – not moralising (in a pejorative sense) but personally exemplifying moral values. The problematic nature of that function in a relativistic postmodern age is precisely the point, for while critics of postmodernism have decried its amorality, in fact and on the contrary it necessitates a truly free and therefore moral agenda. Bereft of externally imposed moral structures, historians are left to formulate their own. In the first place, they have to establish (or re-establish) a shared moral code in terms of which historical work can continue to be done – showing *how* it can be done. In the second place, they are left with the huge responsibility of determining the moral function of historical study, of deciding what is to be derived from the past in relation to their vision for the future – thereby demonstrating *why* we have to bother with it.

Notes

1 Diane Elam, quoted in Keith Jenkins (ed.), *The Postmodern History Reader*, London, Routledge, 1997, p. 67.

2 Alun Munslow, *Deconstructing History*, London, Routledge, 1997, p. 178.

3 Cited as one of Freud's favourite quotations, and attributed to Charcot, by D. M. Thomas, *The White Hotel*, Harmondsworth, Penguin, 1981, p. 111.

4 Keith Jenkins, ' "After" History', *Rethinking History* 3, 1999, p. 7; quotations in the following paragraph are from p. 8.

5 Keith Jenkins, 'Why bother with the Past?', *Rethinking History* 1, 1997, p. 64.

6 Paul Valéry, 'De l'histoire' (1931), quoted by Hayden White, *Tropics of Discourse*, London, Johns Hopkins University Press, 1978, p. 36.

7 See Jenkins, 'Why bother?'

8 Thomas Arnold, inaugural lecture as Regius Professor of History at Oxford, 1841, quoted by J. B. Bury in Fritz Stern (ed.), *The Varieties of History*, New York, Meridian, 1956, p. 217; Oswald Spengler, *The Decline of the West*, London, George Allen & Unwin, 1926; Francis Fukuyama, *The End of History and the Last Man*, Harmondsworth, Penguin, 1992. For an interesting discussion, see Lutz Niethammer, *Posthistoire: Has History Come to an End?*, transl. Patrick Camiller, London, Verso, 1992.

9 Lord Bolingbroke, 'The Substance of Some Letters . . . to M. de Pouilly' (*c.* 1720), in *The Works*, 4 vols, Philadelphia, Carey & Hart, 1841, 2.491; *Letters on the Study and Use of History*, London, A. Millar, 1752, pp. 98–9.

10 Michael Oakeshott, *Experience and its Modes*, Cambridge, Cambridge University Press, 1933, p. 107.

11 See Elizabeth Fox-Genovese & Elisabeth Lasch-Quinn (eds), *Reconstructing History*, London, Routledge, 1999, pp. xvi, 50, xvii. Postmodernism's incompatibility with historical study is maintained in particular by Gertrude Himmelfarb, who is convinced that postmodernism is 'not so much a revision of modernist history as a repudiation of it' (p. 75).

12 Keith Jenkins, *Why History?*, London, Routledge, 1999, p. 5; Lyotard quoted p. 103. Cf. Jonathan Swift: 'Vision is the art of seeing things invisible.' Quoted by Idris Parry, *Animals of Silence*, London, Oxford University Press, 1972, p. 9.

13 Jenkins, *Why?*, pp. 2, 29, 33.

14 John Slater, 'Where there is dogma, let us sow doubt', in Peter Lee *et al.*, *The Aims of School History*, London, Tufnell Press, 1993, p. 45. HM Staff Inspector for history, 1974–87, John Slater is not otherwise renowned for his postmodernist credentials.

15 Ludwig Wittgenstein, *Tractatus Logico Philosophicus*, transl. D. F. Pears and B. F. McGuinness, London, Routledge & Kegan Paul, 1961, 6.41.

16 Matthew Hale, *The Primitive Origination of Mankind*, London, William Shrowsbery, 1677, pp. 57, 129.

17 Hugo Grotius, *The Truth of the Christian Religion* (1624), transl. Simon Patrick, London, R. Royston, 1680, p. 21.

18 Hale, *Origination*, p. 143; Grotius, *Truth*, p. 24. Edward Stillingfleet similarly notes Moses' Egyptian education, and his repudiation of rhetoric: he wrote 'not in an affected strain of Rhetorick . . . but with . . . innate simplicity and plainness'; for he was concerned 'not to court acceptance, but to demand belief.' *Origines Sacrae*, London, Henry Mortlock, 1662, pp. 137–8.

19 Edward Stillingfleet, *Letter to a Deist*, London, Richard Cumberland, 1677, pp. 19, 21.

20 Marcel Proust, *Remembrance of Things Past*, Harmondsworth, Penguin, 1985, vol. 1, p. 404.

21 Thomas Haskell, 'Objectivity is not Neutrality: Rhetoric versus Practice in Peter Novick's *That Noble Dream*', reprinted in Brian Fay, Philip Pomper, and Richard T. Vann (eds), *History and Theory: Contemporary Readings*, Oxford, Blackwell, 1998, pp. 299–319.

22 Percy Bysshe Shelley, 'A Defence of Poetry' (*Oxford Dictionary of Quotations*).

23 Francis Bacon, *The Advancement of Learning*, London, Oxford University Press, 1951, II. 4, 1. The corresponding passage in the 1640 translation of *De Augmentis* previously cited is at p. 105; and cf. p. 77.

24 Richard Rorty, *Contingency, Irony, and Solidarity*, Cambridge, Cambridge University Press, 1989, p. 20.

25 William Walsh, *The Use of Imagination*, London, Chatto & Windus, 1959, p. 87.

26 John Keats, quoted by Walsh, *Imagination*, p. 90.

27 Ludwig Wittgenstein, *Blue and Brown Books*, 2nd edn, New York, Harper & Row, 1969, p. 59; *Culture and Value*, ed. G. H. Von Wright, Oxford, Blackwell, 1994, 65e, 24e. My thanks to Martyn Keys for these references.

28 T. S. Eliot, *The Use of Poetry and the Use of Criticism*, London, Faber & Faber, 1933, p. 146.

29 Quoted by Michael Bentley, *Modern Historiography: An Introduction*, London, Routledge, 1999, p. 27.

8

Postmodern history and the future

. . . History may be servitude,
History may be freedom.
T. S. Eliot[1]

Introduction

Cease to tremble!
Prepare yourself to live!
Friedrich Gottlieb Klopstock[2]

Those words inspired Gustav Mahler, after a blockage lasting some six years, to complete his second 'Resurrection' symphony. Used by him as a part of the text for his final movement, they may serve for us to put a positive spin on a resurrected postmodern history for the future; for, as the employment agency advertisement puts it, 'Certainties are a thing of the past. They've been superseded by possibilities.'[3]

Postmodernism, as we have seen, has often appeared to historians as a terrible threat – as something that threatens not only their subject but their selves, as something negative, if not positively evil, and as something therefore to be resisted to the end. In the eyes of such critics, postmodernism entails above all a repudiation of authority and a cynical relativisation of morals; and that results, they claim, in an attitude of 'anything goes' – both in the context of historical study, where we are left with a multiplicity of special pleaders making of the past whatever suits them, and of morality, where humanity is betrayed and we are reduced again to anarchy. For such critics, to be deprived of the old order, with its assumptions of externally imposed authority and structures, is tantamount to a return to a Hobbesian state of nature where all that matters is survival and the only motivation is self-interest; and we owe it to succeeding generations to maintain traditional standards and keep the flickering flame of civilisation alight. Thus Felipe Fernández-Armesto has recently launched a tirade against postmodernism, from which, he insists, 'we now have to prise ourselves free', so as not to leave our children as abandoned 'victims of delusion or doubt'. As a Catholic, he aligns himself with those who defer to 'the authority of the Church, as superior to whatever my own reason or experience might tell me'; so for him (and no doubt for others of similar persuasions) the barbarians are again well and truly at the gates, with postmodernists appearing as nothing less than 'truth vandals'.[4]

That, again, is hardly surprising, if postmodern theorists are understood as undermining history to such an extent as to deprive it of any value or meaning, validity or point; and admittedly some might seem to have gone that far. But, while some postmodernists may indeed have heralded 'the end of history', it's possible to see the future for historical study in a much more positive light. As traditionally conceived, the subject has (as we have argued in chapter 6) sometimes reduced its practitioners to what is essentially a form of (voluntary) 'servitude'. But, as the lines of T. S. Eliot heading this chapter indicate, history may also be conceived quite differently – not as enslaving at all, but as actually liberating, or as 'freedom'. So I'll conclude by indicating a few ways in which this may be the case.

New narratives and histories

There might be lovers whose gift it was to choose out the elements of things and place them together and so, giving them a wholeness not theirs in life, make of some scene, or meeting of people (all now gone and separate), one of those globed compacted things over which thought lingers, and love plays. – Virginia Woolf, 1927[5]

Narratives have often had a bad press. Displaying what Robert Musil called 'the look of necessity'[6], they have seemed to constitute a part of historians' enforced 'servitude', defining as they do the parameters (albeit contingent) within which historical descriptions and explanations are expected and allowed. However arbitrary, a narrative structure imposes limits, implies evaluations and devaluations, exclusions as well as inclusions. And with its need for comprehensibility and communicability, a narrative, even when it includes, can be seen as a violation of those particular experiences which, for the individual, defy inclusion in any collectively established and accepted mould. The integration of some historical events into an historical narrative can be seen as an affront: by their very inclusion within a meaningful whole, they become domestic-ated, sanitised, normalised – and thence ultimately trivialised. There are some things, perhaps, which not only cannot be reduced by narrativising history to public understanding, but which *should* not be. Claude Lanzmann explained how, in producing his own excruciating treatment of the Holocaust in *Shoah*, he had throughout maintained '*not to under-stand* [as] my iron law', so that his film could never be structured within any conventional narrative.[7]

Nevertheless, Carlyle had a point when he observed: 'Cut us off from Narrative, [and] how would the stream of conversation, even among the wisest, languish into detached handfuls!'[8] Even postmodernists need their narratives, to compact the otherwise detached handfuls of their thoughts. Their repudiation of 'metanarratives' – or of some supposedly external direction-giver to history – does not imply the elimination of any chosen narrative (which no less gives a sense of direction), so long as its contingency is recognised and made explicit. This implies some commitment, even some love, on the part of historians for their chosen subject, and what they fashion is a work of art. 'Really', as Henry James explained, 'universally, relations stop nowhere, and the exquisite prob-lem of the artist [or, we might add, the historian] is eternally to draw, by a geometry of his own, the circle in which they shall happily *appear* to do so.'[9] Like the hypothetical lovers described above by Virginia Woolf, historians will need to choose their stories' elements – individuated (and now separated) people and events – and form them into 'one of those globed compacted things' that we call a coherent narrative.

Coherence may sound too strong a word, or too modernist a goal, for historians currently engaged in their plethora of particularities. During the last few decades, at a time of increasing acceptance of internationalism and of our shared and interlocking destinies in a so-called 'global village', historians have paradoxically tended to reaffirm their particularities, and have reverted to a less than global parish pump, which they've used sometimes selfishly to irrigate their own chosen patches. Frank Füredi has described how feminists, blacks, post-colonialists and other minority groups with an 'exclusivist cultural point of view' and a 'particularist epistemology . . . [demanding] an absolute monopoly on its own culture', have typified an increasingly fragmented discipline, whose practitioners are determined above all to avoid any imputation of proposing 'metanarratives'.[10]

As an antidote to the increasing incoherence of historical study, it's worth considering the alternative model of 'collage', proposed for the discipline by Elizabeth Deeds Ermarth.[11] In the context of the visual arts, collage involves bringing together diverse and heterogeneous material in unexpected ways, so when applied to history it would have the benefit of similarly enabling unusual and unexpected juxtapositions: materials (data) can be exposed and utilised in ways that provoke new visions from alternative perspectives; with conventional usages and contextualisations ignored or deliberately overturned, everything can be made to be seen (as we say) 'in a new light'.

That challenge to our habitual and unthinking way of seeing things can be applied, then, not only to the visual arts and artefacts, but also to historical data and narrative procedures. And in that latter context, it might help to satisfy a requirement proposed by Alex Callinicos, that narratives should avoid the necessity of *closures*.[12] By admitting the validity of alternative materials (data), usages and configurations, historical collage might serve to reveal not so much a seemingly inevitable linear development, as turning-points and moments of choice and decision; and that revelation of the past's contingency (it could have been different) might encourage emancipatory approaches to the future (where again we have a *choice*).

Even for collage, however, (in history as in art) a requirement does remain for some aesthetically pleasing form, and so for some imposed coherence; and coherent synthesis is surely not impossible in a postmodern world (though it may initially seem to deny the very essence of postmodernism). History may now require, in George Eliot's words, 'freedom from the vulgar coercion of conventional plot'[13], but that does not rule out the more refined unconventionality of a *self-imposed* structure. That has recently been shown by Annabel Patterson in her exemplary study of early-modern liberalism – a work in which specific and detailed examples are used to illustrate a universalisable theme and thereby make a moral point. In an opening sentence that must have induced apoplexy in Lord Acton's purportedly purposeless followers, Annabel Patterson writes: 'This book is *not* a disinterested academic investigation'; and thus the tone is set by a writer who explicitly describes herself as 'in the missionary position'. Her study of the birth and growth and transmission of a dissenting liberal tradition in the face of official repression utilises numerous 'elements of things' – letters, memoirs, court transcripts and all the usual (and unusual) data that constitute historical evidence. They are given a 'wholeness' that could not possibly have been 'theirs in life', if only on account of their geographical and chronological diversity. But they have been deliberately moulded into 'one of those globed compacted things' – a coherent historical narrative and argument – because they seem to the author (and this reader) to relate to 'our own prospects for toleration' today. Over such narratives, thought might well linger – not because they reveal some truth about how things were (they don't: their 'wholeness [was] not theirs in life'), but because such 'historical knowledge' has a point for the present and the future, in continuing to inform 'courageous political critique'.[14] That's why we bother with it.

New chronologies and structures

There is no history without dates. – Claude Lévi-Strauss[15]

Lévi-Strauss may seem to have been presenting a platitude in the quotation above, expressing something so obvious that it hardly needed repetition; and indeed many others have previously made that rather basic point about history's dependence on chronology. Some three hundred years earlier, for instance, the author and antiquary Thomas Baker observed that, without the structures provided by chronology (and geography), history inevitably 'lies in confusion'[16]; and few historians would disagree.

However chronologically remote from one another, the rationales for the conclusions arrived at by Baker and Lévi-Strauss, are in essence intriguingly similar: for both, a body of history that lacked a chronological skeleton would simply crumple; it would lack the bones which enable any narrative to stand. What would be left, in Baker's words, is 'only a heap of indigested matter, flat and insipid', which would provide neither the 'profit nor delight' that justifies historical study in the first place. And for Lévi-Strauss similarly, a chronologically structureless history would just descend into 'chaos' – a chaos that would of itself lack any value.

There, though, the resemblance between the two may end. For despite his overt scepticism towards the chronologies utilised by previous historians, and towards their various partial narratives, Baker would probably have conceded the possibility of at least imposing some minimal framework of accepted dates on the potential 'confusion' of the past – or some of it. But Lévi-Strauss is more aware that any such structure is, even then, only contingent, in the sense of being chosen by historians from a host of alternative possibilities. Clocks may chime the hours, but, as Carlyle had earlier put it, 'no hammer in the Horologe of Time peals through the universe when there is a change from Era to Era'.[17] And since our eras are contingent, there can be different 'codes' of dates, or different modes of dating and ordering chronologies; and each of these may provide an internally consistent framework, without necessarily being consistent with any or all of its competitors.

One obvious example of such a coherent chronological framework, imposed upon the whole of time, is that provided by Christian historians (and their sometimes less than Christian successors in the western tradition), who have selected one key date (that of the assumed birth of their religion's founder) as the corner-stone of their whole system. 'This was the moment when Before/Turned into After, and the future's/ Uninvented timekeepers presented arms.'[18] As history's pivotal point, the birth of Christ facilitates a division into epochs, years, centuries and millennia – even though it requires a facility for counting backwards for anything that happened antenatally. The simplicity of the Christo-centric system must have outweighed any conservative nostalgia for pre-Christian and non-European alternatives: at least it was no longer necessary to remember the names of otherwise obscure Greek and Roman annually appointed officials (who lent their names to years), or the intricacies of Egyptian and Chinese dynasties.

But, while something was undoubtedly gained by uniformity, something may well have been lost. It's possible that the universal imposition of a Christian chronology not only confirmed the historical centrality of Christianity, but also de-emphasised some aspects of the past which seemed to fit ill with the newly evolved orbit; or at least it may have put a somewhat different complexion on those wayward items. In terms of individual biography, St Augustine's conversion to Christianity encouraged him to re-assess his earlier life: thenceforth it was to be seen as a progressive development, culminating in conversion; so that previous peccadilloes – whether of scrumping pears or living 'in sin' with a mistress – had to be re-appraised in terms of his new theological agenda. And similar adjustments were needed on the larger scale of Christianity. Greek philosophy, for instance, came to be viewed 'as a kind of preparatory discipline'[19] for the new religion, providing convenient stepping-stones towards the finally revealed truth – with the result that such intellectual anomalies as Epicureanism (which didn't fit that narrative) were decried and as far as possible erased. In more political terms, the Roman Empire was seen as a necessary precursor for the then new religion: by imposing (so far as possible) its universal peace – the *pax Romana* – it provided the framework (not least of international trade and transport) within which Christianity could grow and be widely diffused, and it could accordingly be assigned its proper purpose.

Antiquity is thus defined in terms of what came later: it is made to serve, in various respects, as a 'seed-bed' for the more important ideas and events that follow; and a similar point could be made about the 'Middle Ages'. As used in history (though not, alas, in personal life), the very term denotes a time of potential, rather than of realisation. Wedged as they are between the glorious achievements of antiquity and their belated (and self-conscious) resuscitation at the 'Renaissance', the 'Middle Ages' are not quite one thing or another; they are in between, and awaiting their fulfilment at a later date. With that rather negative role assigned by historians, whose chronology was determined by other enthusiasms, it's not surprising that the Middle Ages' numerous achievements have often been undervalued or neglected.

Chronologies, then, are determined by one's focus; and, once established, they tend in turn to determine that focus. Historians can't expect to see everything equally clearly: the use of one sight-line precludes the use of another (at least at the same time); and, by focusing on one thing, we necessarily relegate others to the background. There's nothing wrong with that: it's just the case; without focusing, we can't see (and nor can we do history). But problems do arise when we get so caught within the constraints of one focus, that we become blind to everything else: that is one thing T. S. Eliot might have meant by 'servitude'. We may (like Elektra and Franco and Proust) be enslaved by the past, and so become unable to extricate ourselves from what *has been*, in order properly to confront what *is*. Or we may similarly be enslaved by the present, leading one-dimensional lives with no more thought for the morrow than the past. Or we may be transfixed by the future, unable ever to settle or feel at home where we are or have been, but constantly fantasising about what and where we might be. A balance between all three, it has been suggested, constitutes 'normality', or at least facilitates an ability to cope; and the challenge remains to avoid enslavement by any one of them.

Time can, after (or before) all, be ordered differently: its relativism is a matter of common experience, by which I mean that our apprehension (or experience) of time is highly personal and indeed perverse. Years can go by 'in a flash', when we're happy, whereas stressful situations can generate a feeling of having lived half a lifetime in what turns out to have been only minutes or even seconds, as measured by someone else's clock. With personal experience of the defence of Stalingrad, Vasily Grossman described how 'time – measured by the most accurate of watches – had suddenly begun to bend, to stretch and flatten', and how the chaos of battle 'tore into shreds any sense of the passing of time'; and one historian of the American Civil War has written of how the intensity of their experience gave participants 'the sense of living a lifetime in a year'.[20]

Even 'past', 'present' and 'future' are categories which (as we have seen in terms of memory and identity) cannot be too rigidly maintained; and, whether through mysticism, drugs or electronic media, would-be escapees from the constraints of linear time have not infrequently sought that 'timeless moment' when, in Nicholas of Cusa's words, 'future and past are one with the present' and 'all succession in time coincideth in the same NOW of eternity'.[21] Constantly intruding on each other through the most permeable boundaries, past, present and future are not even recognised as separate entities (through the use of different tenses) by some languages, and they can come even in English to be seen, in the words of the poet e. e. cummings, as 'a few trifling delusions . . . much too small for one human being'.[22]

As such they can inconvenience those historians who dissent from any 'scientific' model for their subject. Modern scientifically derived rationality and objectivity assist in only one mode of perception (at a time). But there are alternatives; and the more 'romantically' inclined have often favoured a more poetic approach to knowledge, including knowledge of the past. Then the historian requires not only intellect but also, and no less, the sort of 'creative sympathy' that is often associated more with artistic sensibilities; and, from such a standpoint, starts and finishes – the incisions we necessarily make into time's seamless web – become no more than 'convenient human conceptions, products of our thirst for definition [as] we edit the shifting particles of our experience into comforting form'.[23] It's no wonder, then, that Jacob Burckhardt 'even felt it to be a nuisance that the historian, in presenting his historical narrative, was bound by the chronological order compelling him to tell one thing after another, when the true order "could only be represented as a picture" '.[24]

Thus, the delusive order imposed by an overly constraining structure of past, present and future, is too small not only for cummings's human being, but even for the great Swiss historian; and how much more so, in both pagan and Christian traditions, for god – to whom the three are all one anyway. The Roman god Janus, as Alexander Ross reminded his seventeenth-century readers, 'is said to have had two faces, because he saw two worlds'.[25] Living at the time of Noah, he had seen the world both before and after the great flood. So he had the benefit of more than one perception: he had personally witnessed a changing vision of reality, and he therefore represented an ability to embrace more than a single perspective. Nor were the perspectives involved only geographical or spatial: Janus not only knew that the earth had changed; he also knew that the change had taken place in time, so that his varying perspectives were also chronological. His memory enabled him to retain a grasp of the past as well as the present. For him, the past had not been forgotten and lost; nor was it something simply to be jettisoned. Rather it was something to be held within one's present vision, something to keep one eye on, while looking with the other eye into the future. With his double face, Janus signifies the wisdom of blending the tenses, and retaining the past as contemporaneous with present and future.

In the Christian tradition, similarly, St Augustine concluded that past, present and future must all be always in God's mind. They may appear to our finite human minds as distinct and separable entities, but in fact 'neither the future [which still awaits existence] nor the past [which no longer exists] exist'. As too for the Presocratic philosopher Parmenides, the present subsumes both past and future; and the Christian God, in his omniscience, holds all together. 'If God's knowledge contains these things, they are not future [or past] to Him but present.'[26]

That theological point was applied much later specifically to historiography by Sir Francis Palgrave, who noted in the mid-nineteenth century that 'The events appearing to us as consecutive are essentially consentaneous . . . the beginning and the end are simultaneous in the designs of Him who is Alpha and Omega, the First and the Last.'[27] Carlyle, too, defining history as 'a looking both before and after', recognised that 'only by the combination of both is the meaning of either completed'[28]; and the German Romantic author August Wilhelm von Schlegel was clearly in agreement when he proposed that 'the historian is a prophet looking backwards',[29] seeing, in Tennyson's poetic words (describing an artistic depiction of King Arthur's wars), 'New things and old co-twisted, as if Time/Were nothing . . .'[30]

Time's incessant flow, then, may seem to be best represented in a literary style that mirrors a stream of consciousness – a stream with eddies, swells and whirlpools, and surface currents that go for a while against the deeper flow. Descriptions of such watery chaos may deliberately deny logic as an irrelevant and inappropriate constraint: T. S. Eliot's 'freedom' may imply the breaking free from old structures – including even chronological structures – that have been self-imposed through nothing more authoritative than habit and have long since just been accepted as natural. 'Time', one historian has proposed, 'is *not* essential to history'[31]; by which he presumably means that he lays less importance on a chronological sequence of events, or on a narrative thread that progresses, or unravels, *through* time, diachronically, than on an attempted understanding of a specific *moment*, in all its thickness and with its inestimable wealth of *synchronic* relationships.

One potential advantage of focusing on specific moments in that way is that it may encourage awareness of what Goethe referred to as 'the historic moment'. The historic moment is the moment in the present, the moment with which we are confronted right now, when we recognise that moment (this moment) as being a moment in the ceaseless flow of time, and as a potentially transforming moment. The moment is 'historic' in the sense that it arrives for each of us in the present as the culmination to date of what has happened in the past, and as the point from which the future will proceed. It is a moment of infinite potential, infinite possibilities. The only question is: what do we do with it?

We are confronted, of course, by a succession of such moments, and by a successive need to respond in one way or another. Most of the time, or all of it, we allow habit to have its way – responding to each moment as we have responded to all its predecessors, as we have been taught to respond, as convention requires. That way, we don't have to think, or make decisions. That way we can drift through life quite comfortably, with a minimum of angst. But for Goethe that constitutes failure, because it implies a refusal to grow, a refusal at each and every moment to change and develop, a refusal to recognise and realise each moment's infinite potential. And it implies a tacit self-satisfaction – a satisfaction with what and how we are; it implies that our identities are fixed, complete, that we are (unashamedly) what we are. Which is the very reverse of Goethe's own prescription: that 'we must *be* nothing, but desire to *become* everything'.[32]

A similar desire to realise our human potential underlies the recommendation of Elizabeth Deeds Ermarth that we liberate ourselves from modernist 'linear time', with all its attendant narrative strait-jacketing, in favour of a postmodern 'rhythmic time' that better represents the innumerable interweaving threads from which that strait-jacket is designed to keep us. Rather than proceeding straightforwardly along one single track, which is how we tend to think of the time of our lives as we pass from birth to death, we can more likely have the time of our lives by 'swinging', as it were, across chronological planes, keeping 'alive . . . an awareness of multiple pathways and constantly crossing themes', and being all the richer for it.[33]

Nevertheless, coming down to earth where it is still widely believed that 'sanity is perhaps the ability to punctuate'[34], our liberated visions still need to be communicated; so, while recognising the essential unity of times past, present and future, and the chaotic chronologies concealed by any narrativisation of the past, postmodern historians will need again to take responsibility for imposing some form and structure, in order to convey to their readers the message that they think worth bothering about.

New perceptions and perspectives

Each time I've been to Jouy I've seen a bit of canal in one place, and then I've turned a corner and seen another, but when I saw the second I could no longer see the first. I tried to put them together in my mind's eye; it was no good. But from the top of Saint-Hilaire it's quite another matter – a regular network in which the place is enclosed. Only you can't see any water . . . To get it all quite perfect you would have to be in both places at once; up at the top of the steeple of Saint-Hilaire and down there at Jouy-le-Vicomte. – Proust[35]

Proust's character, who finds that he can't have his Madeline and eat it, introduces another potential constraint on history. Narrativity and time are not the only problems: being caught in the chains of a single story or chronology is only one aspect of historians' potential 'servitude'; we are also inevitably snared by the limitations of our perceptions and our inability to enjoy more than one perspective at a time. At ground level, we can see first one canal and then another, but have no idea of the whole canal system; from the higher vantage point of the church steeple, we can appreciate the pattern of the entire canal network, but (unable any longer to discriminate water) we lose any sense of there being *canals* at all. (They could be anything.) Ideally, we need to be in two places at the same time, to enjoy the complementary perspectives that contribute to the whole; but of course we can't be. The best we can do is to minimise the effects of our inevitable limitations, by putting together the various perceptions we have from those various perspectives. That is what postmodern history will need to do, if it is to attain any sort of 'freedom'.

But of course it's not as simple as Proust's example might seem to indicate. There, the impression is given that, by putting together two experiences, the totality is revealed: we may still feel frustrated that we can't actually synthesise two chronological/geographical frameworks, and take in the whole at once; but the intellectual/epistemological problem (of knowing what's there) at least seems to be solved. In the case of history, though, it's not just two perspectives that are needed, but quite literally an infinity – each one necessarily limited but contributing to a fuller (though never completable) whole. 'History', writes Macaulay, 'has its foreground and its background . . . Some events must be represented on a large scale, others diminished; the great majority will be lost in the dimness of the horizon.'[36] That great but inevitable loss remains as one of history's main problems.

Recognition of that problem, of course, long pre-dates Macaulay. 'Every-thing', wrote the German Justus Moser in 1767, 'everything has *its per-spective* in which it *alone* is beautiful; as soon as you change it, as soon as you cut into the entrails with an anatomical knife, the previous beauty evaporates with the changed perspective.'[37] As others have noted, the seamless web of the past does have to suffer the knife, in order to have any sense made of its entrails at all; and each incision provides a marker from which new perceptions can be generated. But, while that cut is made, the surrounding areas must be anaesthetised; what facilitates one perception, denies the possibility of others. At any one time we are necessarily caught within the bounds of a single perspective, so the 'beauty' of coherence is bought at the price of partiality and of another form of 'servitude'.

As an example, we might take one notable historical event: the drop-ping of the atomic bomb on Hiroshima in 1945. How can we possibly wield our surgical knife in such a case? From what perspective can we start? For the physicist the bomb proved an undoubted technical tri-umph; it demonstrated 'superb physics'. For the aircrew there was the professional satisfaction of having carried out their mission; it was a job well done. For the politicians (on both sides, but from rather different standpoints), that playing of a new trump card for ever changed the rules of diplomatic and military games. For the people on the ground, the explosion's immediate victims, John Hersey perhaps adopted the only practicable approach by describing what happened to six named individuals: the clerk Miss Toshiko Sasaki, Dr Masakazu Fujii, the tailor's widow Mrs Hatsuo Nakamura, the German Jesuit priest Father Wilhelm Kleinsorge, Dr Terufumi Sasaki, and the Reverend Kiyoshi Tanimoto – these serve to represent over a hundred thousand people (a number beyond comprehension).[38] And for the other side, the historian Richard Cobb famously (and making an historiographical point) explained that the bomb's effect was to enable his earlier demobilisation; while similarly an American marine described to me how he had been on his way to a prospective invasion of Japan when news of Hiroshima came through, and how he had watched the shadow of the ship's mast traverse the deck as they did a U-turn in mid-ocean, their services no longer required.

Such individual accounts are obviously in one sense inadequate; they are attempts to embrace the unimaginable by contributing perspectives – technical, practical, deliberately individualised, tragic, ironic – to an event before which the historian might well feel helpless. Any internal consistency or 'beauty' they might have depends on their exclusion of infinitely more than they include; and maybe their juxtaposition (revealing incompleteness) challenges their integrity and so (in Moser's terms) threatens to evaporate their beauty. But at least they indicate that there's no end to the perspectival possibilities; and they contribute to some hypothetical 'whole' which may never have existed as a whole, but which stands for an event that undoubtedly occurred.

To deny the 'reality' of that event or that past (as with the Holocaust again) is far less 'ethical' than (by admitting those personalised accounts as contributions to a history) to accept some hypothetical 'violation' of unrepresented interests. Though mutually exclusive in their own terms, each perspective can be seen as a thread ready to be woven into an intriguing tapestry. Once we are liberated from our chronological and geographical constraints – the need to see everything at once, from a single stance, and within a single framework – we are freed to weave those diverse threads in any way, and without necessarily compromising the beauty of any. We may never be able to stand simultaneously on the ground and at the top of the church steeple, but we can flit between them and other possible locations, and then (to revert to Virginia Woolf's previous metaphor) we can compact our various perceptions into something over which thought may linger, and love play.

New ideals and aspirations

I am aware that this is to blaspheme against the sacrosanct school of what these gentlemen term 'Art for Art's sake', but at this period of history there are tasks more urgent than the manipulation of words in a harmonious manner. – Proust[39]

Postmodern history is sometimes seen as reducing everything to 'textuality'. Denying any concrete reality to any unitary past, and denying any possibility of reaching any such past even if there were one, postmodern history evolves into a purely literary construction – a matter of aesthetics, and of manipulating, not so much data, as *words* 'in a harmonious manner'. But that paradoxically, as Proust's character hints in the quotation above, is to endanger history with a reversal to an 'art for art's sake' (or history for its own sake) treatment of the sort espoused by some of postmodernism's greatest opponents. And in fact there do, at this period of history, appear to be 'tasks more urgent'.

Decades ago, J. H. Plumb wrote of fostering an identity that is not national, not 'as Americans or Russians, Chinese or Britons, black or white, rich or poor, but as man'.[40] That aspiration to some sort of *universal* 'humanity' – as distinct from (if not as opposed to) the current obsession with fostering *national*, or even narrower sectional identities – is nothing new. In the eighteenth century, Lord Bolingbroke decried the 'ridiculous and hurtful vanity' of a nationalism which encouraged the members of each country to claim their own superiority. The common belief that one's own customs, opinions and values are the absolutes by which others should be judged is, Bolingbroke accused, often actually engendered by education. But it is of course nothing but 'folly', and that folly is to be remedied by historical study, which should serve 'to purge the mind of those national partialities and prejudices'. For 'a wise man', after all, 'looks on himself as a citizen of the world'.[41]

Since Bolingbroke's day, numbers have spoken out on behalf of such enlightened cosmopolitanism, and even of Plumb's ideal of a universalised humanity. The Romantic poet Coleridge came to the conclusion that 'assuredly the great use of History is to acquaint us with the nature of Man'.[42] And, as another thinker in the Platonic tradition, the nearly contemporary philosopher Schopenhauer recommended for historians a study of 'what for ever *is* and never *develops*'; for underlying 'all those endless variations and turmoils, we have before us merely the one cre- ature, *essentially* identical and unchangeable, busying itself with the same things today, and yesterday, and forever...' That prospective agenda sounds hardly likely to capture the imagination – let alone the intellect – of any practising historian, but in fact Schopenhauer's thought proved a direct influence on Jacob Burckhardt. 'We shall study what is recurrent, constant and typical', proclaimed Burckhardt; and what that implied for him was the centrality in his history of 'man', the human being, 'this suffering, striving and active being, as he is and was and will be for ever'.[43]

That sort of universalism may sound like something long outmoded, and especially in the context of postmodernity. But here I'm not propos- ing a search for something supposedly already existing as an unchanging entity, whether in religion or philosophy or history. Rather, on the assumption that God's death – against the advice of d'Holbach – has been widely reported, I'm assuming widespread nihilism, and an inabil- ity to define that central term of 'man' or 'human'. And then, I suggest, what we need is, if not an antidote, at the very least a prescription; and that's to be provided, not by any superhuman doctor or magician, but by our very human selves.

In other words, the subject-matter of our postmodern histories might (or must) be chosen with our own model of humanity in mind. Sound- ing like a previous incarnation of Richard Rorty, Henry Brougham in 1828 wrote to Lord John Russell, advocating just such a history: 'What I am above all things anxious to see is such a narrative as may . . . inculcate a hatred of cruelty and perfidy';[44] and much more recently Denis Shemilt (in 1992) has described 'good history teaching [as] the enemy of the undemocratic, the bigoted, the irrational and the cruel'.[45] There are those who might want to question Shemilt's unquestioning advocacy of demo- cracy and rationality, but a residue of motherhood and apple-pie is likely to remain as an historical common denominator.

In practical terms, then, the claims of 'humanity' might today be met in Annabel Patterson's work (mentioned above) on early modern liber- alism, or (more controversially, perhaps) Daniel Goldhagen's study of *Hitler's Willing Executioners* (1996). However different, those two books have an important feature in common: they are not written 'for their own sake', from an affectedly 'detached' standpoint, but they embody an agenda. In other words, they have a practical point, and that point is not to wallow self-indulgently in the past, either to glorify or to deny it, but to use it as a starting-point from which positively to set out on our future. A concept of 'humanity' is implicit in both, so that in neither case are we in any doubt as to why we need to bother.

Doubt itself, though, and uncertainty (as we have already noted above à propos Keats's ideal of 'negative capability') may be no bad things to aim at in the context of postmodern historical study. John Casey has recently criticised contemporary dogmatism, and in particular the 'dogma of our own time: that we differ markedly from our ancestors' and are morally superior to them. It is such conviction in our own superiority, he argues, that prompts late twentieth-century Christians to apologise for the Crusades. Unable to enter imaginatively into the experience of past peoples, they judge them from their own parochial standpoints, and show themselves to be no less convinced of the absolute rightness of their cause than the disgraced crusaders were. An injection of doubt inspired by historical study might spare the pain (or spoil the fun) of such self-flagellation, and such an injection has already been sensibly prescribed by David Andress, who proposes 'leaving students uneasy about their relation to the world (and the construction of their "self")'; 'the production of doubt', he suggests, might well be an appropriate educational aim for historians. David Harlan similarly has written about the possibility of turning 'impoverishing certitudes' into 'humanising doubts', and many might agree with Yeats that, even in an anarchic world where the centre no longer holds, it is still indeed 'the best [who] lack all conviction'.[46] Although advocates of 'conviction', whether in politics or elsewhere, will express their own uncertainty about such a goal, dogmatic certainty is surely a 'folly', as Lord Bolingbroke long since noted, that might well be remedied by histories (designed, as we might need to add, to make just that moral point).

That such follies are hard to remedy might be another lesson to be learnt from history before its end, but that's no argument against ideals and aspirations. Postmodernism poetentially (my word-processor is less banal than its user, who had meant of course to type 'potentially'; but the mistake may not be impertinent) expands the range (or definitions) of what it *means* to be human. It leaves *open* what has traditionally been foreclosed in various, but all contingent, ways; and that applies not least to definitions of humanity. As in the case of Heraclitus's river, we may not be able to step (or, more humanely, look) on the same individual twice: even as we gaze, the object of our gaze is undergoing transformation (and that applies also to the past). So that our descriptions – our very language – needs constant (poetically inspired) updating and renewal; and the creative act of writing history emerges from an interplay between a past that surely once existed and a present human being – self-defined, but never therefore static or complete, and never purposeless.

Conclusion

We want to serve history only to the extent that history serves life ... Let us at least learn better how to employ history for the purpose of life! – Nietzsche[47]

The ideally 'purposeless' history, with which we started our discussion of history's point in chapter 1, is profoundly conservative, inasmuch as it accepts – and therefore presumably approves – things (whether of past or present) as they are. 'Being adult', claims Geoffrey Elton, 'means being able to accept people and things as they really are';[48] and being 'realistic' is of course (supposedly) an unquestionable virtue. Paradoxically again, postmodernism might seem to lead us towards Elton's apparently liberal (but actually conservative) position: a tolerant acceptance of people and things as they are, might seem to characterise the postmodern position. But Elton's 'really' gives the game away: for what 'really' are we, or they? The dissolution of a simplistic 'reality' is one of the most important consequences of postmodern thought, and its importance lies precisely in the fact that we don't have to believe it's 'adult' (and therefore incumbent on us as responsible people) to accept things 'as they are'. People and things are not fixed as unchangeable entities for ever: they have infinite potential, which we can help to realise – that is, *make* 'real'. Identities are formed, not only from our pasts, our histories, but also from our visions for the future. That's why our history needs to be informed by such vision, and why Nietzsche's point can help us towards a practical conclusion. Why bother with history? Why indeed, unless we can learn better how to employ it 'for the purpose of *life*!'[49]

Notes

1 T. S. Eliot, 'Four Quartets', in *Collected Poems, 1909–1962*, London, Faber and Faber, 1974, p. 219.
2 Friedrich Gottlieb Klopstock (1724–1803), 'Resurrection Ode'.
3 Advertisement for the Brook Street Bureau, seen on the London Underground, December 1999.
4 Felipe Fernández-Armesto, *Truth: A History and a Guide for the Perplexed*, London, Bantam, 1997, pp. 7, 8, 162, 226.
5 Virginia Woolf, *To the Lighthouse* (1927), London, J. M. Dent, 1978, p. 223.
6 Robert Musil quoted by Frank Kermode, *The Sense of An Ending. Studies in the Theory of Fiction*, New York, Oxford University Press, 1967, p. 127.
7 Claude Lanzmann quoted by Michael S. Roth, *The Ironist's Cage: Memory, Trauma, and the Construction of History*, New York, Columbia University Press, 1995, p. 209 (my emphasis).
8 Thomas Carlyle, 'On History' (1830), in *English and Other Critical Essays*, London, J. M. Dent, 1915, p. 81.
9 Henry James, Preface to *Roderick Hudson*, quoted by Kermode, *Sense*, p. 176.
10 See Frank Füredi, *Mythical Past, Elusive Future*, London, Pluto, 1992, esp. pp. 241ff.
11 Elizabeth Deeds Ermarth, *Sequel to History: Postmodernism and the Crisis of Representational Time*, Oxford, Princeton University Press, 1992, p. 8.
12 Alex Callinicos, *Theories and Narratives: Reflections on the Philosophy of History*, Cambridge, Polity, 1995, p. 210.
13 Quoted by Christina Crosby, *The Ends of History*, London, Routledge, 1991, p. 30.
14 Annabel Patterson, *Early Modern Liberalism*, Cambridge, Cambridge University Press, 1997, pp. 1 (my emphasis), 250, 287.
15 Claude Lévi-Strauss, *The Savage Mind*, London, Weidenfeld and Nicolson, 1966, p. 258.
16 Thomas Baker, *Reflections upon Learning*, 3rd edn, London, A. Bosvile, 1700, p. 121. This work, which includes a chapter on history, ran to seven editions, and was a main source of Baker's contemporary reputation.
17 Carlyle, *Essays*, p. 84.
18 U. A. Fanthorpe, 'BC: AD', in *Selected Poems*, Harmondsworth, Penguin, 1986, p. 66.
19 So Clement of Alexandria, c. AD 200, quoted in Henry Bettenson (ed.), *The Early Christian Fathers*, Oxford, Oxford University Press, 1969, p. 168.
20 Vasily Grossman, *Life and Fate*, London, Harvill, 1985, pp. 79, 49; James MacPherson, quoted by Callinicos, *Theories*, p. 46.
21 Nicholas of Cusa (1401–64), quoted in F. C. Happold, *Mysticism*, Harmondsworth, Penguin, 1964, p. 306.
22 e. e. cummings, quoted by Lewis W. Spitz, *The Reformation: Education and History*, Aldershot, Variorum, 1997, p. 152. cummings always wrote his name in lower case.
23 Idris Parry, *Animals of Silence*, London, Oxford University Press, 1972, pp. 22, 16–17.
24 Erich Heller, *The Disinherited Mind*, Harmondsworth, Penguin, 1961, p. 65. This is an interesting precursor of Elizabeth Deeds Ermarth's postulation of collage as a

model for historical narrative (see n. 11 above); and cf. the pointilliste approach advocated by such historians as Theodore Zeldin.

25 Alexander Ross, *Mystagogus Poeticus, or the Muses Interpreter* (1647), ed. J. R. Glenn, New York and London, Garland, 1987, p. 383.

26 Saint Augustine, *Confessions*, transl. R. S. Pine-Coffin, Harmondsworth, Penguin, 1961, p. 269; and as quoted by J. W. Burrow, *A Liberal Descent*, Cambridge, Cambridge University Press, 1983, p. 224. For Parmenides on time, see G. S. Kirk and J. E. Raven, *The Presocratic Philosophers*, Cambridge, Cambridge University Press, 1971, pp. 272–5.

27 Sir Francis Palgrave, quoted by Burrow, *Liberal Descent*, p. 224.

28 Carlyle, *Essays*, p. 80.

29 August Wilhelm von Schlegel (1767–1845), quoted by Spitz, *Reformation*, Preface. Cf. Hazlitt's description of the historical novelist Sir Walter Scott, as 'a *prophesier* of things past': *Lectures on the English Poets and The Spirit of the Age*, London, J. M. Dent, 1967, p. 223.

30 Alfred Tennyson, 'Idylls of the King: Gareth and Lynette'. Tennyson's typically Victorian intermingling of ages is expressed also in 'The Princess', where he writes of 'the first bones of Time;/And on the tables every clime and age/Jumbled together . . . '

31 Paul Veyne (1984), quoted by Thomas R. Flynn, *Sartre, Foucault, and Historical Reason*, vol. 1, London, University of Chicago Press, 1997, p. x.

32 Goethe, quoted by Parry, *Animals*, p. 68. See pp. 68–75 for the essay 'Goethe and the Historic Moment', to which I am here indebted.

33 Ermarth, *Sequel*, p. 53. See Keith Jenkins' helpful exposition of Ermarth's thought in *Why History?*, London, Routledge, 1999, ch. 7.

34 Idris Parry, *Animals*, p. 63.

35 Marcel Proust, *Remembrance of Things Past*, vol. 1, Harmondsworth, Penguin, 1983, pp. 114–15.

36 Macaulay, quoted by Crosby, *Ends*, p. 170. Professor Crosby notes (p. 58) that Macaulay believed that 'the historian must understand the general principles governing a series of events in order to represent the facts in the proper [*sic*] perspective'.

37 Justus Moser, 'Concerning the Moral Perspective', quoted by Füredi, *Mythical Past*, p. 231.

38 See John Hershey, 'Hiroshima', in *Here to Stay*, Harmondsworth, Penguin, 1962, pp. 236–316.

39 Proust, *Remembrance*, p. 510.

40 J. H. Plumb, *The Death of the Past*, London, Macmillan, 1969, p. 145.

41 Lord Bolingbroke, *Letters on the Study and Use of History*, and *Reflections upon Exile*, London, A. Millar, 1752, pp. 25–7, 444–5.

42 Coleridge, quoted by Mary Anne Perkins, *Coleridge's Philosophy*, Oxford, Clarendon Press, 1994, p. 258.

43 Schopenhauer and Burckhardt are quoted by Erich Heller, *Disinherited Mind*, pp. 67–8. Heller concludes that 'Schopenhauer's philosophy pervades the whole work of Jacob Burckhardt', citing many of the historian's letters, as well as the Introduction to his *Reflections on World History*.

44 Henry Brougham, quoted by Patterson, *Liberalism*, p. 225.

45 Denis Shemilt, in Peter Lee *et al.*, *The Aims of School History*, London, Tufnell Press, 1993, p. 5.

46 John Casey, *The Daily Telegraph*, 1 April 1999; David Andress, 'Beyond Irony and Relativism: what is postmodern history *for?*', *Rethinking History* 1, 1997, pp. 324, 316; David Harlan, quoted by Jenkins, *Why?*, p. 189; W. B. Yeats, 'The Second Coming', in *The Collected Poems*, London, Macmillan, 1950, p. 211.

47 Nietzsche, *Untimely Meditations*, transl. R. J. Hollingdale, Cambridge, Cambridge University Press, 1983, pp. 59, 66.

48 Geoffrey Elton, quoted by Füredi, *Mythical Past*, p. 212.

49 Since concluding this, my attention has been drawn again to William Stubbes' Inaugural Lecture as Regius Professor at Oxford, 7 February 1867, where he asserts: '...We want to train not merely students but citizens...to be fitted not for criticism or for authority in matters of memory, *but for action*' (my emphasis). Perhaps the gap between 'proper' and 'postmodernist' historians need not be unbridgeable? Stubbs is quoted in Gordon Connell-Smith and H. A. Lloyd, *The Relevance of History*, London, Heinemann, 1972, p. 28 – a reference for which I am grateful to John Tosh.

Bibliography

Anderson, Judith H. (1984) *Biographical Truth: The Representation of Historical Persons in Tudor–Stuart Writing*, New Haven and London: Yale University Press

Andress, David (1997) 'Beyond Irony and Relativism: what is postmodern history for?', *Rethinking History* 1, pp. 311–26

Anon, *Anglo-Saxon Chronicle*, transl. James Ingram (1912) London: J. M. Dent

Anon (n.d.) *The Great Army of the London Poor*, London: Charles H. Kelly

Appleby, J., Hunt, L. and Jacob, M. (1994) *Telling the Truth about History*, New York: W. W. Norton

Augustine, Saint (1961) *Confessions*, transl. R. S. Pine-Coffin Harmondsworth: Penguin

Bacon, Francis (1951) *The Advancement of Learning*, 1605, London: Oxford University Press

Bacon, Francis (1640) *Of the Advancement and Proficience of Learning*, Oxford: Robert Young and Edward Forrest

Bacon, Francis (1960) *The New Organon*, 1620, ed. F. H. Anderson, Indianapolis: Bobbs-Merrill

Baker, Thomas (1700) *Reflections upon Learning*, 3rd edn, London: A. Bosvile

Bayle, Pierre (1710ff) *An Historical and Critical Dictionary*, 1697, 4 vols, London: C. Harper

Beattie, A. (1987) *History in Peril*, London: Centre for Policy Studies

Bede, The Venerable (1958) *The Ecclesiastical History of the English Nation, etc*, London: J. M. Dent

Bellow, Saul (1977) *Mr Sammler's Planet*, Harmondsworth: Penguin

Bentley, Michael (1999) *Modern Historiography: An Introduction*, London: Routledge

Bettelheim, Bruno (1979) *Surviving and Other Essays*, London: Thames and Hudson

Bettenson, Henry, ed. (1969) *The Early Christian Fathers*, Oxford: Oxford University Press

Blundeville, Thomas (1574) *The true order and Methode of wryting and reading Hystories . . .*, London: Willyam Seres

Bodin, Jean, transl. B. Reynolds (1945) *Method for the Easy Comprehension of History*, 1566, New York: Columbia University Press

Bolingbroke, Henry St John, Lord (1752) *Letters on the Study and Use of History*, and *Reflections upon Exile*, London: A. Millar

Bolingbroke, Henry St John, Lord (1841) *The Works*, 4 vols, Philadelphia: Carey and Hart

Boyle, Robert (1690) *The Christian Virtuoso*, London: John Taylor

Bradley, John L., ed. (1965) *Selections from London Labour and the London Poor,* London: Oxford University Press

Braithwait, Richard (1638) *A Survey of History,* London: Jasper Amery

Briggs, Asa, ed. (1962) *William Morris: Selected Writings and Designs,* Harmondsworth: Penguin

Brooks, R., Aris, M. and Perry, I. (1993) *The Effective Teaching of History,* London: Longman

Brown, Norman O. (1959) *Life Against Death: The Psychoanalytical Meaning of History,* London: Routledge

Buchanan, George (1690) *The History of Scotland,* London: A. Churchil

Burrow, J. W. (1983) *A Liberal Descent,* Cambridge: Cambridge University Press

Butterfield, Herbert (1973) *The Whig Interpretation of History,* 1931, Harmondsworth: Penguin

Cahoone, Lawrence, ed. (1996) *From Modernism to Postmodernism: An Anthology,* Oxford: Blackwell

Callinicos, Alex (1995) *Theories and Narratives,* Cambridge: Polity

Cannadine, David (1999) *Making History Now,* London: University of London Institute of Historical Research

Carlyle, Thomas (1908) *On Heroes, Hero-Worship and the Heroic in History,* London: Cassell

Carlyle, Thomas (1915) *English and Other Critical Essays,* London: J. M. Dent

Carlyle, Thomas (n.d.) *Past and Present,* London: Ward Lock

Casaubon, Méric (1665) *To J.S. (the Author of Sure-Footing) his Letter, lately Published . . . ,* London: Timothy Garthwait

Castiglione, Count Baldassare (1928) *The Book of the Courtier,* 1561, transl. Sir Thomas Hoby, London: J. M. Dent

Cheng, Nien (1995) *Life and Death in Shanghai,* London: Flamingo

Connell-Smith, Gordon and Lloyd, H. A. (1972) *The Relevance of History,* London: Heinemann

Cressy, Hugh (1647) *Exomologesis,* Paris

Croix, Geoffrey de Ste (1981) *The Class Struggle in the Ancient Greek World,* London: Duckworth

Crosby, Christina (1991) *The Ends of History: Victorians and 'the woman question',* London: Routledge

Curthoys, Ann and Docker, John (1997) 'Metaphor in English Historiographical Writing', *Rethinking History* 1, pp. 259–73

Davies, Norman (1997) *Europe: A History,* London: Pimlico

Descartes (1985) *The Philosophical Writings,* transl. John Cottingham, Robert Stoothoff and Dugald Murdoch, 2 vols, Cambridge: Cambridge University Press

Dicks, Henry V. (1972) *Licensed Mass Murder: A Socio-Psychological Study of Some S.S. Killers,* London: Heinemann

Dix, Dorothea Lynde (1967) *Remarks on Prisons and Prison Discipline in the United States,* 2nd edn 1845, ed. Leonard D. Savitz, Montclair, New Jersey: Patterson Smith

Dryden, John (1911) *The Poetical Works,* ed. W. D. Christie, London: Macmillan

Duroselle, Jean-Baptiste (1990) *Europe: A History of its Peoples*, transl. Richard Mayne, London: Penguin

Eliot, George (1947) *Middlemarch*, 1871–2, London: Oxford University Press

Eliot, T. S. (1933) *The Use of Poetry and the Use of Criticism*, London: Faber and Faber

Eliot, T. S. (1974) *Collected Poems, 1909–1962*, London: Faber and Faber

Elton, G. E. R. (1969) *The Practice of History*, London: Fontana

Elton, G. E. R. (1991) *Return to Essentials*, Cambridge: Cambridge University Press

Ermarth, Elizabeth Deeds (1992) *Sequel to History: Postmodernism and the Crisis of Representational Time*, Oxford: Princeton University Press

Ermarth, Elizabeth Deeds (1998) *Realism and Consensus in the English Novel: Time, Space and Narrative*, 2nd edn, Edinburgh: Edinburgh University Press

Eusebius (1965) *The History of the Church from Christ to Constantine*, transl. G. A. Williamson, Harmondsworth: Penguin

Evans, Richard J. (1997) *In Defence of History*, London: Granta

Fanthorpe, U. A. (1986) *Selected Poems*, Harmondsworth: Penguin

Fay, Brian, Pomper, Philip, and Vann, Richard T. eds (1998) *History and Theory: Contemporary Readings*, Oxford: Blackwell

Fernández-Armesto, Felipe (1997) *Truth: A History and a Guide for the Perplexed*, London: Bantam Press

Fisher, H. A. L. (1936) *A History of Europe*, London: Edward Arnold

Fitzgerald, Frances (1979) *America Revised: History Schoolbooks in the Twentieth Century*, Boston: Little, Brown

Flynn, Thomas R. (1997) *Sartre, Foucault, and Historical Reason*, vol. 1, London: University of Chicago Press

Foot, Sarah (1999) 'Remembering, Forgetting and Inventing: Attitudes to the Past in England at the End of the First Viking Age', *Transactions of the Royal Historical Society*, Sixth Series, 9, pp. 185–200

Fox, Adam (1999) 'Remembering the Past in Early Modern England: Oral and Written Tradition', *Transactions of the Royal Historical Society*, Sixth Series, 9, pp. 233–56

Fox-Genovese, Elizabeth and Lasch-Quinn, Elisabeth, eds (1999) *Reconstructing History*, London: Routledge

Freeman, E. A. (1884) *The Office of the Historical Professor*, London: Macmillan

Froissart, Jean (1968) *Chronicles*, ed. Geoffrey Brereton, Harmondsworth: Penguin

Froude, J. A. (1907) *Short Studies on Great Subjects*, 5 vols, London: Longmans, Green

Fukuyama, Francis (1992) *The End of History and the Last Man*, Harmondsworth: Penguin

Füredi, Frank (1992) *Mythical Past, Elusive Future*, London: Pluto

Gasquet, F. A., ed. (1906) *Lord Acton and his Circle*, London: George Allen

Gildas (1978) *The Ruin of Britain*, AD 540, ed. Michael Winterbottom, London: Phillimore

Glanvill, Joseph (1665) *Scepsis Scientifica*, London: H. Eversden

Gombrich, E. H. (1960) *The Story of Art*, London: Phaidon

Gott, Samuel (1648) *Nova Solyma, the Ideal City: or, Jerusalem Regained*, London: John Legat

Grossman, Vasily (1985) *Life and Fate*, London: Harvill

Grotius, Hugo (1680) *The Truth of the Christian Religion*, 1624, transl. Simon Patrick, London: R. Royston

Hale, Sir Matthew (1677) *The Primitive Origination of Mankind considered and examined according to The Light of Nature*, London: William Shrowsbery

Happold, F. C. (1964) *Mysticism*, Harmondsworth: Penguin

Hartley, Cecil (1820) *British Genius Exemplified*, London: Effingham Wilson

Harvie, Christopher, Martin, Graham, and Scharf, Aaron, eds (1970) *Industrialisation and Culture, 1830–1914*, London: Macmillan

Hay, Denys (1977) *Annalists and Historians: Western Historiography from the Eighth to the Eighteenth Centuries*, London: Methuen

Hayward, Paul A. (1999) 'The *Miracula Inventionis Beate Mylburge Virginis* attributed to "the Lord Ato, Cardinal Bishop of Ostia"', *English Historical Review*, 114, pp. 543–73

Hazlitt, William (1967) *Lectures on the English Poets and The Spirit of the Age*, London: J. M. Dent

Heinsius, Daniel (1943) *The Value of History*, c. 1613, transl. G. W. Robinson, Cambridge, Mass.: privately printed

Heller, Erich (1966) *The Artist's Journey into the Interior, and Other Essays*, London: Secker and Warburg

Heller, Erich (1961) *The Disinherited Mind*, Harmondsworth: Penguin

Hershey, John (1962) *Here to Stay*, Harmondsworth: Penguin

Heywood, Thomas (1973) *An Apology for Actors*, 1612, facsimile New York and London: Garland

Hitchin, N. W. (1999) 'The Politics of English Bible Translation in Georgian Britain', *Transactions of the Royal Historical Society*, Sixth Series 9, pp. 67–92

Hobbes, Thomas (1914) *Leviathan*, 1651, London: J. M. Dent

Hobbes, Thomas (1679) *Behemoth; or an Epitome of the Civil Wars of England from 1640 to 1660*, London.

Hobsbawm, Eric and Ranger, Terry, eds (1983) *The Invention of Tradition*, Cambridge: Cambridge University Press

Hughes, John (1706) *A Complete History of England*, 3 vols, London: Brab. Aylmer

Hume, David (1985) *Enquiries concerning Human Understanding and concerning the Principles of Morals*, 1777, ed. L. A. Selby-Bigge, revised P. H. Nidditch, Oxford: Clarendon Press

Hume, David (1987) *A Treatise of Human Nature*, 1739, ed. L. A. Selby-Bigge, revised P. H. Nidditch, Oxford: Clarendon Press

Hunter, Robert Wiles (1965) *Poverty*, 1904, ed. Peter d'A. Jones, New York: Harper and Row

Huxley, Aldous (1955) *Eyeless in Gaza*, Harmondsworth: Penguin

Jacobs, Michael (1985) *The Presenting Past*, Milton Keynes: Open University Press

Jenkins, Keith, ed. (1997) *The Postmodern History Reader*, London: Routledge

Jenkins, Keith (1997) 'Why Bother with the Past?', *Rethinking History* 1, pp. 56–66

Jenkins, Keith (1999) '"After" History', *Rethinking History* 3, pp. 7–20

Jenkins, Keith (1999) *Why History? Ethics and Postmodernity*, London: Routledge

Josephus, Flavius (1906) *The Wars of the Jews*, transl. William Whiston, London: J. M. Dent

Kelley, Donald R., ed. (1991) *Versions of History from Antiquity to the Enlightenment*, New Haven and London: Yale University Press

Kelley, D. R. and Sacks, D. H., eds (1997) *The Historical Imagination in Early Modern England: History, Rhetoric, and Fiction, 1500–1800*, Cambridge: Cambridge University Press

Kermode, Frank (1967) *The Sense of An Ending: Studies in the Theory of Fiction*, New York: Oxford University Press

Kirk, G. S. and Raven, J. E. (1971) *The Presocratic Philosophers*, Cambridge: Cambridge University Press

Kümmel, W. G. (1973) *The New Testament*, London: SCM Press

Kundera, Milan (1983) *The Book of Laughter and Forgetting*, London: Faber and Faber

Lacey, Robert (1973) *Sir Walter Ralegh*, London: Weidenfeld and Nicolson

Lee, Peter, Slater, John, Walsh, Paddy, and White, John (1993) *The Aims of School History: The National Curriculum and Beyond*, London: Tufnell Press

Le Goff, Jacques (1992) *History and Memory*, New York: Columbia University Press

Lévi-Strauss, Claude (1966) *The Savage Mind*, London: Weidenfeld and Nicolson

Lipstadt, Deborah E. (1994) *Denying the Holocaust: The Growing Assault on Truth and Memory*, Harmondsworth: Penguin

Locke, John (1690) *An Essay Concerning Humane Understanding*, London: Thomas Basset

Locke, John (1809) *Some Thoughts concerning Education*, 1690, London: Sherwood, Neely and Jones

McCourt, Frank (1997) *Angela's Ashes*, London: Flamingo

McHoul, Alec and Grace, Wendy (1995) *A Foucault Primer: Discourse, Power and the Subject*, London: UCL Press

Maier, C. S. (1997) *The Unmasterable Past: History, Holocaust, and German National Identity*, Cambridge, Mass: Harvard University Press

Moorehead, Alan (1968) *The Fatal Impact*, Harmondsworth: Penguin

Munslow, Alun (1997) *Deconstructing History*, London: Routledge

Newman, John Henry (1915) *On the Scope and Nature of University Education* (1852), London: J. M. Dent

Newton, Isaac (1966) *Principia Mathematica*, 1687, ed. Florian Cajori, 2 vols, Berkeley and Los Angeles: University of California Press

Niethammer, Lutz (1992) *Posthistoire: Has History Come to an End?*, transl. Patrick Camiller, London: Verso

Nietzsche, Friedrich (1974) *The Gay Science*, transl. Walter Kaufmann, New York: Vintage

Nietzsche, Friedrich (1983) *Untimely Meditations*, transl. R. J. Hollingdale, Cambridge: Cambridge University Press

Oakeshott, Michael (1933) *Experience and its Modes*, Cambridge: Cambridge University Press

Osborne, Francis (1656) *Advice to a Son*, Oxford: Thomas Robinson

Parry, Idris (1972) *Animals of Silence*, London: Oxford University Press

Patterson, Annabel (1997) *Early Modern Liberalism*, Cambridge: Cambridge University Press

Perkins, Mary Anne (1994) *Coleridge's Philosophy: The Logos as Unifying Principle*, Oxford, Clarendon Press

Plumb, J. H. (1969) *The Death of the Past*, London: Macmillan

Plutarch (1803) *Lives*, transl. J. and W. Langhorne, 6 vols, London: Lackington, Allen

Popkin, Richard H. (1979) *The History of Scepticism from Erasmus to Spinoza*, Berkeley and Los Angeles: University of California Press

Priestley, Joseph (1788) *Lectures on History and General Policy*, Birmingham: J. Johnson

Proust, Marcel (1983) *Remembrance of Things Past*, vol. 1, Harmondsworth: Penguin

Raleigh, Sir Walter (1614) *The History of the World*, London: W. Burre

Rauschenbusch, Walter (1964) *Christianity and the Social Crisis*, 1907, ed. Robert D. Cross, New York: Harper and Row

Rawlinson, Richard (1728) *A New Method of Studying History*, 2 vols, London: W. Burton

Rorty, Richard (1989) *Contingency, Irony, and Solidarity*, Cambridge: Cambridge University Press

Ross, Alexander (1987) *Mystagogus Poeticus, or the Muses Interpreter*, 1647, ed. J. R. Glenn, New York and London: Garland

Roth, Michael S. (1995) *The Ironist's Cage: Memory, Trauma, and the Construction of History*, New York: Columbia University Press

Roth, Michael S. (1995) *Psycho-Analysis as History: Negation and Freedom in Freud*, London: Cornell University Press

Rowse, A. L. (1946) *The Use of History*, London: Hodder and Stoughton

Sacks, Oliver (1985) *The Man Who Mistook His Wife for a Hat*, London: Duckworth

Sacks, Oliver (1995) *An Anthropologist on Mars*, London: Picador

Salmon, Nicholas, ed. (1996) *William Morris on History*, Sheffield: Sheffield Academic Press

Sampson, R. V. (1956) *Progress in the Age of Reason*, London: Heinemann

Sarpi, Paolo (1620) *The History of the Council of Trent*, transl. Nathaniel Brent, London: Robert Barker and John Bill

Schmitt, C. B., Skinner, Q., and Kessler, E., eds (1988) *The Cambridge History of Renaissance Philosophy*, Cambridge: Cambridge University Press

Sergeant, John (1665) *Sure-Footing in Christianity*, London

Sergeant, John (1688) *Fifth Catholick Letter*, London: Matthew Turner

Sergeant, John (1696) *The Method to Science*, London: W. Redmayne

Shakespeare, William (1943) *The Complete Works*, ed. W. J. Craig, London: Oxford University Press

Skinner, Quentin (1998) *Liberty Before Liberalism*, Cambridge: Cambridge University Press

Smiles, Samuel (1890) *Self-Help*, London: John Murray

Sophocles (1979) *Electra*, transl. Kenneth McLeish, Cambridge: Cambridge University Press

Southgate, Beverley C. (2000) 'Blackloism and Tradition: from theological certainty to historiographical doubt', *Journal of the History of Ideas*, 61, pp. 97–114.

Spencer, Herbert (1910) *Education*, London: Williams and Norgate

Spender, Stephen, ed. (1958) *Great Writings of Goethe*, New York: Mentor

Spengler, Oswald (1926) *The Decline of the West*, London: George Allen and Unwin

Spitz, Lewis W. (1997) *The Reformation: Education and History*, Aldershot: Variorum

Stannard, David E. (1992) *American Holocaust: Columbus and the Conquest of the New World*, New York: Oxford University Press

Stern, Fritz, ed. (1956) *The Varieties of History from Voltaire to the Present*, New York: Meridian

Stillingfleet, Edward (1662) *Origines Sacrae*, London: Henry Mortlock

Stillingfleet, Edward (1677) *Letter to a Deist*, London: Richard Cumberland

Suetonius (1957) *The Twelve Caesars*, transl. Robert Graves, Harmondsworth: Penguin

Swan, John (1698) *Speculum Mundi, or A Glass Representing the Face of the World*, 4th edn, London: W. Whitwood

Swift, Graham (1992) *Waterland*, London: Pan

Tacitus (1959) *The Annals of Imperial Rome*, transl. Michael Grant, Harmondsworth: Penguin

Tacitus (1873) *History*, transl. A. J. Church and W. A. Broadribb, London: Macmillan

Tennyson, Alfred (1953) *Poetical Works*, London: Oxford University Press

Thomas, D. M. (1981) *The White Hotel*, Harmondsworth: Penguin

Thomson, E. P. (1977) *William Morris: Romantic to Revolutionary*, London: Merlin

Tillotson, John (1666) *The Rule of Faith*, London: Sa. Gellibrand

Tolstoy, Leo (1941) *War and Peace*, transl. Louise and Aylmer Maude, London: Oxford University Press

Toynbee, A. J. (1924) *Greek Historical Thought*, London: J. M. Dent

Trevor-Roper, Hugh (1971) *Queen Elizabeth's First Historian: William Camden and the Beginnings of English 'Civil History'*, London: Jonathan Cape

Walsh, William (1959) *The Use of Imagination*, London: Chatto and Windus

Wheare, Degory (1685) *The Method and Order of Reading both Ecclesiastical and Civil Histories*, 1635, transl. Edmund Bohun, London: Charles Brome

White, Hayden (1978) *Tropics of Discourse: Essays in Cultural Criticism*, London: Johns Hopkins University Press

White, Thomas (1659) *The Middle State of Souls from the Hour of Death to the Day of Judgment*, London

White, Thomas (1661) *Devotion and Reason*, Paris

Wittgenstein, Ludwig (1961) *Tractatus Logico Philosophicus*, transl. D. F. Pears and B. F. McGuinness, London: Routledge and Kegan Paul

Wittgenstein, Ludwig (1969) *Blue and Brown Books*, 2nd edn, New York: Harper and Row

Wittgenstein, Ludwig (1994) *Culture and Value*, ed. G. H. Von Wright, Oxford: Blackwell

Woolf, D. R. (1990) *The Idea of History in Early Stuart England*, London: University of Toronto Press

Woolf, Virginia (1978) *To the Lighthouse*, 1927, London: J. M. Dent

Yeats, William Butler (1950) *The Collected Poems*, London: Macmillan

Index